FOCUSING ON TRUTH

Focusing on Truth explores the question of what truth is, balancing historical discussion with issue-orientated discussion. The book offers a comprehensive survey of all the major theories of truth. Lawrence Johnson investigates a number of closely related matters of truth in his inquiry. What sorts of things are true or false? What is attributed to them when they are said to be true or false? What do facts have to do with truth? What can we learn from previous theories?

The book opens with an analysis of the coherence theory of truth and then the correspondence theory of truth, as developed by Moore, Russell and Wittgenstein. Through a study of the semantic conceptions of truth, the author reveals that an adequate theory of truth must take account of the pragmatics of person, purpose and circumstance. A full understanding of facts and truth bearers is considered central to Johnson's criticism of the opposing truth theories of J. L. Austin and P. F. Strawson.

Drawing on the merits of these theories and others, while identifying their deficiencies, Johnson presents a new account of truth, based on the correlation of referential foci and the use of linguistic conventions. This account is defended as being adequate to meet the legitimate demands made on a theory of truth. It is argued that the account leaves scope for statements of many different sorts to be true in their own widely varying ways, without there being a need to posit fundamentally different kinds of truth.

Focusing on Truth will be of interest to all those concerned with the philosophy of truth, and will provide a central textbook for all students of philosophy.

FOCUSING ON TRUTH

Lawrence E. Johnson

London and New York

First published 1992
by Routledge
11 New Fetter Lane, London EC4P 4EE

Simultaneously published in the USA and Canada
by Routledge
a division of Routledge, Chapman and Hall Inc.
29 West 35th Street, New York, NY 10001

Typeset in 10 on 12 point Garamond by
Florencetype Ltd, Kewstoke, Avon
Printed in Great Britain by
T J Press (Padstow) Ltd, Padstow, Cornwall

British Library Cataloguing in Publication Data
Johnson, Lawrence E.
Focusing on truth.
I. Title
121.4

Library of Congress Cataloging in Publication Data
Johnson, Lawrence E.
Focusing on truth/Lawrence E. Johnson
p.   cm.
Includes bibliographical references.
1. Truth.   2. Truth—Correspondence theory.   3. Truth—Coherence
theory.   I. Title.
BD 171.J59   1992
121—dc20   91-35743

ISBN 0–415–07252–2   ISBN 0–415–07253–0 (pbk)

This book is dedicated to my children
FREJA K. JOHNSON
and
NICHOLAS A. JOHNSON
to whom I have tried to present the truth.

CONTENTS

ACKNOWLEDGEMENTS

I would like to thank all who have contributed to the genesis of this book. In particular I would like to thank Avrum Stroll, Piero Ariotti, Stanley Malinovich, Graham Nerlich, Christopher Mortensen, Ted Honderich, anonymous referees, and inquiring and argumentative students. Thanks to Jill Rawnsley for editorial help and advice. Thanks to many about me for their patience.

1

INTRODUCTION

I sketch the scope, purpose, and intended value of this inquiry. My aim, broadly, is to elucidate what it is for that which can be true or false to be true. There may be different sorts of things which can be true and different ways in which they can be true, some of which (e.g. true grit) may not be relevant to our inquiry. Part of the problem is to focus the inquiry without begging questions in the questions we ask. I shall approach the matter through discussion both of historical theories and of central issues, attempting thereby to bring the inquiry into focus.

Truth is a matter of interest not only to philosophers but to all those who desire to know about anything whatsoever. This being so, our interest in truth is by no means recent. No one could presume to say when, in the mists of the past, people – or perhaps our pre-human ancestors – first took an interest in what was true and what was not, but the question would arise in some form for any being which took an interest in the world and could wonder whether things were one way rather than another. Certainly any beings which could develop a language would have, would *have* to have, a basic concern for whether things said were so. People may not be concerned with truth on every occasion, but if they never were, there could be no understanding of things said, nor could anything be said at all.

While truth has long been of concern to us, almost always our chief concern has been in determining which things are true and which are not, rather than in attempting to determine just what truth is. Until relatively recent times there has been comparatively little attempt, with a few noteworthy exceptions such as that of Aristotle, to do the latter. Evidently it was felt – and certainly with justification for most purposes – that we understand what truth is well enough, and that the important problems lay in finding out what is true about various matters of interest to us. Still, it would be gratifying to know more about truth, if only as a matter of interest in its own right, and in the last century or so there has been renewed philosophical interest in the subject.

I propose to contribute to the discussion of what truth amounts to, eventually presenting my own account. Such an inquiry may have its uses, a matter about which I shall subsequently have some things to say. At the very least, an improved philosophical understanding of truth might have the value of keeping us from wandering lost in theoretical blind alleys, as has often been done. I think, though, that developing a better understanding of truth, like being a truthful and honest person, or enjoying beautiful music, is something which is of value in its own right, quite apart from any further considerations.

NARROWING THE FOCUS: WHAT THINGS ARE TRUE?

Broadly, my goal is to determine, as nearly as possible, what truth is. That *is* to put it broadly, and without precision. At this stage, precision might be neither possible nor desirable. Even so, before we attempt to find answers, it would be wise to try to get clear what it is we are trying to answer. We do not want to run the risk of getting poor answers through asking poor questions. Conceivably, we might say that we are trying to determine what it is for something to be *true*, or even that we are trying to determine the *meaning* of truth. That sounds very grand and, if possible, well worth accomplishing. Putting it this way might get us off on the wrong foot, though. For one thing, it asks for an abstraction which applies to all of the various different things which are true. Perhaps we would then be looking for something which does not exist. Perhaps true things are true in various different ways. We should not pre-judge these issues at the outset. As it happens, very different things can be said to be true or not true, and we cannot just assume that the word 'true' means the same thing when applied to each of them. Beliefs and statements can be true or false, but so can friends, and various other things. Is truth the same thing in each case? I think not. Whereas a false belief is still a belief, just as much as is a true one, a false friend is not really a friend. Truly being a friend entails being a true friend, certainly not being a false one, yet even a false belief or statement can truly be a belief or statement. Moreover, not being a true friend does not necessarily entail being a false friend. One may be a nodding acquaintance or a total stranger. Yet beliefs and statements implicitly make truth claims – statements are stated to be true and beliefs are believed to be true – and there is normally a strong presumption that those which are not true are false. Evidently, then, different things can have very different ways of being true or false.

There is a thread which runs through this diversity. True things are those in which we can safely repose our confidence. The etymological origins of the English word 'true', deriving from Middle English *trewe* and Old English *trēowe* (loyal, trusty), appear to be connected with Old English *trēow* (loyalty, fidelity) and with *trēow* and *trēo*, the roots of our word 'tree', giving us the sense of 'as firm and straight as a tree' (Partridge 1958: 740). There is something reliable about a tree. In contrast to true things, false things, be they an incorrect belief, a treacherous friend, or a false (fake, imitation) pearl, are such that we cannot accept them at face value and repose confidence in them. There is something crooked, something infirm about false things. Different things may merit or betray our confidence in different ways, but at root there is some element of dependability in things which are true. Even so, there are *different* elements of dependability in different sorts of cases. True pearls have a different sort of dependability than do true pearls of wisdom. There is no one type of dependability which is common to all things which are said to be true.[1]

In the following, I shall not be concerned with truth as it applies to everything which might properly, in some way or another, be described as true or not true. That would take us in too many directions at once. Instead, I shall concentrate on a problem which is quite broad enough in its own right and which is fundamentally concerned with our knowledge of our world. It is a question which I hinted at earlier. What I am trying to ask, *roughly*, is what is it for something which we do or could say or think to be true or false. That would include that which we might assert, believe, doubt, conjecture, or wonder about, whether or not it is ever actually stated. (After all, we may well have beliefs, true or false, which we never utter. We may wonder about the truth of something which we never state, not even internally. Indeed, one would think that some things might be true, or false, which no one has ever thought about

3

at all.) It is in this direction that I want to develop our lines of inquiry.

It may seem that I am, exasperatingly, just beating around the bush here, that, obviously, what I am trying to get at is truth/falsity in the case of real or potential statements (rather than friends, pearls, or whatever). That is right, of course. That is approximately what I am getting at. Yet it is only an approximation, with a number of loose ends, and we must be very careful how we frame the question we are trying to answer. To start with, what is a statement? Not just anything we say or utter (or think) is a statement. We ask questions, make requests or promises, and sometimes we curse. What makes something we say a statement? (Why is it *saying* and not just uttering or noise-making?) Is not a statement something that is, . . . well, true or false? There is a different but related difficulty concerning this business of things which we say. Do we say words, or do we use words to say things (what things?) which are true or false? We may do both. Just what are those things we say which are true or false, the truth-bearers? Some writers take them to be sentences, some take them to be propositions (said to be the 'contents' of our thoughts or linguistic expressions), some take them to be beliefs or statements – whatever statements are – and there have been other candidates. In the following we shall have to look more closely at such matters.

Perhaps, for now anyway, we should just take it that the truth-bearers with which we are concerned are those things which are (or could be) said/stated/asserted. This looks somewhat promising, as what we know, believe, doubt, conjecture, wonder about, say, or think are things which are (or could be) said/stated/ asserted. Other things, from which we wish to distinguish the truth-bearers we are concerned with, while they may be true or false in some sense, cannot be said/stated/asserted. Pearls, whether they be true ones, generated by oysters, or false ones, generated by human contrivance, are never said. Whatever we may say about them, we never say them. We may say things about friends as well and, unlike pearls, a friend may say various things, and even claim to be true, yet even the truest of friends are never said/stated/asserted. What, then, we ask, is it for what is (or could be) said/stated/asserted to be true?

This approach, asking what it is for that which is (or could be) said/stated/asserted to be true, seems good enough to get on with. We have not fully characterized truth-bearers, to be sure, but at least we can generally recognize them in practice. At this stage, we may not wish to try to characterize them too precisely. Different theories of truth have presupposed different truth-bearers, and one would not wish to pre-empt the issue before we give different theories a hearing, else we might drift into premature commitments. For now, a truth-bearer will be taken to be that which is (or could be) said/stated/asserted, and for convenience we can say that the statement says/states/asserts that such-and-such. Later, we shall consider the question of what truth-bearers are in more detail. At this stage, that is not the most critical problem.

As we take it now, truth-bearers are (or could be) said/stated/asserted in some way, and so serve to say/state/assert something-or-other – and one would presume that true statements are those wherein this is done correctly. Put that way, the question seems virtually to answer itself. The thought that there is not really a very serious question about truth is no doubt a major reason why so few philosophers, until relatively recently, have concerned themselves with the topic. As we shall see, though, there are problems. As noted, to have an adequate account we will have to work out what truth-bearers are, and how words and contents fit in if they have anything to do with it. There are also questions about what merely could-be sayings/statings/assertings have to do with actual truth. Very importantly, there are questions about what saying/stating/asserting amounts to – and perhaps about what it is to say/state/assert something *about* something. Answers here are unlikely to be either simple or unitary, for language performs many different functions. (What is uttered may be true or false in some sense, being perhaps false cheerfulness or true defiance, but it is not with such utterances and their truth or falsity that we are to be concerned here.) And, of course, one would think that there is a lot that is true which has not, or not yet, been uttered. As we go along we shall continually reconsider the questions we ask.

To answer these and related questions we would have to find out quite a lot – to say the least – about language and about truth-related uses of it. Why bother? Instead of going into all of that, why can we not just accept that truth-bearers are true if things are as they are (or could be) said/stated/asserted to be, and false otherwise? Then we could get down to the business of trying to determine which beliefs, statements, or the like, are or are not true. If we did that, though, we might miss out on discovering some interesting things about truth. They might be useful things as well. A better understanding of truth might help us better to understand and deal with such difficult subject-matters as ethics, science, metaphysics, or mathematics. It might help us better to understand what we are using language to do when we pursue these subjects. In any case, giving truth theory the quick brush-off is unsatisfactory unless we are content, as I am not, to not know what is special about truth-bearers when what they say/state/assert is so. Why is truth to be prized but not falsity? How is it that truth is thought to be different from being interesting or being *zilch* if we know no more about things being as they are said/stated/asserted to be than we know about their being *zilch*? That taking such an approach leaves us with nothing can be seen by taking a look, as we do in the next section, at one notable attempt to get by in this fashion. We shall also see that trying to give it some content raises problems.

ARISTOTLE'S CONCEPTION OF TRUTH

As well as telling us about what he thought was true, Aristotle was one philosopher who did try to give us a quick gloss – and a quick brush-off – on truth. In his *Metaphysics*, he tells us that

> To say of what is that it is not, or of what is not that it is, is false, while to say of what is that it is, and of what is not that it is not, is true; so that he who says of anything that it is, or that it is not, will say either what is true or what is false.
>
> (1011^b 26–9)

One presumes that it is what is said rather than the saying of it which is held to be true. This analysis seems like simple and indisputable common sense, and a way of disposing of the topic with minimal bother. That would seem pretty well to settle the matter so that we can turn our attention to the really serious business of working out what is true or not true about various things which are important or interesting to us. There are difficulties to be faced here, however. For the moment, let us remain with Aristotle.

In his commentary on the passage, Christopher Kirwan (1971: 117) notes that the ' "is" could mean "exists", "is so-and-so", or "is the case" (and "is not" similarly)'. The first of these alternatives seems much too restrictive. It would evidently allow us to say truly that dogs exist, for instance, but not that they wag their tails. That

6

would rule out much too much. (The only way around it would be to take what exists as being not just the dog but the wagging of its tail, or the fact of its wagging its tail. That would be to take what exists as the dog's being so-and-so, or else as the being the case of something about the dog, which amounts to one or the other of the remaining alternatives.) The remaining two alternatives certainly seem much more plausible. They also seem, at first glance, to be about the same. I think, though, that there is an important difference. For example, according to the alternative wherein 'is' means 'is so-and-so', to say of what is white that it is white is true. To say of snow that it is white is true because snow is white. How does that work out according to the 'is the case' alternative? To say of what is the case that it is the case is true, then, but what is said to be the case here? *That* snow is white? Or something else? According to the 'is so-and-so' alternative, we are saying something about snow, that it is white. According to the 'is the case' alternative, we are saying that something – what kind of a thing? – is the case. It is the latter alternative, obviously, which is the hardest to nail down. Is the thing said to be the case snow's being white, or is it a statement or proposition or sentence or some other thing? How is that thing, whatever it is, tied up with our saying that it is the case? Opinions on such matters have varied, generating some involved discussions in truth theory about intricate issues. These discussions have sometimes been misleading, or misled.

That there is a difference between an 'is the case' approach to truth and an 'is so-and-so' approach is worth bearing in mind. We might profitably see many subsequent theories of truth as being primarily concerned with explaining truth in terms of what it is for something of some sort to be the case, while many other theories are primarily concerned with explaining truth in terms of what it is for something properly to be described as being so-and-so. Each approach has its characteristic problems. I think it would be mostly correct to say that the former approach was the more popular among theorists of truth until recent decades, and that this is the approach which led to the most colourful theories, such as those of coherence and correspondence. I suspect that the other, 'is so-and-so', approach has tended to suggest that the thing to do is to bypass theorizing about truth in favour of inquiring into what is true. It is only in recent times that explicit theories of truth along such lines have been widely promulgated. Among their number I would count Tarski's semantic theory of truth, and also Austin's very different account. My own account, which I present later, also tends to be along 'is so-and-so' lines.

Certainly this is not the time to accept or reject any particular approach – and I hasten to add that I suggest the above classification only as a rough rule of thumb, claiming for it neither precision nor exhaustiveness. By no means do I make the absurd suggestion that subsequent theories of truth are properly to be characterized as expressions of divergent schools of Aristotelian interpretation. I think, though, that it would be worth our while to note some of the problems faced by those general approaches. As has been noted (e.g. Williams 1976: 67), taking truth to be a matter of saying of what is so-and-so that it is so-and-so has the effect of tying truth exclusively to subject–predicate statements. We state truth, then, when we predicate some description of something of which it is properly predicated. But what is the subject of predication of an existential statement, such as 'There are black swans'? (There is no particular swan to serve as a subject for predication. Moreover, if we treat the statement as 'Black swans exist', and try to treat existence as a predicate, we get into a great many philosophical difficulties.) What about cases like 'Caesar crossed the Rubicon', where there is no longer a subject of predication? Again, suppose we are not dealing with simple predication, saying that something is so-and-so, but are dealing with a two or more place relationship, saying that something has some relationship to some other things. For example, we might have 'Juliet loves Romeo more than Paris'. Here we are no longer dealing with simple predication, and – as Bertrand Russell found out – this raises very formidable logical problems. There are other difficulties with the 'is so-and-so' approach as well, all of which in some way revolve around whether we can take truth as centring on some sort of predication. Much later we shall look at whether these problems can be resolved. Unless we can resolve them, any such account would have inadequate content and would not apply to many things which we do want to hold to be true or false. Now, though, let us briefly look at some of the difficulties with the other approach.

A major problem with the 'is the case' approach – that which gives truth theory the quickest brush-off – is that it does not seem to be saying very much, if anything at all, since 'is the case' seems more or less equivalent to 'is true'. Are we being told only that it is true to say of what is true that it is true? We would be getting somewhere only if we could independently characterize what 'is the case' means. That could be difficult. We might perhaps try to do it in two stages. We could take what is or is not the case to be a truth-bearer, perhaps a statement, e.g. that snow is white. Then our formula would tell us that it is true to say of what is the case (that snow is white) that it (that snow is white) is the case. The next thing would have to be to explain what it is for it to be the case that snow is white. Perhaps it corresponds to the facts, or perhaps something else is going on. Saying just what is going on will be difficult, if we want to do more than just say that the statement is true if it is true. There are severe problems which show up as we try to give the 'is the case' account some real content. Is it the case because of something else in the world to which it relates, or because of some special way of relating to it? What else? What way of relating? Terms such as 'fact', 'representation', and the like often get involved, but they have to be explained themselves and cannot just serve, without further ado, as part of the explanation. There have been many answers to these and related questions, answers which frequently seem to lead us into tangled metaphysical thickets populated by strange relationships and dubious entities dubiously conceived.

If we try to get by on the cheap, then, resting on something like the claim that a statement, or truth-bearer, is true if what it says is so, we have only a hollow conception of truth – if it is a conception of truth at all. (Much later it was suggested that truth is only a pseudo-concept, for which there is no need to try to find a content. As we shall see, though, there is good reason to think that this is not the correct approach.) If we try to give the concept content, we find that there is no safe and simple way of doing so. Any way of giving it content, whether or not it proves viable, will involve intricacies and problems. Instead of giving up, though, or taking refuge in triviality, let us face up to it and try to develop a viable account of truth which does have significant content.

TOWARD AN ACCOUNT OF TRUTH

We have not yet sufficiently well determined what we are asking for in a theory or account of truth and what we will accept as an answer. Much of this book will, in one way or another, attempt to improve our focus on the nature of the issues of our inquiry. This, rather than just a desire to write most of a book between now and then, is why I will not present my own account until a much later chapter. Answers do not amount to much without an intelligible question, one which is a good question. Being told that the answer is 'forty-two' does not tell us much if we do not know what the question is, and the better we understand the question the better we can understand – and evaluate – the answer. Before I attempt to present my own account of truth, I hope to clarify further just what the question is which I am trying to answer, what it is not, and why that question came to be posed in that way rather than in some other way. Only then can I hope to explain why I attempt to answer it as I do. Those who are not convinced by my account will, I hope, profit from my development of the topic, and I also hope that by the end of the book they will have a useful understanding of where and why we differ.

That pearls and such like have different ways of being true or untrue than do statements (or whatever our relevant truth-bearers are) is only one difficulty with asking for the *meaning* of truth – or for *the* meaning of truth. It may be that there is more than one way for a statement to be true. It may be, for instance, that true universal statements are true in a way different than are true particular statements. That all mammals have four-chambered hearts may not be true in the way that it is true that Lassie has long hair. It is not at all obvious that truth is the same thing in each case, and certainly they are verified in quite different ways. Again, perhaps the truth of positive statements differs from that of negative statements, and perhaps empirically true statements have a significantly different sort of truth than do logically true statements. Perhaps truth has different meanings (what is a meaning?) in different sorts of cases. We cannot just adjudicate such matters by prior assumption. Nor can we even just tacitly assume that there is some particular number of ways in which statements can be true. Looking for the essences of truth is as questionable as asking for the essence of reality. It may be that instead of there being a number of specific ways of being true, there is a continuously differentiated range. Is there some very broad something which makes them *all* cases of truth? Or is there some collection of 'family resemblances' loosely linking them together. We cannot answer such questions now. I merely warn that we must be wary of building tacitly presupposed answers into our questions. Instead of asking what it is to be true, or asking for the meaning of truth, it might be better to ask what we say about a statement when we say that it is true. If we do that, we must recognize that we may get other than one precise answer. Our answer might not be fully precise, and we might get more than one answer. We might even get no answer at all, since the question assumes that calling a statement true is to say something about it – an assumption which has been hotly disputed. It might turn out to be that the concept of truth is illusory and that there is no worthwhile question we can ask about it at all. That would be a valuable result in its own right. Perhaps we should just ask in what way(s) we use the word 'true', or ask what we use it to do. At this stage I think it would be unwise to define our inquiry into truth too rigidly or more precisely. We know roughly what we are trying to do. Let us proceed cautiously, bearing in mind throughout that we are developing questions as much as we are developing answers. As we probe, we shall learn to bring the issues into better focus. Only then shall we be able to find worthwhile answers.

The inquiry we are proposing to pursue did not arise in an historical vacuum. Truth theory has a history of change and development, particularly since it became a major topic of philosophical investigation during, approximately, the last hundred years. Those changes and developments have been for reasons, good or bad, and it would be profitable for us to consider some of this history. Accordingly, I shall begin my approach to the topic by critically reviewing several of the major theories of truth which have been developed. I shall do so for the sake of what we have learned and can learn from them in developing better understandings of the relevant questions and of how, formally and substantively, we can effectively go about trying to answer them. We can learn both from their successes and from their failures in answering the questions which they asked and in meeting the difficulties which they faced.

Truth theory no more occurs in a philosophical vacuum than it occurs in an historical vacuum – and these points are by no means unconnected. It influences, and most assuredly is influenced by, the other branches of philosophy, and develops with them. Indeed, it is misleading to refer to the 'branches' of philosophy as if they were separate entities connected only at an extremity. The interconnections are much more complex and integral than that. Often the relationship is closer than that of interconnection. For instance, as we shall note in the next chapter, the coherence theory of truth that was advocated in one form or another by so many of those who upheld an idealist metaphysics was not merely connected with their metaphysics. Rather, it was an integral component of their metaphysics. It was thereby a coherence theory of a quite different hue from that offered by certain logical positivists, who developed their own coherence theory precisely because they refused to countenance metaphysics in any form whatsoever. Again, the correspondence theories developed by Russell and Moore stemmed from their rejection of idealist philosophy, and were expressions of their own views about the nature of the world and our knowledge of it. Logical atomism manifested itself in characteristic theories of truth, culminating in the system of Wittgenstein's *Tractatus*, and those theories declined with the rest of logical atomism. And so it goes. The semantic conception of truth is tied to many matters in logic and linguistics, and to many other things as well. Again, that approach to philosophy which stressed linguistic analysis, and which was so influential in recent times, developed its own style of approach to truth theory. Through it all, theories of truth have been closely associated with theories of meaning, though the pursuit of meaning has not been the same pursuit as that of truth. In one way or another, various and changing theories about metaphysics, epistemology, logic, language, and even ethics have been involved with truth theory, and there are other connections as well.

A complete discussion of twentieth-century truth theory would involve a discussion of most of twentieth-century philosophy. That, I cannot offer. What I do have to offer will therefore be incomplete – as will any other book about philosophy, including any book about the history of philosophy. In the following I shall primarily concentrate directly on truth theory, but not as if truth were an independent feature of reality or truth theory an independent pursuit. Rather, I shall attempt to conduct the inquiry as if I were shining a spotlight onto a stage, illuminating as best I can the key features and their immediate surroundings. I do not suggest, and one is not to imagine, that only what is within the circle of illumination is real or that what is within the circle is truly separate from what is without. It is all intimately interconnected and, in truth, all the world is the stage.

A FINAL PRELIMINARY WORD

I believe that we should expect something of our investigations into truth theory. We can ask what it is for that which is true to be true – or we can ask whatever turns out to be a better question about truth. If it were to turn out in the end that we cannot answer, or develop, a worthwhile question, then in finding that out, and finding out why, our investigations would have come up with something well worth knowing. I shall argue that we can develop a worthwhile positive result. It would be a mistake, though, to expect truth theory to determine something unexpected and spectacular about truth – the equivalent, perhaps, of discovering that $E = mc^2$. A viable account of truth is apt to seem tame by comparison. After all, we deal with truth and falsity on a day to day basis. We deal with energy on a daily basis too, of course, but we need not *understand* it in order to deal with it. Yet we often understand that something is true and why it is true, and certainly we understand many things we know to be true. It would be strange, then, if a correct account of truth were to appear totally foreign to us. To be sure, that it was correct might not be recognized by everyone immediately, or at all. One would expect it to be built from reasonably familiar components, however, even if one had not thought of them before in quite that way. Being a spectacular novelty is not necessarily what is needed. An account of truth should be informative, theoretically useful, and, not least, true.

The account of truth which I shall eventually give is influenced by several historically preceding accounts. It responds, I hope successfully, to considerations and difficulties which became apparent only through historical attempts to develop an account of truth. I shall claim, with considerable elaboration, that in the making of a statement something-or-other is said about some other something-or-other, and that true statements are those where whatever it is that is said to be some way is that way. If there is anything startling about that at all, it is only because some true statements (e.g. 'There are no green swans.') seem not to be about anything at all. I shall argue that even there, something is said about something. We must bear in mind that there are statements of many different sorts, which work in many different ways, and all of them, in their own way, say something about something. As we might put it, they have different ways of being true or false according to their different ways of saying what they say. Anything very exciting that we concluded about one sort of statement would likely not be true of all of them. Even so, I believe that the conclusions which I will offer you are worth the effort, yours and mine, involved in obtaining them. Like most conclusions in philosophy, they are as important for *why* they are, and for why they are to be preferred to alternatives, as they are for *what* they are. En route to the conclusion, we can better see how it fits into the general terrain. Moreover, not only is the scenery along the way worth looking at, there are things to do once we get there. The conclusions for which I argue do not just shift the emphasis from truth in the abstract to the question of what it is for a statement to be true. They further shift the emphasis to a consideration of what it is for various different statements, functioning as they do, to say what they say about whatever they say it about. I am not suggesting, nor do I conclude, that there are different kinds of truth which statements might have. Rather, I suggest that there are many different ways in which different statements can be true, just as there are many different ways in which statements can function. Understanding that, we may better understand their different ways of being true. Via truth theory, then, we come to put the emphasis back to where it has usually been: not on truth *per se*, but on those things which may or may not be true. Via truth theory we will then, I believe, have a *better* understanding of how those different sorts of things are or are not true or false – and of what the significance is of their being one or the other.

In beginning our inquiry with an investigation of the leading traditional theories of truth, we shall be concerned to assess them for their strengths as well as for their weaknesses. The coherence, correspondence and pragmatic theories will be investigated, as will the semantic conception of truth and various other alternatives. In the course of our inquiry we shall try to focus more closely on the question of what truth-bearers are, and we shall also consider other things, such as facts, sometimes supposed to be involved. Along the way certain related issues, important to truth theory, will arise and be discussed (though they cannot adequately be introduced at this point). Further, we shall pay particular attention to the very important Austin–Strawson debate about truth. From there, I shall go on to develop my own conclusions, and to elaborate them in the light of alternative theories. Subsequently, I shall discuss truth in connection with mathematics, theoretical science, and certain other subject-areas, asking whether they require a different conception of truth. Finally, I shall offer an overview. In truth, I shall do my best to make our inquiry profitable.

2

COHERENCE

The coherence theory of truth *is explained and criticized, and found
to be incorrect. The purpose of the chapter, however, is not just to
refute that theory but to find what it has to offer us which is of value,
and to develop a better understanding of what we are to require
of a theory of truth. Certainly it is worth bearing in mind, as the
coherentists stress, that truths do not exist on their own as independent and isolated units.*

The basic core of the *coherence theory of truth* is the conception that
beliefs (or judgements, or whatever truth-bearers are taken to be)
are true or false according to whether or not they fit in, that is,
cohere, with the body of other beliefs (or whatever) that are true.
This may seem a little strange at first approach, as it appears to
reduce truth to being a subjective matter of our mental states. One
might well think, instead, that truth or falsity must be dependent on
a reality which is external to and independent of our mental states.
Things are not true or false because thinking makes them so. The
problem with that, though, is the notorious difficulty of reaching
beyond our thoughts, perceptions, etc., to some reality of things-in-
themselves untainted by our awareness of them. Indeed, it may be
that we cannot even know that there are any such things. Hume
gave us considerable reason to be sceptical about our possible
knowledge of such things, and Kant pointed out that our knowledge of the world is given shape, whether or not it is given all of its
content, by our own mind. Our knowledge, then, all of the truth
that we can ever know, is relative to our own phenomenal world.

This is not to say that truth is whatever we please it to be, any
more than phenomena are. These things are resistant to our wishful
thinking, whether the source of the resistance be external reality, the

subconscious depths of our own mind, or some combination of other factors. Be that as it may, according to the idealist coherence theorists truth is inherently a matter of things mental (whether or not it is tied with specific minds). This being so, the coherence theory has characteristically been the theory of truth espoused by *idealists* – those who maintain that reality, at least in-so-far as we can be aware of it, is of an inherently mental nature. There have been other exponents of the coherence theory, for instance those logical positivists who were afraid of lapsing into metaphysics if they posited an independent reality for things to be true of. However, we shall primarily be concerned with the coherence theory as developed in its classical form by the idealists of this and the last century. I shall first discuss the coherence theory in the context of idealism, and then proceed to a more direct discussion of its strengths and weaknesses.

IDEALISM AND COHERENCE

Idealists[1] take reality, or at least knowable reality, to be mental or ideal[2] in character, but that is not to say that it must be thought or experienced by someone. Reality is not dependent on minds. Minds are only part of reality. Being mental, though, reality is such as to be thinkable by the mind. Indeed, since it is taken to be an organically interconnected whole, all of reality is held to be completely accessible to the rational mind. That is in principle, of course, rather than in practice. Since we are not omniscient, we can know only a portion of reality. Some of reality may never be known by anyone, but that neither affects its reality on the one hand nor implies that there is a reality beyond the accessibility of mind on the other.

That portion of reality which we are able to know is not a separate or separable part but only a fragment. It is incomplete and cannot stand on its own metaphysically or epistemologically. Central to the idealist philosophy is the conception that a thing is what it is only in relationship with the rest of the universe. Any change in any part of the web in some way, to some degree, changes everything else. This is the doctrine of *internal relations*, according to which all of a thing's relationships with everything else is essential to its nature. It may not make very much of a difference to the moon whether or not there is a coffee cup on the table in front of me, but it does make some difference. (There would be a very slight mutual gravitational influence, for instance, and no doubt there would be other links as well.) It would be a slightly different moon if the coffee cup were somewhere else or did not exist at all, and it will make some sort of a difference to the cup whether the moon is directly overhead or somewhere else. I cannot fully know the coffee cup, then, unless I know it in its connections with the moon and, for that matter, with everything else. The coffee cup I know is only partially the cup which really is, and my knowledge of it is only a distorted fragment of that one whole truth which spans the one whole reality. Indeed, as we shall see, truth not just spans reality but *is* reality. So far as the idealists are concerned, the question of truth is not one of whether one of our ideas corresponds to or correctly describes reality, but whether it is part of the fabric of reality as a whole.

If there were any non-internal relations, if there were so much as one purely *external* relation, we would be admitting the existence of brute facts which were not entirely integrated with the rest of the world. Thus, some part of reality would not be entirely accessible to the mind, and so would not be part of *our* world. Given that all relations are internal, by thoroughly studying the nature of any one particular thing one could in principle determine all the properties of any other thing. It was something like this which the poet had in mind who wrote

> Flower in the crannied wall,
> I pluck you out of the crannies,
> I hold you here, root and all, in my hand,
> Little flower – but *if* I could understand
> What you are, root and all, and all in all,
> I should know what God and man is.
>
> Tennyson, *Flower in the Crannied Wall*

The idealists, it will be clear, maintain that all of a thing's character is essential to it , and so entirely reject the traditional distinction between essential and accidental properties (and with it the distinction between physical and logical necessity). In sum, reality is viewed as a whole, experiential (whether or not actually experienced) in nature, which is intricately interconnected in such a fashion that any portion is what it is only in virtue of all the rest, and such that no portion can be adequately defined by itself or in any way taken as wholly discrete. This whole is wholly accessible to the mind, in principle, there being no brute facts – unless the One is said to be the one such fact. Metaphysically, there is only one thing, the all-encompassing *Absolute*, with anything less being an incomplete fragment without identity in its own right. Epistemologically, there is really only one truth, with anything less having identity only as a fragment of the whole truth.

Our words, our languages, our schemes of conception and perception – all of these tend to limit, distort, and confuse our awareness. Through them we associate or distinguish things according to our own limited ideas and particular values, dividing reality along lines of our own drawing. We thereby miss the true depth of things. We think in terms of names and forms as if they reflected the essential nature of reality, yet what we are really seeing in them are reflections of our own mentality. As Bradley (1893) tells us, our linguistic and mental apparatus divorces the *what* from the *that*. This is not to deny that we can ever know anything about anything. While our knowledge may be distorted and fragmentary, it can serve very nicely for limited purposes. We do not know all about ourselves, coffee, or coffee cups, but we know enough to be able to take a drink of coffee, getting results sufficiently in accordance with our intentions. The same applies, with respect to higher degrees of precision, to the supposedly exact sciences. Yet ultimately there is only one truth, the universal Absolute, wherein the *what* properly coincides with the *that*. Finite humanity can never achieve that, which could only be at the end of a never-ending road. Our progress in awareness nevertheless lies along this road of understanding things more and more nearly as they are, which is as they are in their interconnection.

THE COHERENCE THEORY OF TRUTH

We now turn to the coherence theory itself (first concentrating on its idealist versions). As Blanshard put it,

> That view is that reality is a system, completely ordered and fully intelligible, . . . at any given time the degree of truth in our experience as a whole is the degree of system it has achieved. The degree of truth in a particular proposition is to be judged in the first instance by its coherence with experience as a whole, all-comprehensive and fully articulated, in which thought can come to rest.
>
> (1939: vol. II, 264)

Coherence, which is not to be confused with mere consistency, is a relationship of mutual dependence and entailment over the whole body of reality. No particular proposition within the coherent whole can be false while all the rest are true, nor can any be quite true without the truth of all the rest. None can *be* independently, so none can be true or false independently. A proposition, then, is true when, and only when, it coheres with the rest of the system. Of course Blanshard's reference to 'particular propositions' is only a figure of speech, for nothing can exist in particularity. Ultimately there is only *the* proposition, the Absolute, one and self-coherent, which is reality as a whole. Anything less is only partially coherent and partially true, being true to the degree that it expresses the whole. Short of the whole universe there is no fully coherent whole, and short of it there is no proposition, or *judgement*, to use the term normally preferred by coherence theorists, which is completely true. It is important to bear in mind that the coherence theory, in the idealist's versions, combines two different claims: that coherence is the nature of truth, and that truth is a matter of degree with nothing short of the Absolute being absolutely true. While related, these points are separable and require individual consideration.

Let us start with coherence as the nature of truth. It is worth noting that we very often use coherence as a criterion of truth. Whether what we are evaluating fits in with other things we know or believe to be true, and whether it 'hangs together' internally, are highly important determinants in our evaluation of it. In Shakespeare's *Measure for Measure* (V, i, 60–3), the Duke was so evaluating Isabella's account of things when he mused that 'If she be mad . . . her madness hath the oddest frame of sense, such a dependency of thing on thing, as e'er I heard in madness'. To be sure, mad people can be highly rational – once we grant them an assumption or two – but one is inclined to think that a prime difference between truth and fantasy is that sooner or later the latter will be in conflict with the indubitable truth, whereas truth must be compatible with truth. Certainly if we are jurors in a court of law we cannot compare statements directly with external facts. All we can do is hear the sometimes conflicting testimony and try to determine what fits together and what does not. If we are historians we must proceed similarly, as we cannot directly compare claims with past events. Indeed, any time we are dealing with that which is not immediately present we can only reason on the basis of what we do have at hand. This applies as well to the forming of scientific hypotheses. We consider the available facts and arrive at a conjecture which takes them into consideration and which seems to give a coherent and plausible account.

While it is generally recognized that coherence often serves as a valuable criterion of truth, those who reject coherence as the nature of truth will reply that there is still the question of whether a given coherent account is true. Hypotheses must be tested against the facts, and what the jury decides may or may not be factually correct. As it happens, the idealists are quite prepared to agree wholeheartedly that, as Bradley (1883: 2) puts it, 'truth and falsehood depend on the relation of our ideas to reality'. Yet we must bear in mind the idealist conception of reality and our awareness of it. When we check a judgement of some sort against the facts we are, according to the idealists, checking its coherence with facts which are themselves ideal in character. Being true to the facts, then, is a matter of cohering with them. If it is true that the cat is on the mat, it is true because that judgement is coherent with other true related judgements (whether or not entertained by a mind) which are part of reality as a whole. Our true judgements and the facts to which they are true are all true by virtue of coherence. As Bradley put it

> facts . . . are true, we may say, just so far as they work, just so far as they contribute to the order of experience. . . . And there is no 'fact' which possesses an absolute right. . . . It is all a question of relative contribution to my known world-order.
>
> (1914: 210–11)

Idealist metaphysics will not appeal to everyone, to say the least. However, I shall not evaluate the coherence theory on metaphysical grounds. While I do not reject metaphysics out of hand, I think that a discussion of metaphysical issues would be neither necessary nor useful in this connection. That the universe is a totally interconnected whole, and that it is ideal in character, may or may not be true, but these are not really necessary presuppositions of a coherence theory of truth. Indeed, certain of the logical positivists, who most assuredly did reject metaphysics out of hand, accepted the coherence theory of truth (e.g. Hempel (1935), as one among several). After all, as these positivists argued, since we cannot reach beyond our perceptions to any hypothetical underlying reality, we clearly cannot check our beliefs against any such thing. The positivists specifically tied truth and meaning to real or possible verification, and held that we can only check our beliefs, observations, experiences, and whatever, against one another.[3] Whether or not reality at large is ideal, our awareness of it is so. The key question about a statement's truth, then, is still one of how it fits into a general body of truths. So, according to these positivists as well as the idealists, the coherence theory provides not just a criterion but the definition of truth. Whatever their views on metaphysics, checking a statement against the facts is still a matter of coherence.

HOW FIRM A COHERENCE?

Before going on to consider objections, let us first take a closer look at what coherence is supposed to amount to. By way of entry, I shall start by asking whether a coherence theory rules out all indeterminacy in the world. Does quantum mechanics, for instance, run counter to the coherence theory in claiming that certain events, such as certain changes of energy levels in electrons, are indeterminate? Whatever the electrons do would appear to be consistent among themselves and with the rest of our knowledge, but the type of coherence required by the coherence theory amounts to much more than apparent consistency. Some sort of cohesiveness and comprehensiveness is involved. As to what more is specifically required, I suggest that idealist and logical-positivist coherentists have different conceptions of coherence, which give us different answers about truth. As Bradley explains the idealist conception of coherence,

> Truth is an ideal expressive of the Universe, at once coherent and comprehensive. It must not conflict with itself, and there must be no suggestion which fails to fall inside it. Perfect truth in short must realize the idea of a systematic whole.

> (1914: 223)

Truth, then, is an organic whole which, as Joachim puts it,

> is such that all its constituent elements reciprocally involve one another, or reciprocally determine one another's being as contributory features in a single concrete meaning. The elements thus cohering constitute a whole which may be said to control the reciprocal adjustment of its elements, as an end controls its constituent means.

> (1906: section 22)

Somewhat later Blanshard sums it up for us, saying that truth is

> coherent in a double sense, first in being consistent through-

21

out; in spite of apparent incongruities, secondly in being interdependent throughout, that is, so ordered that every fact was connected necessarily with others and ultimately with all.

(1962: 91)

Seemingly, then, if we really did understand that flower in the crannied wall, we would know about all quantum events. All truth or falsity would be necessary truth or necessary falsity, with apparent contingency really being misunderstood logical/material determinacy.

Some would find such a conclusion objectionable, and some would not. However, we could not justly conclude that the claims of the coherence theory are refuted on the grounds that there really are indeterminacies in the world, on the quantum level or otherwise, even if such indeterminacies could be established. There may well be such indeterminacies, but that would merely indicate that the one and only fact, the totally interconnected Absolute, was undergoing indeterminable change as a whole. Every time that an indeterminate quantum event occurred, our exemplar flower and the whole universe would spontaneously change its identity. It does seem rather strange that we should change our identity every time that an electron did something unpredictable in the Andromeda Galaxy. (Do identities change instantaneously, or do identity-changes only propagate outwards at the speed of light? Do not ask *me*.) Strict determinism seems much less startling, and so does the idea of a less rigidly structured universe, yet this tale is not logically absurd. At best, though, it could show only that the truth of certain soon-to-happen quantum events is coherent not with this reality but only with a system which does not yet exist and which is not fully coherent with this one. Whatever we decide about such things, I think it would be risky to tie our definition of truth to any particular theory of the nature of reality. Setting aside speculations about spontaneous and indeterminable future events, though, the fact remains that on the idealist conception of coherence, all present truth, to be truth, must be necessary truth, with apparent contingency being only a measure of our ignorance.

In their own way the logical-positivist coherentists also stressed cohesiveness and comprehensiveness as well as consistency, though for them questions of determinacy – particularly metaphysical questions – posed no real problems. Nothing rests on any doctrine of internal relations, nothing on a claim that things, events, and judgements/sentences have, individually or collectively, only limited and incomplete identity and even that only with reference to all the rest of the universe. Our judgements about flowers in walls have to fit into a truth structure which is consistent, and as comprehensive as is feasible, and mature consideration may lead us to conclude that we had been hallucinating when we thought we saw a flower in the wall. Yet there is no claim that we could derive the whole truth about the rest of the universe given the flower, nor is there even a claim that we could derive the whole truth about the flower (let alone about quantum events) from the rest of the universe. While truths, including those about the flower, must fit together with other truths, there is no claim made one way or another about whether the truths are *completely* mutually determining. It may be that while we can make quite a shrewd guess about what is on one piece of the jigsaw puzzle, given the surrounding pieces, we cannot know *exactly* what is on each particular piece except by looking at it. It may be that certain truths, or, more realistically, certain bodies of truths, are only loosely determined by surrounding truths. They are contingent, and we can know their truth, if at all, only by checking on them (or their very near neighbours). If we cannot look at a problematic piece of the puzzle, or cannot see it well enough, then that is that.

Interpreted this way, the positivists are allowing, though not specifically advocating, a view of truth and reality which is rather less rigid than that of the idealists. For the latter, reality has a determinate nature and our knowledge of it becomes increasingly determinate as it increasingly approaches reality. In contrast, the looser scheme suggested above has, as it were, not the rigid structure of a perfect crystal but the flexible yet coherent structure of a working ecosystem. Truths are true in context, according to this scheme, but some truths are much more localized. Now, it does seem at least possible that it is possible that some truths (or falsities) might not be rigidly tied to everything else in the universe, even though true or false in context as a matter of local coherence. Whether reality actually is that way is a matter which need not detain us.

What is a relevant question is whether there can be any truths apart from coherence – which would of course be fatal to any coherence theory. Like the idealist, the logical positivists answer in the negative, though not quite for the same reasons. With their verificationist principles, there is no question of reality independent of our real or potential knowledge of it. However, this seems to leave 'holes' in the system in the sense that some seemingly meaningful statements about things are not true or false or even meaningful at all, though they would be meaningful and true or false were verification procedures possible. Even so, that our knowledge about some things is somewhat indeterminate does not indicate in positivist-coherentist eyes that there is a gap between coherent knowledge and actual fact, with coherence therefore not being the *whole* story about truth. To them, the idea that there was such a thing as *the* truth, independent truth, would be metaphysical nonsense. If more than one possible fact fits in with our (real or possible) observations, and with whatever else we have adequate warrant in believing, then the alternatives have equal claim and it is meaningless to ask which one is really true. If we must choose, we might as well go along with what other people, particularly scientists, have opted for, but it is silly, according to the positivists, to imagine that there is truth beyond the reach of verification.

As it happens, few people accept logical positivism these days, fewer, I should think, than those who accept idealism. One problem is that of giving an account of the verification principle that holds water. (Is the principle that meaning depends on possible verification logically true? Is it otherwise verifiable? What, in fact, does it mean? Etc.) In whatever form, their reduction of meaning to verifiability does seem somewhat facile. While many philosophers were happy enough to agree with the logical positivists in ruling out metaphysics as illegitimate, there has been considerable reluctance to accept the far less attractive implication that scientific theories are never true.

There are other awkward cases as well, such as those concerning the inaccessible past: at just what minute did the last trilobite die? Is there some unknowable truth about that? Was there ever one? Suppose there were some truths which were not verifiable. Would that demolish the coherence theory by indicating that some things were true or false, though not cohering with the system as a whole? Only if we equate cohering with verifiably cohering, but it is not evident that we need go that far. A scientific theory might be true even though we could never verify it conclusively, being true because of its actual coherence with the general scheme of things. We might have good reason to believe it on the evidence, because it fits with everything we can check. It could be tied coherently with all sorts of things. That does not seem far-fetched, but what about the last trilobite? It must have died at some time, from some cause – or so I cannot help believing – though it might be utterly impossible to determine when or why, particularly if quantum indeterminacy has been eroding the traces of causal chains over the intervening several million years. Could the truth of the matter still be a matter of coherence? It could on the idealist account, and even apart from idealism, I should think it might perhaps be possible to contrive some conception of coherence which would allow such a thing to be true by virtue of coherence with its surrounding truths. However, that would take coherence a long way from us and our awareness, and from any possibly useful criterion of truth. At this point, let us turn to questions about what criteria of truth have to do with truth.

CRITERIA AND TRUTH

It has been suggested by many (e.g. by Russell (1910), who made such suggestions in connection with both coherentists and pragmatists, and more recently by Rescher (1973)) that the coherence theory gives the, or at least a, criterion of truth, while the nature of truth is said to be something else, usually correspondence with fact. Things are true, then, if they correspond with facts (or whatever else is called for), and checking for coherence is how we find out whether that is so. Accordingly, it is often charged that coherence theorists mistake sign for substance, criterion for what it is a criterion of. As we shall see, a similar charge is frequently made concerning the pragmatists. Coherentists and pragmatists alike quite deny that they are guilty of confusing anything. Rather, they stoutly maintain that they are refusing to separate that which is, when properly understood, inseparable. About the pragmatists and their ideas about truth, I shall have more to say subsequently. Now, I shall consider the point in connection with the coherence theory of truth.

I am not convinced that coherence is the only criterion of truth, and I suspect that it may sometimes not be workable in cases where other criteria do work, though many would not share my doubts. Of that, more later. In any case, it is generally agreed that coherence is at least frequently decisive. We know, for example, that there is a cup of coffee on the table because that judgement coheres with the world of our awareness as a whole. A similar judgement based on qualitatively similar sensory experiences might be determined to be an illusion or hallucination or dream, because of a different relationship with its own wider context. Whatever the apparent facts, or apparent correspondence with them, coherence settles the matter. Against the coherence theory of truth, however, there remains the claim that while coherence is how we determine that the cup is really on the table, its really being there is what constitutes the truth of the matter. Blanshard argues in reply (1939: vol. II, 268) that coherence could not be such a universally satisfactory criterion of truth, as he claims it is, unless the criterion actually constituted truth. If something else, perhaps correspondence, constituted truth, why would the judgement which coheres *always* be the one which is true?

Some criteria are clearly stronger than others. In response to Blanshard's argument, Nicholas Rescher (1973: 29–31) distinguished *guaranteeing* criteria and *authorizing* criteria, as he calls them, of which only the former are foolproof. The latter may have their uses, however, often being largely reliable and much easier to apply. Of course, any definition will yield a correlative guaranteeing criterion, the criterion being that of whether the definition is met. For instance, if being acid is defined as having a pH less than exactly 7, then whether it has a pH of less than that is obviously a guaranteeing criterion. Yet whether it turns litmus paper red is an authorizing criterion which is almost (though not quite) invariably correct, and very much easier to apply in practice. Similarly, any definition of truth yields a correlative guaranteeing criterion, whether or not it is one which can easily be used. It might for instance be maintained that correspondence defines truth and provides the only guaranteeing criterion, though not a criterion which can always easily be applied directly, whereas the authorizing criterion of coherence is very useful in practice. That is Rescher's position. According to his diagnosis, Blanshard has mistakenly taken as a guaranteeing criterion what is really an almost but not quite invariably correct authorizing criterion. Now, whether coherence is a universally applicable criterion is one of the points at issue. If in some cases we could not appeal to coherence as a criterion of truth, then we might well suspect that there is something more to truth than coherence, even though coherence might be a very useful authorizing criterion in a great many cases. Yet if coherence must invariably be a guaranteeing criterion of truth, then as Blanshard observes it would be most remarkable, to say the least, if the nature of truth were anything different. In the next section we shall consider whether considerations concerning coherence can always give us the right answer about truth. I shall conclude that in some cases this is not sufficient.

I might add that while Rescher holds that coherence does not constitute truth, he offers a detailed discussion of how coherence-analysis offers a widely useful and very effective means of determining what is true. He points out that in our attempts to deal with the world around us, we often find ourselves in the position of having to deal with very imperfect data or presumptive data, which may be incomplete or inconsistent. Where data are incomplete we can explore further. Where (presumptive) data are inconsistent, as when we must sort through rival accounts or competing theories, we must attempt to pull together a maximally plausible coherent story. As Rescher puts it (1973: 41), 'this organization of discordant data into a coherent system of truths is akin to finding the "right" solution to a jigsaw puzzle with excess pieces.' He offers some interesting and worthwhile ideas about how we can go about getting the data to add up sensibly. To start with, we must find maximally consistent subsets (m.c.s.) of the discordant data (these being subsets to which we cannot add further members from the data-base in question without generating inconsistency). That in itself does not solve the problem, however, as there may be several mutually incompatible m.c.s. of the data-base we are trying to sort out. The problem is to determine which story to believe. Not all consistent stories are equally plausible. What we must do is to assess the plausibility of each m.c.s. as a function of the plausibilities – not to be confused with probabilities – of its component members. At some length, Rescher discusses various strategies for doing this. This is not a topic which we can pursue here, though I do think that he makes a significant contribution to a neglected subject, that of inference from imperfect premisses.[4] Here we have yet further reason to believe that coherence offers useful means for determining truth – or at least for getting closer to it. Whether or not it is the only criterion, or the only authorizing criterion, it is a useful criterion. Let us now turn to objections which have been levelled against the coherence theory as an account of the nature of truth.

SOME OBJECTIONS

An apparently very strong objection against the coherence theory is that there might be more than one coherent system, equally consistent, equally interconnected by mutual implication, and both of sufficiently wide scope (White 1967; Woozley 1949). This is a problem frequently faced by historians, scientists, and members of juries. When more than one story hangs together, how are we to chose between them? If the two stories are compatible there is no problem, as they can be united in a wider coherence. The problem comes when different seemingly coherent systems are incompatible. Are we to say that *both* of two incompatible systems are each true? Maybe so, but those would be two totally independent worlds having absolutely nothing to do with one another, and the question would remain of which world we actually live in. Something must be true in *this* world, and it cannot be two incompatible things. We cannot rest with just reaching incompatible yet internally coherent conclusions, claiming that they are all true in some world. If we are to avoid an *embarras de choix* between different systems, we must find some method for distinguishing *the* real system from other possible systems. In one way or another, coherence theorists have referred us to experience or observation as the final determinant. The question is not one of what might be true in the abstract, but one of what is true, coherent with the reality of which we are aware. The abstract is not where we live. The Absolute, to be real and true, must cohere with the world, as it is, of which we are aware.

It is often thought that in referring us to experience or observation, coherentists are having recourse to something other than coherence, something quite like correspondence to fact, as being definitive of truth. This impression is reinforced by Bradley (1914: 325) when he writes that 'Truth to be truth must be true of something, and this something itself is not truth'. This seems to concede that, sooner or later, coherence must be validated by something more substantive than mere coherence. His remarks have often been interpreted this way (e.g. Haack 1978). But what is this something of which truth is true? Bradley warns us that we must be careful not to misinterpret this. Certainly, it is a fact about us that we are limited beings whose beliefs and awareness of the world are limited and incomplete. We cannot span the whole of reality. Whatever may be true of the Absolute, our much-smaller-scale judgements (the great bulk of them, anyway) do not wear their truth or falsity on their sleeve. So long as our *whats* fall short of being *thats*, and so lack a sufficient degree of clarity, we cannot just determine the truth or falsity of judgements by directly inspecting them. Nor can we exhaustively trace out their coherence or the lack of it with the rest of reality, which is really the same thing so far as the idealists are concerned. The reality of it is all right in front of us, but we cannot grasp it as it is. So, instead of determining their truth or falsity by tracing out their interrelationships with the rest of reality, we directly compare our judgements with fact. The coffee cup, whatever it is in detail, is on the table, whatever that amounts to in detail. As Bradley tells us a few pages later,

> From a better point of view . . . No judgement can refer to anything beyond itself, since in every judgement the ultimate Reality is actually present. In any judgement on the other hand this Reality is incomplete, and there will therefore be a difference between the Reality present and the truth actually reached in the judgement. But this difference remains within the object, and for truth to pass on or to refer beyond that is impossible.
>
> (1914: 331)

So, we might say that while for practical purposes correspondence with fact is an indispensable criterion of truth, coherence is none the less the nature of truth.

There is – there can be – one and only one ultimate reality, and that is the world of our experience as it truly is. It may be that there is more than one system partially conceivable by us which is, or which appears to be, coherent and consistent with the world of our limited awareness. If so, we can decide between them only by extending our awareness by thought and experience. However, it is asking too much of the coherentist to ask to be provided with a test by means of which we can tell how it will all turn out in the end, before we have traced it all out. We might just as well, and just as unfairly, demand of the correspondence theorist that we be given a test by means of which we can decide between different propositions which might correspond with the facts, before we have actually checked them out. For the coherence theorist as well as for the correspondence theorist, and, indeed, for anyone in their right mind, the real world is the one in which we happen to live.

So far, objections appear not to have overturned the coherence theory. Yet can it actually be that easy? Why is it that we pay attention to those facts, apparently simple and apparently brute, of direct awareness? Perhaps they will serve as the foundation for our eventually much more coherent awareness of the world, but can that *really* be why we concern ourselves with them in the first place? The plain fact is that we do not pay attention to them initially because they serve to verify coherence or are a first step toward it. As infants we pay attention to our mother because she is important to us, and we think 'Mummy there' or something of the sort because that, at that time, is very important for us, not because it is a clue to the ultimate nature of the universe. The infant does not think about coherence or truth, but about its mother. Most of us most of the time do not think about whether our judgements meet some definition of truth – few of us have a definition – or about whether they are validated by some systematic test. Rather, we think about those things we do think about, and accept some judgements as true while rejecting others as false. The reasons why we do one or the other, when we do, have to do with the judgement and what it is about, not because of something further. In such cases, then, to all appearances, coherence provides neither conception nor test of truth. Can we conclude on that basis that the coherence theory does not give us the nature of truth?

May it nevertheless be that the coherence theory gives us the nature of truth in the sense that coherence is what makes true things true, even if we are not aware of that at the start or ever after? We might believe that the cup is on the table, believing it because we can see it there, and we might be correct, even though we were totally unaware that ultimately this amounts to coherence. Amount to coherence it most assuredly does, the coherentists urge, because all facts are theory-laden (and therefore coherence-laden). That which is true or false has meaning only in context and is true or false only in context. The cup has a role as a cup and is recognizable as being one only in terms of a wider system, and the like applies to everything else involved. There are no bits in isolation, no independent truths. We cannot avoid facing up to this contextual dependence by taking the line that it is only judgements, including those about our basic experiences, which are context-dependent, while our basic experiences themselves are simply given, serving as an independent foundation for coherent superstructures. As we have already noted, since Kant philosophy has grown to recognize that, perceptually as well as conceptually, facts, including our most basic experiences, are context-dependent to some degree. In spite of the best efforts of many subsequent thinkers, the myth of the incorrigibility and the atomicity of sense-data remains only mythical. Bradley tells us that

I do not believe that we can make ourselves independent of these non-relational data.

But . . . no given fact is sacrosanct. With every fact of perception or memory a modified interpretation is in principle possible, and no such fact therefore is given free from possibility of error.

(1914: 203–4)

Evidently, there is no way in which we can break through the circle of contextual dependence to immutable fact.

Even so, Bradley did have to concede that 'I do not believe that we can make ourselves independent of these non-relational data'. That remains the rub for the coherence theory. As I would put it, while our facts, to be our facts, are system-dependent, our systems to be true must none the less be fact-dependent. We cannot pull ourselves up by our bootstraps, no matter how coherent they may be. Just what is it we are fitting, or attempting to fit, into a coherent system? We start, as we have remarked, with the fact that *the* system of truth and reality is the one in which we are living – that which we are seeing from the *inside*. That we are inside *this* reality is the given fact upon which truth stands. In however inchoate a form it is given, it is given. While reality is undoubtedly consistent, and coherent to at least a considerable degree, its givenness is more than mere coherence. That is true even if our awareness of it must eventually cohere with it.

This needs some elaboration in connection with the non-idealist coherentists. As I have presented it, consideration of these objections was primarily phrased with reference to the idealists. Their overall position demanded that, so to speak, the *whats* which cohered (and corresponded) with *thats* would, were our awareness to advance that far, eventually merge with them. The logical-positivist coherentists with their anti-metaphysical stance could hardly take that line. The line they did take, however, came to pretty much the same thing in effect. According to them, we start with the truths of immediate awareness which we augment with the reports of others including, in particular, the findings of the scientific community. As Hempel tells us,

the occurrence of certain statements in the protocol of an observer or in a scientific book is regarded as an empirical fact, and . . . the concept of truth may be characterized . . . as a sufficient agreement between the system of acknowledged protocol-statements and the logical consequences which may be deduced from the statement and other statements which are already adopted.

(1935: 54)

Of possible coherent systems, the best selection is that which best coheres with our knowledge in the state to which we have been able to advance it. The positivist cannot tell, any more than anyone else, what the final truth will turn out to be, but as we expand our knowledge we come closer to the ultimate coherent truth. The idealists maintain on metaphysical grounds that there can be only one ultimately coherent reality. The positivists maintained the same thing on epistemological grounds: if we cannot decide between two possible systems on the grounds of some possible experience, they are really not different after all. Either way, there is only one coherent reality: this one. What it is we are still trying to find out. Since our knowledge of the world is incomplete, the systems we develop are incomplete and admit of alternatives, but this is so whether or not we maintain a coherence theory.

None the less the same insuperable problem arises here for the coherence theory, the problem of distinguishing a true coherent system from other coherent systems, though it arises in logical positivist form. Where do those protocol-statements come from, and why should we pay particular attention to those of scientists? Hempel, with reference to two of his fellow positivist-coherentists, writes:

What characteristics are there according to Carnap's and Neurath's views, by which to distinguish the true protocol statements of our science from the false ones of a fairy tale?

As Carnap and Neurath emphasize, there is indeed no formal, no logical difference between the two compared systems, but an *empirical* one. The system of protocol statements which we call true, and to which we refer in every day life and science, may only be characterized by the historical fact, that it is the system which is actually adopted by mankind, and especially by the scientists of our cultural circle; and the 'true' statements in general may be characterized as those which are sufficiently supported by that system of actually adopted protocol statements.

(ibid.: 56–7)

It appears to me that the positivist-coherentist thesis self-destructs at this point. The case rests, we are told, on an empirical fact. Not, as we might expect, the empirical fact that certain empirical statements are known by observation (our own or that of others) to be true, but the empirical fact that they are the ones which are part of our socio-scientific culture. On this account there is the given fact that we live in this culture and not some other one we might coherently imagine. That is a given fact. Moreover, we ask, why do we accept the testimony of scientific experts and not that of witch-doctors (or metaphysicians)? In part, the answer given is that this is because what scientists say more generally coheres with the facts of observation. We have also to take into account the fact that individual observation-statements are corrigible and can be wrong for one reason or another. We must assess how they fit with other statements – an undertaking to which scientists and logicians contribute. Yet the fact remains that we are in this world. Other systems might also be coherent but they are not to the point. We must try to achieve a maximal fit with empirical reality. While individual observation-statements are corrigible, the mass of experience is insistent. We must come to an accommodation with the empirical world in which we are. We may sort statements out largely or entirely on the grounds of coherence, but it is this world with which we must deal, and it is this on which our true statements rest. So, while coherence may provide a criterion for which statements to accept, we accept some and reject others as being true of *this* world.

On balance, then, I am inclined to think that there is something more to truth than the coherence theory, in whatever version, provides for. At some point truth must rest on the alogically given. This is so even though coherence theorists do us a valuable service in pointing out that true beliefs and statements (and what they are true of) can only be, and be what they are, in a system. Before we go on to consider alternative theories, though, I think it would repay us to consider some further points in connection with the coherence theory.

DEGREES OF TRUTH – A SIDE-ISSUE

Let us now take time to consider the controversial doctrine that truth is a matter of degree. Degree of truth is not to be confused with probability or plausibility. It is not a question of how probable or plausible it is that a judgement is true, but of how true it is. Historically, this doctrine has closely been associated with the coherence account of the nature of truth as expounded by the idealists. While objections have been raised against the coherence theory on this score, it is, as I shall argue, essentially a side-issue. The doctrine of degrees of truth is not a necessary component of a coherence theory of truth, and was not a doctrine of the logical-positivist coherentists. Nor is the doctrine even a necessary component of a coherence theory held by Absolute idealists. Those coherentists who held the doctrine of degrees of truth could have maintained quite the same substantive points about truth without formulating them in terms of degrees of truth. Not only is it a side-issue, it is one which has become quite confused. By looking into the matter we can, I believe, gain a clearer understanding of the coherence theory and of truth itself.

Why did they maintain the doctrine of degrees of truth? The idealist coherentists are concerned to deny that either reality or our knowledge of it is composed of distinct units, like individual bricks combined to form an edifice. Metaphysically, it is held that the world is one whole, with no separable or independent parts. Given the ideal nature of that whole, this implies that epistemologically, truth is one whole, with no separable or independent parts. But granted that only the Absolute can stand alone, why proclaim that an individual judgement is a scrap of truth which can be only partially true? Must something be the whole truth in order to be wholly true? The central issue here is that of what is involved in being, or not being, wholly true. We must be careful. For the idealist coherentist the whole truth is not something *in addition* to the scrap of truth – there *is* nothing in addition to it. Rather, whole truth is that scrap of truth in its full truth and reality. Scraps are scraps only in the incompleteness of our understanding. Partial truth is partially understood truth, not an understood part distinct from other parts. Now, to take an example, an advanced geometer and a beginning pupil might each accept the postulates of Euclidean geometry, yet their understandings would be vastly different. They might both believe that figures formed by the diagonal and two adjacent sides of a parallelogram are proper triangles. However, the geometer's understanding of *that* truth is much deeper than that of the pupil, though we use the same words to describe their belief(s). The pupil might at the same time even think it possible that some triangles, perhaps large ones or small ones or funny-shaped ones, might have interior angles that added up to a bit more or a bit less than two right angles. The geometer could no more think this than think that one plus one might equal seven. In general, the geometer's beliefs about figures formed by taking the diagonal of a parallelogram, and all other beliefs about triangles, have greater *depth* than do the nominally similar beliefs of the pupil. The concept of triangularity has greater meaning for the former than for the latter. A belief about triangles, as understood by the geometer, has a much greater degree of coherence with the system of which it is a portion. It is not just that it is more rigidly tied with system, but that there is greater interpenetration of meaning. Similarly, while I may believe, correctly, so far as that goes, that a given plant is an *idiospermum*, my belief has not the same depth of coherent truth as the nominally similar belief of the trained botanist. Flowers in crannied walls are less informative to me. The more deeply coherent belief, so it is claimed, is the more true.

Yet why must we accept the claim that the more deeply understood truth is the more true? Why not just take truth as a yes or no matter of whether a particular judgement meets its particular criterion? To start with, there are no particular truths. Truth is not a one-at-a-time thing, but involves the system as a whole. Nor can truth be a matter of whether some abstract criterion is met. Truth is not an abstract matter. Rather, truth is a matter of how a concrete judgement fits into an entire system, and fit is a matter of degree. If truth is coherence, then, seemingly, degree of coherence is degree of truth.

We have come to what I believe is a question of labelling, a matter of whether it is preferable to describe degree of coherence as degree of truth. I think that to do so obscures important distinctions. Not only is coherence (and incoherence) a matter of degree, it is a matter of kind. Coherence, as understood in the coherence theory of truth, requires both consistency and comprehensiveness, and a judgement may prove inadequate either by being inconsistent with surrounding truth or by falling short of comprehensiveness. The pupil's belief that some (Euclidean) triangles might add up to other than two right angles suffers from the first of these failings, while his or her knowledge of what a Euclidean triangle *is*, which permits such an error, suffers from a lack of comprehensiveness. The two different failings here are subject to two different remedies: in one case we improve things by getting rid of incompatibility among our ideas, in the other we increase our depth of understanding of significance. It seems to me to be sweeping important distinctions under the rug to use the same label, 'largely false', for both beliefs.

Those who maintain the doctrine of degrees of truth, however, make a further claim. Not only are our judgements incomplete but, it is claimed, they distort the truth. We distort by wrongly limiting. There are limits to the understanding even of the advanced geometer and the learned botanist. The truths of geometry, for instance, may be expressions of higher-order logical truths – ultimately, The Truth – with which the geometer is not exhaustively familiar. With our limited understanding, everyone's judgements, falling short of the Absolute, presuppose unreal boundaries and distorted distinctions. Indeed, all boundaries are ultimately unreal and all distinctions distorted. Accordingly, idealist coherentists will proclaim that even the advanced geometer's knowledge of triangles is only partially true (and partially false) in that it treats triangles (or geometry) as if it were a distinct and separate subject-matter. This seems to me to be too severe. To employ certain distinctions for the purposes of a given judgement is not to assert that the world actually divides that way, nor is it to claim that what we say captures the full nature of anything. 'Euclidean triangle' may not be an independent category, or the best one for all purposes. We need not claim so when we find it useful to talk about them. As I see it, our means of reference and description is like a spotlight which we shine on a stage (this is discussed in a later chapter). What we see within the circle of illumination will depend on the nature and angle of the light, and it will also depend on what is there in that area of the stage and also on things which are out of sight. We need not think, and we do not falsely claim, that the stage actually divides along the line of illumination. Some lights are less illuminating than others, but they are not false because they fail to light up the entire universe. It seems that the idealist coherentists are again over-stressing the whole. While there can be no part without the whole, portions of the whole must have some shape, even if a purely dependent shape, for there to be the whole. We can say meaningful and true things about what shape they have. Even though I find the doctrine of partial truth and partial falsity more obscuring than clarifying, however, I think that little damage is done so long as we bear in mind the different ways in which judgements are said to be partially true or partially false.

While I reject the doctrine of degrees of truth, I must also reject an objection to the coherence theory which centres on that doctrine.

Bertrand Russell (1910: 133), following the standard philosophical tactic of trying to turn an argument or conclusion back upon itself, argued that if only the Absolute is absolutely true, then the claims of the coherence theory are themselves not entirely true and need not be accepted. The coherence theory of truth, then, evidently refutes itself. Setting aside the question of whether a coherence theory of any stripe really does demand a doctrine of degrees of truth, let us consider the reply of those who accept that doctrine. The idealist-coherentist reply is that Russell confused different ways in which truth can be merely partial (e.g. Bradley 1914: 114–18, and elsewhere). Some partial truths are only conditionally true, and so ultimately require revision. Newtonian mechanics provides a good example. While largely true in most of its applications, it requires revision for general application. On the other hand, that there is a coffee cup on the table before me as I write this is (take my word for it) unconditionally true, as far as it goes. It is merely partially true, but only in the sense that it is incomplete (and because it naively suggests that the cup is a separable and independent item), and not because it requires revision to be unconditionally true. It does not give the whole coherent picture, which is to be found only in the Absolute as a whole. As we noted above, since I do not know all about that coffee cup – else I *would* know the Absolute as a whole – *my* knowledge that there is a coffee cup on the table before me is only a partially understood scrap of incomplete information. None the less, that partial truth is true within the limits of our understanding. The situation with respect to the coherence theory of truth is, the coherentists insist, analogous with the case of the coffee cup rather than that of Newtonian mechanics. The coherence theory is said to be unconditionally true, yet a statement of it does not encompass the Absolute in its whole nature, and therefore it is said to be only partially true. The more we understand it and so the more we understand reality at large, the more meaning it has for us and the truer it is in our understanding. (And what truth does it have in itself? Everything in itself is the Absolute, and so is absolutely true in itself.) Yet while a statement of the coherence theory is only partially true in this sense, this does not impeach the content which it does have. The theory is not self-refuting, therefore, it just calls on us to understand it better. Russell's objection misses the mark. For a further discussion of degrees of truth, from a coherentist point of view, see Joachim (1906: sections 30–44).

While I have concluded that the coherence theory of truth does not provide an adequate account of the nature of truth, I think we should recognize those things concerning which the theory is correct. Certainly we would do well to try to accommodate its insights into our eventual conclusions. It is quite correct that there can be truths only in context. It is also correct that portions of reality are, and are what they are, only in context. Moreover, considerations of coherence very often provide us with a criterion of truth and means of verification. And as Rescher points out, coherence-analysis can help us to proceed in the face of imperfect data, and to broaden our understanding and discover new truths. Again, I would also concede that the idealist coherentists were moving in a right direction with their claim that the truth-value of a proposition is at least in some part a function of what its meaning is for the one who entertains it, though I would make something else out of the insight. Even so, while coherence theories have these things to be said for them, I think that we must somehow accommodate part as well as whole, independent fact as well as integrated system. But it must be *as well as* rather than *in place of*. Certainly we must be wary of treating facts as being so individual and self-contained that they lose both their relatedness to us and their place in the whole world. Let us now turn to consider correspondence theories, which conceived of individual truths being true by virtue of their relation to independent fact. One of the questions we would do well to keep in mind is that of whether the correspondence theorists pushed the philosophical pendulum too far in another direction.

3

CORRESPONDENCE

The correspondence theory of truth, *as developed by Moore, Russell, and Wittgenstein (in the* Tractatus), *is investigated. In its different versions it has severe difficulties concerning the nature of the correspondence relation. It is concluded that accounts based on structural similarity are not viable. Pictorial or other similarities rest on the truth-stating function of language, and not the truth-stating function on the similarity. Correspondence theories not only have difficulties in explaining the correspondence relation, but also in explaining those things which are supposed to be joined in the relationship.*

Let us now take it that coherence theories do not provide an adequate account of the nature of truth, and consider the view that the nature of truth lies in some sort of a relation between those things which are true or false and facts which make them true or false. We are to suppose that our experience provides us with brute facts which can validate some of our beliefs and serve as the foundation for our knowledge of the world. As William James viewed the matter,

> Bradley . . . at the dividing of the ways, where thought gives out, instead of coming back and taking up the alogically given, *tel quel*, as an absolute element of knowledge, . . . says 'that' kind of knowledge is . . . not for the 'philosopher', whose escape from the intellectual incomprehensibilities can only be further flight in the foreward direction, where an Absolute must do the work.
>
> (1909a: 328)

While the idealists continued to pursue the universal Absolute, James and many others opted for the alogically given and absolute element of brute facts. This I believe to be the correct option, as I have said, because if nothing else, we must at least start from the fact that we live in this world, the one we experience from the inside.

The *correspondence theory of truth* is one of those theories which have tried to account for truth in terms of a relationship between those things which are true and the brute facts which make them so. There are other accounts as well, such as the pragmatic theory favoured by James. We shall subsequently consider the other major theories of truth, after reviewing the correspondence theory. Certainly there is a great deal of intuitive plausibility to a correspondence theory in that it tells us that what is true is true because it fits (corresponds to) the facts. If I state or believe that a coffee cup is on the table, what I say or believe is true because it fits the fact that there *is* a coffee cup on the table. If I say that there is an elephant on the table, that does not fit the facts. These things are true or false by virtue of how what they say fits with what they say them about. What could be simpler or more obvious? The coffee cup is or is not on the table, without our having to concern ourselves with how that fits in with everything else or with some ineffable Absolute. Even so, while the correspondence theory as so presented may appear to be obviously correct, it comes to appear much less plausible and much less meaningful when we try to work out just what it actually amounts to. What, to start with, is this correspondence relationship which, when it obtains, makes true things true? That needs to be explained. Moreover, we must ask what is related in the correspondence relationship. True beliefs and statements (or propositions, or whatever the relevant truth-bearers are said to be), we are told, correspond to the facts. But what *are* facts? What do they have to do with coffee cups and other things in the world? If my belief corresponds to the *fact that* there is a coffee cup on the table, that seems to make the fact that which is stated, which is then true because it is true. Moreover, if we are to explain truth in terms of correspondence, we must give some account of what those things are which may or may not correspond to the facts. There are severe problems here. Indeed, as we shall see, much of truth theory, and not just the correspondence theory, has been undermined by conceptual muddles about what is related and about how they are related. In this chapter my primary concern shall be on the relation of correspondence.

40

G. E. MOORE AND CORRESPONDENCE

After a brief initial dalliance with idealism, Moore became disenchanted with it because of what he saw as its obscurities and absurdities. He wanted a philosophy which was more consistent with straightforward common sense and accordingly he led a philosophical revolt, later joined by Russell, against idealism. As one would therefore expect, he wanted a theory of truth which would not get us lost in (to put it pejoratively) the infinite fog of an ineffable Absolute. Moore presented the first modern version of a correspondence theory of truth in a series of lectures which he delivered in 1910–11.[1] According to his theory, whether a belief about some feature of reality is true depends on reality and the relation to it of the belief. Whether my belief that the coffee cup is on the table is true is not just a matter of the nature, in depth, of my belief, but depends on the cup and the table and their relationship in the factual state of affairs. Of course Bradley and just about everyone else would agree to that much, give or take a few possible quibbles about wording. If that were all there were to the correspondence theory, it would be as uncontroversial as it would be empty and useless. The key question is that of just how it is that the factual world makes a belief true – or, alternatively, how it is that true beliefs relate to the factual world. According to Moore,

> Every belief has the property of *referring to* [later he uses the term 'corresponding to'] some different fact, every different belief to a particular fact; and . . . *the* property which we name when we call it [the belief] true, is the property which can be expressed by saying that *the* fact to which it refers *is*.
>
> (1953: 267)

Such an account still leaves us with many unanswered questions. To start with, what are facts, and what is the nature of this relation of referring/corresponding between a true belief and the fact which makes it true? For that matter, just what is it which is said to be true or false?

Facts, whatever they are, give truth a solid grounding in the world and thereby make true beliefs true. While they do not exist in the way that physical objects do, they objectively are physical objects, Moore tells us (ibid.: 306–9), and that they are gives truth its worldly purchase. Trying to give an account of facts, though, gives Moore and other correspondentists some serious problems.

41

Standing as they do at the junction of words and world, facts seem to be tied to our cognition and yet seem to be independent. On the one hand, facts are stated, and it may be a fact *that* whatever. Yet again, facts are thought to be hard features of the world, whether or not stated or even known. Moore points out that the belief, the proposition believed, and the fact which make it true, all have the same name. If I believe of a given tree that it is an oak tree, the proposition believed is that it is an oak tree, and, if my belief is true, the fact is that it is an oak tree. Even so, he distinguishes the fact from other things which have the same name, as we may have the fact without the others, or vice versa. Yet confusingly, Moore prefers to call facts 'truths', in honour of their cognitive significance, though he distinguishes these more independent truths from those things, beliefs and propositions, which are said to be true. No doubt this having a foot in each camp is one thing which makes facts so attractive to him and to other correspondence theorists as the link between words and world. (Indeed, coherence theorists would find much comfort in facts which are cognitively significant, and yet are objective features of reality.) Yet it seems a remarkably lame theory which tells us merely that a belief is true if and only if there is a certain truth-fact (having the same name) to which it refers/corresponds. At best, such a theory would appear to tell us no more than that a belief is true when what is believed is (or names) a truth. Historically, one of the greatest problems for the correspondence theory is to arrive at a formulation which actually asserts something substantial.

Moore gives us very little help here. *Belief* is left as an unanalysed term in the correspondence relationship (ibid.: 266). The same goes for *facts* and *truths* (ibid.: 309). We just know that we have various beliefs, some of which are true and some false. The true ones stand to facts in a relationship which is also left unanalysed. He tells us only that

> [a] belief, if true, has to the fact . . . a certain relation, which that particular belief has to no other fact. . . . I propose to call it the relation of 'correspondence'. . . .

> [T]hese definitions . . . define ['correspondence'] by pointing out *the* relation for which it stands; namely *the* relation which certainly does hold between the belief . . . and the *fact* . . . and which does *not* hold between that precise belief and any other fact. . . . The essential point is to concentrate attention upon

the relation *itself*: to hold it before your mind . . . If you are not acquainted with the relation in the same sort of way as you are acquainted with the colour vermillion [when you hold it before your mind], no amount of words will serve to explain.

(ibid.: 276–9)

He later makes it even more explicit by adding that

I confess I don't know how to describe the property which belongs to all truths [facts] and *only* to truths [facts]: it seems to me a property which can be pointed out and seen, but if it can be analysed, I don't know how to analyse it.

(ibid.: 309)

False beliefs, of course, are those which do not have facts as referents, but that is the most we can say about them. What it comes to is that truth is a matter of beliefs and facts, the nature of which is unanalysed, standing to one another in a relation which he cannot analyse. We just notice the relation, fix it firmly in our mind, and we then know, without being able to explain it, what truth amounts to – just as we know, without being able to explain it, what a colour is. If we cannot do any better than that, we might as well give up on truth theory. In order for such a theory to tell us more, we would have to know what sort of thing these fact-truths are, what correspondence is, and, perhaps in the first instance, what it is which is said to correspond with facts.

RUSSELL AND CORRESPONDENCE

Between 1906 and 1912, Bertrand Russell (1907, 1910, 1912) developed an account of beliefs, facts, and the relationship between them when the belief is true, a relationship which we might construe as being one of structural correspondence. (Indeed, it was Russell who first popularized the term 'correspondence theory of truth'.) The basic idea is that a belief is true if what is associated together in belief is also associated together, in just that way, in fact. If not an elaboration of Moore's theory, Russell's multiple relation theory is at least compatible with it, and it offers an analysis of terms which Moore left unanalysed. Russell analysed belief as a multi-term relation between (1) a person who (2) believes that (3, 4, . . .) whatever, where the 'whatever' part of it comprises various things related together by a relating term. For example, perhaps (1) I (2) believe that (3) Jack (4) is taller than (5) Jill. Beliefs are true when terms (3) and beyond are ordered in the belief as they are ordered in the fact which is the object of the belief. In this case, obviously, the belief is true if Jack is taller than Jill. If the terms are ordered in some other way in the fact (if Jill is taller than Jack), or if one of the terms does not exist (Jack is the real Jill's imaginary unicorn), then the belief is false. Beliefs and facts are said to exist, in this account, but only as real things related together into individual units.

Russell's account of truth is subject to a number of difficulties. One line of objection has focused on the question of the status of negative facts. Is it a fact that Jill is not taller than Jack? That Jack is not standing on her left? That he is not sitting on her right? That they are not both made out of green cheese? Seemingly there must be an infinite number of negative facts about Jack and Jill for an infinite number of possible true negative beliefs to be about. So why should that be a problem? Why not just shrug it off with the thought that there are doubtlessly any number of ways in which things in the world are *not* related, which should surprise no one? The problem for Russell is that facts, including all the negative ones, are themselves things in the world. He is quite insistent about that. Facts are what are there that true beliefs correspond to. They are composed of various things in the world, knit together into a unit by the relation named by the main verb among the factual terms –'is (not) taller than', or whatever. While it is not logically impossible that the world should contain an infinite array of such knit-together negative facts, this does seem a somewhat implausible doctrine.

As I see it, the key problem with Russell's account concerns the status of the relating terms in beliefs and facts. The fact, as we have noted, is knit together into a unit by some relation. A belief is knit together into another unit by its being believed, the relation uniting the fact being one term among the others. On the one hand, the relation of being taller than unites Jack and Jill together to make a unit. On the other hand, that relation, together with Jack and Jill, is knit together by being believed to form a belief. Different units – beliefs and facts – are formed in different ways by different relations. The main verb among the factual terms has quite a different character in the fact-unit than it has in the belief-unit, relating in one case and being one of the relata in the other. It cannot be, therefore, that in a true belief terms (3) and beyond fit together in the belief in the same way that they do in the fact, as one of the terms differs radically.[2] Not only does this difficulty in the account threaten the

44

concept of correspondence, it undermines the very possibility of making sense of the world. If in the belief that so-and-so, the so-and-so is not the same so-and-so as in the fact that so-and-so, how could one ever possibly know whether a belief were true?

We cannot just shunt this issue aside as a mere semantic quibble, and get by with just claiming that when a person believes that so-and-so, the belief is true if there is a fact that so-and-so having the same structure as what is believed. That is not enough. Neither a belief nor a fact is just a pile of terms. They have to be structured in some way. It matters who goes at which end of the 'is taller than' relation. But what does the structuring? The belief is structured mentally by the believer, but what structures the fact? Reality? That could be. Whatever it is, the only way in which such a theory could work is that we could in some way independently specify the structure of the fact, and of the belief, and show that they share the same structure. Failing that, we could only say that the belief and the fact share the same structure only if the belief is true. We would then not be explaining truth in terms of correspondence, but just the opposite. This is not a problem we can ignore, nor can we leave the relation unanalysed. Yet Russell's attempt to analyse it is unsuccessful, as he himself came to realize. He conceded

> the impossibility of putting the subordinate verb on level with its terms as an object term in the belief. That is a point in which I think that the theory of judgement which I set forth once . . . was a little unduly simple, because I did then treat the object verb as if one could put it as just an object like the terms. . . .

> (1918: 226)

If a correspondence theory of truth is going to be of any use at all, we will have to develop a better account of the correspondence relation. Also, if it is a matter of correspondence with fact, as usually it is said to be, we shall need a clearer and better account of what facts are. One thing we will have to work out is what, as it were, facts and facts-that have to do with one another. A large part of Russell's problem was that he tried to take facts two different ways. He tried to take facts as features of the world, whose elements are related together in reality, and to which true beliefs must correspond. Yet what makes the belief that so-and-so true, when it is, is the correspondent fact that so-and-so, which is stitched together in the manner of the true belief. The relating term of the worldly fact now functions only as part of the fact *that* the particular terms fit together in a certain way (that being the way in which they are believed to fit together). This gives facts a quite conceptual cast which makes them less plausibly things in the world and more plausibly devices for describing things in the world. My conclusion is that we need to develop a more adequate account of facts (and facts-that), and that to do so we must work out what facts have to do with stating. Perhaps facts will turn out to be only contrived pseudo-entities used for describing how things are. To what, then, would true beliefs correspond? Historically, while it did not happen all at once, it slowly became clear that the issues here had to be extensively re-thought.

LOGICAL ATOMISM

After the First World War, during it in fact, Ludwig Wittgenstein began to develop his logical-atomist philosophy, in which he was subsequently joined by Russell. They both maintained a correspondence theory of truth, though one of a different stripe than that proposed earlier by Russell and Moore. True propositions are still those which correspond to fact, but, for one thing, a different conception of fact was being developed. As late as 1918, Russell held that facts were worldly entities, of some sort, though he repudiated his previous account of what they were. By 1924 he had come to the conclusion, in agreement with Wittgenstein, that 'the symbol for a fact is not a name. . . . The way to mean a fact is to assert it; the way to mean a simple [thing] is to name it' (1924: 335–6).[3] To say that a proposition corresponds to the facts is not to say that there are facts but to say that things are as they are said to be. That requires some elaboration. In elaborating on how it is that things are as they are said to be, questions about language will clearly be important.

Language is our key to understanding the world – and sometimes it is the lock which stops us from doing so. Many of our problems, philosophical and otherwise, have arisen from our being misled by linguistic forms. We have mistakenly thought that unreal things were real because language suggests they are, and we have also missed important features of the world which are linguistically difficult to accommodate. Meinong thought that the fact that 'The golden mountain does not exist' is true indicated that the golden mountain must in some sense be real in order for that to be a true

statement about it. Accordingly, he went off to discover and cata-
logue various sorts of non-existent reals. Even now, people who
should know better sometimes talk about gravity, evolution, or
aggression as if they were things of some sort, since we use nouns
for talking about them. On the other hand, our languages sometimes make it difficult to talk about things which should be talked
about because they lack adequate means. At one time, the notion of
unconscious thought seemed to be a manifest contradiction in
terms, and there are still considerable conceptual difficulties in
talking about that sort of thing. Currently, debates about abortion,
for another instance, are often confused due to the inadequacies of
our categories. Such seemingly familiar categories as human, human
life, person, and non-person, seem quite unable to do justice to the
complexities of the issues. Again, we seem sometimes to have
trouble in thinking about quantum mechanics due to inadequate
linguistic/conceptual apparatus.

To avoid such difficulties we must better understand the language
we use, and sometimes we must find ways to improve language.
Russell did both in solving Meinong's problem about the golden
mountain. He urged that we must not be misled by the superficial
appearances of language, and argued that while the golden mountain
is the grammatical subject of 'The golden mountain does not exist',
it is not the logical subject of the sentence and so need not be real (in
any sense) for the sentence to be meaningful. Properly understood,
that name, and all names, dissolve into component descriptions. The
problematic sentence is to be understood as equivalent to 'It is not
the case that there exists x such that x is golden and x is a mountain',
to 'For all x it is not the case both that x is golden and x is a
mountain', and to 'The propositional function "– is golden and is a
mountain" is false for all x' . These more formal ways of putting it
are thought more clearly to reveal the way things actually are. Not
only does Russell attempt to better understand language, then, he
also attempts to improve it. The ideal is to develop a linguistic
structure which conforms to the world and which allows us to
depict it in the most accurate way. To be sure, we ought not to
disregard the forms and distinctions of ordinary language without
understanding them, but that should not prevent our improving the
situation.[4] The general aim of logical atomism, as an approach to
philosophy, is to develop a superior linguistic apparatus having
atomic units, and complexes of atomic units, which are interrelated
in a way which has the same structure as the interrelationships of

real things and complexes of real things in the world. In the spirit of Russell's earlier views, we can go on to suggest that true propositions are those which correctly reproduce the structure of what they are about. An extremely influential theory along these lines was developed by Wittgenstein in his *Tractatus Logico-Philosophicus* (1921), to which we now proceed.

TRUTH AND THE *TRACTATUS*

We are told in the *Tractatus* (assertion 4.5) that 'The general form of a proposition is: this is how things stand'. A proposition, obviously, is true if things really do stand that way, which is a matter of some relation between the proposition and reality. What relation, we have to ask, and what is at the reality end of it? Let us start with what facts are and are not. We have to be careful not to misinterpret what Wittgenstein says about them. He tells us such things as (keeping the original numbering)

1   The world is all that is the case.
1.1   The world is the totality of facts, not of things.
1.2   The world divides into facts.
1.21 Each item can be the case or not the case while every-thing else remains the same.
2   What is the case – a fact – is the existence of states of affairs.
2.01 A state of affairs (a state of things) is a combination of objects (things).

(Wittgenstein 1921)

If we put 1.1, 2, and 2.01 together, what we get is that the world is composed not of things, but of the existence of combinations of things. That is, the world is composed not *just* of things, but of things combined together in particular arrangements. While the world is said to be the totality of facts, facts are not entities in any bizarre sense, and certainly they are not fact-that entities. They are specific combinations of things of some sort. Some of these things are complex, being combinations of other things, and some are simple, not being combinations though they may be components of combinations. While things may stand in various relationships with one another, and may depend on them in some way, each simple thing has its own identity in its own right, while complex things have their identity in terms of their components and how they are combined. There are no internal relations (1.21). We do not identify each thing in terms of everything. Notoriously, Wittgenstein does not specify the nature of simples at all, leaving it a matter of multiple interpretation. Russell suggested that sense-data might fill the bill, while others have suggested that some simples might be universals, and these are not the only suggestions. Fortunately, we need not settle that question. The point is that these things fit together to form our world.

The central conception of the logical atomist's correspondence theory of truth is that true propositions are those which fit together in the same way as the reality they represent. As Wittgenstein tells us,

2.1 We picture facts to ourselves.

2.12 A picture is a model of reality.

2.21 A picture agrees with reality or fails to agree; it is correct or incorrect, true or false.

2.224 It is impossible to tell from the picture alone whether it is true or false.

4.01 A proposition is a picture of reality.
A proposition is a model of reality as we imagine it.

4.05 Reality is compared with propositions.

4.06 A proposition can be true or false only in virtue of being a picture of reality.

(ibid.)

To the extent that our language is to be useful for talking about the real world, there must be complex propositions to represent complex facts and simple propositions to represent simple facts. True propositions are those which share the structure of the reality they are about, which they picture, while false propositions misrepresent reality by misrepresenting the way in which it fits together.

The *Tractatus* asks us to believe that a true proposition pictures a fact, the proposition and the fact being structurally similar. (One thing we must be clear about is that whatever may be the structural similarity between proposition and fact, it cannot be a matter of *sentential* structure. The same proposition may be expressed by quite widely divergent sentences, as Russell's analysis of the 'golden mountain' case illustrates. Again, the same sentence can express quite different propositions. 'Jack is to the left of Jill' can express a true proposition one minute and a false one the next.) The structure with which Wittgenstein and the other logical atomists were concerned is the logical structure of meaning-relationships. A proposition is said to have the same structure as what it pictures, what it is about, if its logical structure fits together in the same way as does the fact pictured. Intuitively, this conception of truth is quite attractive and quite elegantly simple: a proposition is a picture of reality, and a true one if reality is as pictured. If I say that the cat is on the mat, I pose a picture of a cat on a mat. It is a very schematic picture, to be sure. It is no particular cat, nor of one of a particular colour or kind, nor of one in a particular posture or on a mat of any particular sort. But, then, even the most faithful of photographs does not show every detail. This is a general picture, and could be satisfied by any kind of a cat on any kind of a mat.

In spite of its attractions, this version of the correspondence theory, *the picture theory of truth*, as it is often called, faces serious difficulties. Indeed, Wittgenstein himself eventually came to reject his *Tractatus* theory, and with it this theory of truth. Without getting bogged down in the wider issues concerning the *Tractatus*, which would involve trying to comment on much of recent philosophy, I shall try to explore the main issues directly concerned with truth and the reasons which lead me to reject the picture theory. Some of the difficulties with the theory arise from it being the case that facts have material structure in the real world while propositions have a meaning-structure which is of some radically different nature. After all, while Jack might be taller than Jill, there can be nothing taller than something else in the proposition, though there might be in a photograph of the two. We can compare a photograph with the reality, but how can we compare structures of such widely different sorts as that of a proposition and that of a pair of people? We must take a closer look at what is involved in this supposed structural similarity between meanings and the material world. Other important issues concern the assumption that the world is composed of specific and discrete units of atomic fact. All of these points merit investigation. Let us first investigate the claim that true propositions in some way picture some bit of reality.

CORRESPONDENCE AS PICTURING: STRUCTURAL SIMILARITY

Can a picture be true? While I ultimately reject any sort of picture theory of truth, I cannot give credit to one very common objection which has been raised against it. I cannot accept Austin's *a priori* objection (1950: 25) that propositions are true *of* something, while pictures are true *to* something. According to this objection, while propositions assert things about things – things which are true or false *of* them – pictures merely resemble things and are or are not true *to* them. We may say something about a picture, and about what it depicts, but a picture does not say anything. A picture can be a false picture, as in the case of a trick photograph, only in the same way that a pearl can be a false pearl: by not living up to a claim expressly or tacitly made about it. Pictures themselves claim nothing. So runs the objection. It is more assertion than argument. To be sure, most pictures certainly are not propositions, but it is by no means self-evident that propositions cannot be pictures of a sort – perhaps of their own very atypical sort. At best, this line of objection would have force in so far as we encounter difficulty in accounting for the supposed picturehood of propositions. The primary question remains one of whether propositions *are* pictures. Do they represent the structure of some bit of the world?

The most obvious subjects for comparison in terms of structural similarity are things which have spatial shape. Scale models, blueprints, and photographic images, for instance, are all structurally similar to what they are about. Structural similarity need not be a matter of spatial similarity, however. A tune played on an oboe may have the same structure as one played on a violin, and the theme Tchaikovsky assigns the Sugar Plum Fairy would have something, certainly rhythm, in common with the imagined fairy or her actions. In all of these cases, things are said to be structurally similar in that their components are 'laid out' (whether or not spatially) in such a way that the things have relational properties sufficiently in common. That is the relationship which the *Tractatus* claims holds between propositions and facts. What it is to, sufficiently, have structural similarity in common in the case of propositions and facts – and whether that adds up to truth – is something which requires further inquiry. Before leaping in to ask about the structure of such things, however, let us inquire further concerning structural comparisons.

Is it possible for two things to have *absolutely* identical structure? There might be said to be such cases. Formal systems can have absolutely identical structure even when they appear to be quite different. The classical proof of the relative consistency of certain non-Euclidean geometries involves translating the non-Euclidean geometry into a part of Euclidean geometry in a way which preserves the internal relationships of the geometry. (Any inconsistency in the non-Euclidean geometry would then be translated into a parallel inconsistency in Euclidean geometry.) The principle of translation may be fairly complicated, but the possibility of inter-translation demonstrates that the non-Euclidean geometry and the relevant part of Euclidean geometry have the same structure. Indeed, it could be claimed that they are really one and the same mathematical system merely given different formulations – one formulation rather more complicated than the other. Were this not so, were they not formulations of one system, they would have to have different structure – that being the only substantive difference two formal systems could have.

Formal systems have the structure which is defined into them, and that is all that they have. Things become more problematic when we get to reality. Suppose that we have a formal system, let us say a finite geometry which talks about some number of points and lines and the way they are laid out. We might sketch it on a blackboard, or even make a model of it using wooden knobs for points and dowels for lines. If we do the job properly, the key terms such as 'point', 'line', 'on', and 'between' will be mapped onto the model in a way which preserves the relationships defined in the formal system. The wooden model will have all of the structural properties of the formal system, plus a few of its own, such as those having to do with the structure of cellulose. These it will not share with the formal system itself nor, presumably, with the chalk diagram, which will have its own structural properties. We can ask for *the* structure of the formal system, but in the case of a material model, how its structure is to be described depends on what we are interested in, be it mathematics, biology, or something else.

Suppose next that we take a pair of finite cognate geometries – which really amount to two different interpretations of one and the same mathematical system. The terms of the system are given different semantic meanings, and are correlated with different material models. Two terms may be interpreted as 'point' and 'line' respectively in one model and 'line' and 'point' respectively in the other, and two 'relations' may be interpreted as 'intersect' and 'are on the same line' in one model and vice versa in the other. A theorem for one model will translate into a theorem for the other, given the appropriate interchange of interpreted terms. Knob-and-dowel mock-ups would look quite different, having different shapes, and varying numbers of knobs and dowels. Even so, each is a mock-up of the same mathematical system, and we can translate mathematically from a true proposition about one to a different true proposition about the other. This will be true so long as we are concerned with propositions which are expressed in terms of a certain class of properties and relations, and so long as we use the proper rules of translation. This indicates not only that the two models share a common relational structure, but also that they answer to the same description – given the proper style of description. For each pair of true correlative propositions we can form one general proposition true of both models, something like, for instance,

> There is a class of things x (knobs in one system, dowels in the other) and another class of things y (dowels, knobs) such that there are n number of x and m number of y, and such that each x has at least two y (i.e. each knob is fitted with at least two dowels, and each dowel with at least two knobs).

Given a particular method of description, it can be said that the models share the same structure – even though they do not share *all* the same structure (according to all schemes of description). What the structural properties of the knob and dowel arrangements are, and whether they share the same structure, depends on what sort of properties we are interested in and on what style of description we are using. As is the case with all concrete things, however, any description will not fully capture what is there (though any feature might be captured by one or another description).

It is important to bear in mind that there can be a relation-preserving correlation between radically different things which appear to have nothing in common structurally. Things may be much more widely divergent than the two models of the cognate geometries. An electronic signal which relays a television picture has no evident similarity with what is being televised, perhaps a sporting match, but there are relation-preserving correlations between them. What appears on the picture tube of a receiving set normally resembles what is on the playing field, whether closely or not, but the same can be said of the signal, though it resembles it in what is evidently a different way. We cannot just inspect a signal and find out what is happening on the playing field, no matter how much we know about electronics. We have to know in what manner the signal is being employed. What signal results from what cause, and eventually leads to what result in the picture tube, depends on a convention which is built into the apparatus. Again, a column of chess notation can, conventionally, represent a series of moves even though there is no apparent similarity between the notation and anything on a chess board.

It is possible to construe the chess notation and the chess moves as answering to the same structural description, so long as we use the right style of description, and the same can be said of the electronic signal and the state of affairs on the playing field. With the proper contrivance, *any* two things can be taken to answer to the same description. In the case of chess and chess notation, it is really quite straightforward. The chess board and the notation each have sixty-four units of one sort (squares, letter–number combinations) and thirty-two of another (pieces, names) which fit together into patterns answering the same broad descriptions. Of course we can only get out of the notation what that sort of notation can represent, and only some of the structure is represented. (Each piece is represented only as a chess piece, not as a piece of wood or an example of a cheap import, and there is no indication of how the pieces are designed or whether the black queen is properly centred on her square.) We cannot get out of the notation what is not there, and what is represented is represented by the notation only according to a particular conventional style of representation.

Similar points, with similar qualifications, can be made concerning the electronic signal and the televised object. Indeed, with similar qualifications we can claim that any two things in the universe, say a small pebble and New York City, answer to the same description, with the pebble's particular shape and colour being just the right ones according to that particular and no doubt extremely bizarre descriptive scheme. More to the point, however, so far as we are concerned, is that it is quite correct to say that a proposition and what it is about share the same structure – again subject to such qualifications. To continue a previous example, a proposition about a knob-and-dowel model will share the same description as the model, given an appropriate method of description. The proposition will not have cellular structure, but we might say that it has the same *logical* structure as its object. For instance, if the proposition is that a dowel has two knobs on it, this proposition and any dowel with two knobs on it will answer to the same very general description which we might formulate something like the following:

There is a class of things x (dowels in the model, references to dowels in propositions) and another class of things y (pairs of knobs, references to two knobs) such that a member of x is associated (in the model, in the proposition) with a member of y.

We could extend such a description to apply to a formula (having to do with two Ps and an L) in a formalized geometry. Answering to the same general description (according to our way of describing), they can all be said to have the same logical structure. Here again, we note that structural similarity is relative to a mode of description, one which may be highly conventional, and that the description only captures some of the features of that which is described. This makes it look too easy.

According to the *Tractatus*, a proposition is true if it pictures its fact. But for that to be right, there must be more to a proposition picturing its fact than just sharing a structural similarity with it. If any two things can be said to share the same structural description, then *any* proposition will be structurally similar to any and every fact. Even false propositions will be structurally similar to every fact. For instance, the proposition that a knob has two dowels on it would have the same structure as a dowel with three knobs on it, both answering to the following description:

There is a class of things x (dowels in the model, references to dowels in propositions) and another class of things y (groups of knobs, references to groups of knobs) such that a member of x is associated (in the model, in the proposition) with a member of y.

How do we know that we are omitting essential information if we omit from our description the numerical content of the groups, but not the cellular content of the dowels? Somehow, we know which sort of structural similarity counts. So, there must be something more to truth than just having structural similarity of some sort. There would, if structural similarity of some sort were all there was to it, be no way to separate true propositions from false ones. There would be no false propositions at all. Obviously, for a picture theory to work at all there must be some particular sort – which sort? – of structural similarity which is critical to a proposition's being true. Yet, of all the possible structural similarities which it might share with a particular fact, which one determines whether that fact makes that proposition true? This is not something the proposition can tell us. It says something about its subject-matter, but nothing about the structure it is supposed to share with it. So how are we to know what the structure is supposed to be which is to be shared by a proposition and its fact?

> 4.121 Propositions cannot represent logical form; it is mir-
> rored in them.
> What finds its reflection in language, language cannot
> represent.
> What expresses *itself* in language, *we* cannot express by
> means of language.
> Propositions *show* the logical form of reality.
> They display it.
>
> (Wittgenstein 1921)

How we are to understand a proposition is not something stated by the proposition. Rather, it is what we have to see in order to understand what the proposition does state. Still,

> 4.022 A proposition *shows* its sense.
> A proposition *shows* how things stand *if* it is true. And
> it *says that* they do so stand.
> 4.1212 What *can* be shown, *cannot* be said.
>
> (ibid.)

While the proposition cannot tell us what structural similarity it must, if true, share with its fact, it can show it. We can see and understand this which cannot be said, and understanding it we can understand what *is* said.

We do generally understand propositions, including a great many which we have never encountered before. We know *how* to understand them. Certainly, it would be very convenient were there some one way of seeing propositions which, once learned, would give us a way to understand any proposition which made sense. We do not have such a perspective. Sometimes we just do not know what to make of a proposition. While we may understand the words individually, we still do not see the way in which it all fits together. Different propositions have to be seen in different ways. One thing which has become abundantly and inescapably clear is that propositions do *not* all work the same way. This poses a problem for

Wittgenstein. A basic idea of the *Tractatus* is that a proposition presents us with a model of reality so that we can read off from the logical structure of the model what the structure of the fact is asserted to be. Yet there is no overall *system* of pictorial representation if different pictures are pictures in differing ways. In being told how things are we are shown how to understand the picture, and only in understanding how things are said to be do we see in which way we are to understand the picture. (At one time, the French Impressionists faced an uphill battle in convincing their critics that their paintings in any way resembled their objects. People had to learn to see how it was that they did so. We have to learn how to take a proposition, too.) Instead of the picture showing us how things are said to be, we have to come to understand how things are said to be in order to see how the picture is a picture. The picturehood of a proposition, then, is at best an epiphenomenon of its asserting.[5] This being so, the picture part of the story does no work and might as well be left out. These considerations alone, I believe, give us sufficient reason to reject the picture theory. So far as truth theory is concerned, it would be better to concentrate on what is involved in telling things truly, rather than on what is involved in showing.

ATOMIC FACTS AND UNIQUE ANALYSIS

There are yet other problems concerning the *Tractatus*'s theory of truth, in addition to those having to do with structural similarity and the picturehood of propositions. Central claims are that the world is composed of atomic facts and complexes of atomic facts, and that, properly understood, there is exactly one way in which atomic facts can be analysed in terms of basic simple components. Both of these claims are controversial and, I believe, mistaken. I think it would be useful to explore these matters before we move on to consider other theories of truth.

Elementary propositions – in terms of which we must understand any other proposition – are held to be pictures of particular states of affairs. A state of affairs, recall 2.01, is a combination of objects (things). Facts, then, are taken as the existence of particular arrangements of things. Setting aside for a moment the vital question of whether facts really are the existence or arrangement of something, let us ask why it is that there must be a unique analysis in terms of atomic facts. According to the *Tractatus*, we can be sure of this on logical grounds. The key idea is that in order to be understandable, a proposition must have a definite sense.

> 3.23 The requirement that simple signs [As Wittgenstein called logically proper names] be possible is the requirement that sense be determinate.
>
> 3.24 . . . When a propositional element signifies a complex, this can be seen from an indeterminateness in the propositions in which it occurs. In such cases we know that the proposition leaves something undetermined. . . .
>
> 3.251 What a proposition expresses it expresses in a determinate manner, which can be set out clearly: a proposition is articulated.
>
> (ibid.)

However, descriptions are never fully determinate. No matter how detailed they are, they must always underdetermine reality. Whatever description we might have, if the description could be met by anything at all it could be met by things which were at least slightly different. So long as things are to be understood in terms of descriptions, and descriptions are analysed into further descriptions, then, a proposition can never have a fully definite sense. A proposition can have a fully definite sense only if it can be understood in terms of simple basic facts which are the arrangement of simple basic things – things which are not just described but directly named. These fully definite things provide the material out of which fully definite facts are formed, and these allow us to form propositions with fully definite sense.

What these simple basic things are, Wittgenstein does not tell us. Some have suggested that they are sense-data, while others have suggested that they might include universals. There may be other accounts as well, but no account is definitive. Wittgenstein held that he had established the necessary existence of simple objects (things) on logical grounds, and was content to dismiss the question of what they are as an empirical question in which he took no particular interest (Malcolm 1958: 86). We might question, though, whether he has proven his point. Is it really true that we always mean something with a definite sense when we assert a proposition? If I say 'That is water' I may mean something different and a good deal less precise if I am referring to the campus lake than if I make the same remark in a chemistry lab with reference to the contents of a flask. Seemingly, my remark with reference to the lake turns on a concept of water which is much less definite. But then,

> 3.262 What signs fail to express, their application shows. What signs slur over, their application says clearly.
>
> (ibid.)

Even if my remark was less precise than a chemist's reference to distilled H_2O, for it to be meaningful, so the claim is, there must be some criteria for what is to count as water presupposed in making that remark under those particular circumstances for those particular purposes. Even if the criteria allow considerable leeway, there is still a definite sense in terms of whether those criteria are met. I am inclined to dispute this account. I think that our practices and our thoughts very often underdetermine criteria, that different and incompatible criteria are often consistent with both our actual thoughts and actual practices, and, accordingly, that often the propositions with which we are concerned have a sense which is only partially or relatively definite even though they are quite serviceable for the purposes for which we use them. If propositions do not necessarily have a fully definite sense, then they are not necessarily analysable into fully definite components as demanded by the *Tractatus*.

I am also inclined to doubt that there is always exactly one correct way to analyse a proposition into basic components. Of course we can often reduce complex propositions to simpler ones through an analysis of the meaning relations involved. Thus, the apparently simple 'equality is transitive' might be analysed as the logically complex 'for all a, if a equals b, and b equals c, then a equals c'. Going beyond such logical relations, we can break down things like 'Scott is the Author of Waverley' in the manner described by Russell. With each descriptive scheme we can no doubt analyse in terms of simples and complexes. No doubt we can often integrate one descriptive scheme with another, so that one scheme can be reduced to the other or both to a simpler and more basic scheme. Perhaps a system in which knobs and dowels are simple can be reduced to one in which atoms are simple. I think, though, that such reduction cannot always be done, even in principle. I believe, that is, that sometimes different schemes of description lead to different simples, with some equally valid schemes of description not being interreducible at all. To suppose an example for which there is some evidence, one person or group of people might come to use colour words for somewhat different ranges of colour than do other people. One person might then consider a given object to be blue while another considers it to be green. Through prior habituation, moreover, they come to associate together certain colour ranges so that, now irrespective of colour names, a given shade may appear to one person to be obviously significantly similar to colours of one range and not to those of another, while to another person the opposite might be the case. To one the shade is obviously rather similar to its fellow blues; to the other it is rather similar to its fellow greens. In such a case, one person's colour simples (and therefore propositions based on them) might well be determined to be irreducibly incommensurate with those of another person. Later, in his *Philosophical Investigations* (1953: sections 47–8), Wittgenstein himself seems to have come to a similar conclusion, that what are simple and complex is relative to the 'language-game' with which we are concerned – and that some language-games are just irreducibly different from some other language-games.

AFTER THE *TRACTATUS*

Not everyone would agree with the above criticisms, and certainly not in the form in which I have presented them, but the general verdict of philosophers, and of Wittgenstein himself, was that the system of the *Tractatus* was incorrect. There were other problems as well, with any such theory of truth. For instance, it is by no means clear that such a theory can handle existential, negative, or universal truths. What simples are being pictured if it is said that there are black swans, that there are no green swans, or that all crows are black? Again, it has been severely questioned whether all propositions are either elementary or else are truth-functions of elementary propositions. Whether this is so may depend on the language-game we are employing. Given that the *Tractatus* has not withstood criticism, what then of the correspondence theory of truth? For some time the *Tractatus* was considered to offer the definitive version of that theory, and as the system of the *Tractatus* crumbled – in considerable measure, due to the criticism of Wittgenstein himself – the correspondence theory seemed to crumble with it. But with what should the correspondence theory, or this version of it, be replaced? Before we attempt to answer that, let us pause to quickly take stock of what we can learn from the fall of the *Tractatus*.

The idea that the world is composed of precise units which fit together in precise ways, all of which is describable by a logically proper language which mirrors the structure of the world, had a considerable vogue in the first part of this century. It is expressed not only in the *Tractatus* but in Russell's versions of the correspondence theory as well, and in much of the rest of the analytical philosophy of the period. This conception led to some undeniable successes, as in the fall of the golden mountain. Even so, it appears to me to be a conception of a world composed of Lego blocks to which we are to apply a Lego-language, a conception which I believe to be wrong about the world, about language, and about the relationships between them. In our consideration of the *Tractatus* we have already seen faults in this conception and I shall subsequently have more to say about its faults. I suggest that we would be wise to rule out theories which define truth in terms of picture-hood or any form of structural similarity, which demand that propositions can be analysed in only one way, or which call for a world of atomic facts. More generally, we would do well to be wary of theories which offer a view of truth which is too mechanical, as if propositions had some general form which fit the world in some one particular way. That is much too rigid and restrictive. In this as in most areas of inquiry, a good rule of thumb is that there is no one way in which everything works.

After the *Tractatus*, the correspondence theory, and truth theory in general, could never be the same. Having re-thought the main issues of the *Tractatus*, Wittgenstein in the *Philosophical Investigations* did not offer us a new theory of truth. Instead, he drew vividly to our attention that different propositions describe the world in different ways for different purposes. Instead of rigidly and artificially trying to impose a preconceived structure on language and the world, we must come to terms with language as it is and with linguistic usages as we use them. Only then can we hope to understand truth. Knowing this does not give us a theory of truth, but it is something we must bear in mind if we are to develop one. There will be much to investigate concerning the workings of language and its relations to reality. Wherever we go from here, though, I believe we would do well to try to retain the initial conception that those things which are true are so not just by virtue of themselves, but by virtue of external reality.

If we continue to maintain that truth is a matter of a relationship between truth-bearers and independent reality, there are still options open to us after the fall of the *Tractatus* and theories of truth based on structural similarity. It might even be possible to have some sort of a correspondence theory. Tarski's semantic conception of truth soon came on the scene and offered an important alternative, one which has had a major impact on recent philosophy and which has often been regarded as a version of the correspondence theory. Somewhat later, Austin offered his own version of the correspondence theory, one which followed quite different lines from any of the preceding. As we shall see, critical questions concern what is to count as a correspondence theory, and what is to be required of one. We should note too that one need not accept any version of the correspondence theory at all in order to maintain that truths are true by virtue of external factual reality. One alternative is the pragmatic theory of truth, which has been in the field since well before the *Tractatus* and which still has a following. There are other alternatives as well, and it has even been suggested that there is no need for any theory of truth, since to attribute truth to a statement is not to say anything whatsoever about it. We shall look at some of the major alternatives in subsequent chapters, as we work toward finding a viable account of truth.

4

ALTERNATIVES I

Further theories of truth are considered, these being the pragmatic, redundancy, and performative theories of truth. While they each have their reasons and merits, all are inadequate as theories of truth. Through consideration of these theories we develop a better understanding of what we are to look for in an adequate account of truth. Subsequent versions, or descendants, of these theories are considered in chapter 9, 'Alternatives II'.

While they are historically and theoretically important, there is much more to truth theory than is to be found in the coherence or correspondence theories of truth. There are alternative approaches, and important alternative accounts of what it is to be true. Pragmatic theories take true beliefs to be those which work out well in overall practice. Again, there are theories which maintain that truth is not any sort of property of anything, and so is not in need of definition. These suggest that if anything, what we must concentrate on is giving an account of what it is that ascriptions of truth are used to do. Yet again, there is the semantic conception of truth which takes truth to be specifiable in terms of the structure of a given language. While sometimes, controversially, claimed to be a version of the correspondence theory, it is certainly different from any other version. All of these theories offer insights which repay investigation, and there are other theories as well. Let us now consider some of the major alternative approaches to truth, commencing with that alternative which takes historical precedence, that of the pragmatists.

PRAGMATIC THEORIES OF TRUTH

William James, as we will recall, distinguished theories which rested on brute fact from coherentist theories which lost truth in the unfathomable depths of a universal Absolute. Like the correspondence theorists, James and his fellow pragmatists opted for brute fact. The pragmatists, though, did so in a distinctively different way. Whereas the correspondence theorists joined the coherentists in taking truth as being a matter of that which is true fitting with something else – in whatever way with whatever thing – the pragmatists took truth as being a matter of fitting in with practice. Pragmatic theories of truth are based on the pragmatist's conception of meaning, according to which all meaning is grounded in practice, with all difference in meaning involving some difference in practice. As James (1907: 45) put it, 'there can *be* no difference that *makes* no difference'. In this he followed Charles S. Peirce, who held that (1878: 30) '. . . there is no distinction of meaning so fine as to consist in anything but a possible difference of practice'. Beliefs have meaning in terms of practice, and true beliefs, accordingly, are those which work out well in terms of practice. This conception of truth was given modern currency first by Peirce, and subsequently by John Dewey and William James.

There is more than one formulation of the pragmatist's conception of truth, and they are not equivalent. According to Peirce,

> The opinion which is fated to be ultimately agreed to by all who investigate, is what we mean by the truth . . .
>
> (1878: 38)

Peirce was well aware that the opinion we now find convincing may well prove untrue, and held that the truth is that opinion which we would eventually settle on if we persisted long enough in our inquiries, taking into account a sufficient diversity of factual material and using an adequate scientific method. This is obviously quite uncertain. Still, staunch empiricists are not given to promising certainty in our dealings with the real world, and reality it is which puts constraints on our practical activity and determines the results of scientific inquiry. We must deal with reality as best we can – and the truth, as best we can find it, is that which is, overall, the belief which is most effective in our dealings with reality. That the real world with which we must deal is the ultimate arbiter of truth is a conviction in which pragmatists and correspondence theorists are at one.

Peirce's conception of truth was quite closely tied to scientific methodology and the results of scientific investigation. James wished to widen the pragmatic approach so as to provide a conception of truth which was generally applicable. At the same time he wished to avoid defining truth in terms of the ultimate results of future investigation. According to his formulation,

> *The true*, to put it very briefly, *is only the expedient in the way of our thinking, just as the right is only the expedient in the way of our behaving.*
>
> (1907: 222; reiterated, 1909a: vii)

This was meant to apply not only to truth in science, but to truth in all areas, including metaphysics and religion. James's conception of truth has lent itself to considerable satire and ridicule (e.g. by Russell 1910). For a few people it might be very useful and work out well in their practice to think that the earth is flat, and for some children it may be very rewarding to believe in Santa Claus. That these beliefs are untrue, however, does not refute the pragmatic theory of truth. After all, such beliefs are useful only with respect to a severely limited field of application. The claim is not that true beliefs are the most useful in every instance, nor that the belief which is useful in some instance must therefore be true. The claim is that true beliefs are those which work out well over the generality of experience. Often enough, beliefs are workable and useful for some restricted purposes, yet eventually turn out to be unviable, and therefore untrue, when further considerations are taken into account. (Such, for instance, was the case with the geocentric theory of planetary motion.) In criticizing the pragmatic conception of truth it is much too easy to forget, as many have done and we must not, what James said immediately after the above:

> Expedient in almost any fashion, and expedient in the long run and on the whole, of course; for what meets expediently all the experience in sight won't necessarily meet all farther experiences equally satisfactorily. Experience, as we know, has ways of *boiling over*, and making us correct our present formulas.
>
> (ibid.)

Whatever the version of the pragmatic theory of truth, there is a standard objection raised against it. It is often claimed (e.g. by Russell (1910) and many since) that the pragmatists are guilty of a fundamental error, confusing criteria of truth with the nature of truth. (We recall that a similar charge was raised against the coherentists.) Such things as practical expediency and being the result of scientific inquiry may be good criteria of truth but, it is said, they are good criteria just because there is a reality which makes them so, and it is correspondence to (or maybe coherence with) that reality which constitutes truth. A better line of objection than this is required. It is not that they were too stupid to notice the difference between criteria and essence. Rather, while well aware of the putative distinction, they held that it was not viable in the long run. Difference in meaning must make a difference in real or possible practice, so any difference in meaning between being true and meeting the criteria of truth must indicate some possible difference in practice. Such a difference would serve to define a better criterion, but we can never go beyond criteria. The relevant distinction is not between criteria and essence, but between limited criteria and better ones. To be true *is* to meet the appropriate criteria. It might then be said that each meaningful proposition bears its own truth-nature/criteria with it. To be meaningful a proposition must mean something in practice, and true ones are those which meet the criteria implicit in their meaning. False ones are those which, in real practice, fail to meet the criteria for which they themselves call.

PRAGMATISM AND TRUTH

There are problems for the pragmatist's conception of truth, and we may wonder whether they have successfully balanced the claims of brute reality with the relativity of our experience. James points out on the one hand that:

> To admit, as we pragmatists do, that we are liable to correction (even tho we may not expect it) *involves* the use on our part of an ideal standard. . . . No relativist who ever actually walked the earth has denied the constitutive character in his own thinking of the notion of absolute truth. What is challenged by relativists is the pretence on any one's part to have found for certain at any given moment what the shape of that truth is.

> (1909a: 264–6)

While a matter of relativity, truth is relative to reality. But even so, there is the other hand. It is the reality of our experience to which truth is relative – seemingly a quite relative reality:

> Truth here [according to the pragmatic account] is a relation, not of our ideas to non-human realities, but of conceptual parts of our experience to sensational parts. Those thoughts are true which guide us to *beneficial interaction* with sensible particulars as they occur, whether they copy these in advance or not.
>
> (ibid.: 82)

To be sure, there is something to be said for this relativism. We can never reach beyond experience to an absolute reality. Brute fact for us must be brute fact as we can experience it. James, indeed, invokes what seem very much like coherentist considerations, calling on us to adjust what we take to be truth and what we take to be brute fact so that the world, *our* world, fits together as a coherent whole (1907, 1909a). In consequence, James must face certain of the difficulties faced by the coherentists. Evidently we can never be certain of anything – until, *per impossibile*, we can know all of its consequences and implications for our world-order. Russell argued that it is often easier to determine whether a belief is true than it is to assess the consequences of believing it:

> It is far easier, it seems to me, to settle the plain question of fact: 'Have Popes been always infallible?' than to settle the question whether the effects of thinking them infallible are on the whole good.
>
> (1910: 118–19)

Elsewhere (1946: 853), using a much less controversial example, he remarks that it is easier to know whether one had coffee that morning than it is to assess the comparative long-term effects of believing that one did or did not.[1] Russell thereupon concludes that the pragmatic conception of truth is incorrect.

I do not find such an objection persuasive. To be sure, if asked whether I had coffee this morning I need not and do not assess the comparative benefits of believing one thing or the other. I clearly recall that I did have coffee, and know that the annoying and highly unlikely case of my not having done so would have been prominent in my awareness. As I cannot trace out all the consequences of my beliefs, I cannot be absolutely totally certain on Jamesian grounds. Neither are there Russellian grounds for absolute certainty. We can always imagine various improbable scenarios according to which we are wrong. Even so, by consultation with memory and circumstance, and perhaps the witness of others, I can establish to a very high degree of confidence that I had coffee. Russell would accept that my belief was established beyond any reasonable doubt, without having to consult future consequences. The critical point, though, is that James could accept that just as well as Russell. One consequence of denying that I had coffee would be the conclusion that my memory and self-awareness were radically defective. In the absence of persuasive reason to accept such awkward consequences, the pragmatically most reasonable thing to do would be to accept as true my belief that I did have coffee.

Such virtually conclusive verification as might be achieved in the previous case is by no means universally available. Sometimes we must make do with evidence which is much less compelling. The truth may be that which will or would work out best in the long run, but in the meantime we must get by as best we can. Short of whatever validation the ultimate long run might bring, James recommended that we accept the expedient as the true – at least until we find out that it was not really expedient after all. He seems to be on reasonable ground so long as he is suggesting that we take as provisionally true that which is most expedient, subject to further correction and revision. However, problems arise when it comes to cases, for instance cases having to do with religion or metaphysics, wherein we may *never* be able to find strongly compelling reasons. James recommended that we adopt the expedient as the true, though it may perhaps be only the psychologically expedient. Here we come to a major point of divergence among the pragmatists.

Peirce and Dewey feared that James would admit the *merely* expedient as true. Accordingly, they maintained that the truth is that which is/would be verified (in a scientific or near scientific sense). This allows that some beliefs – or perhaps they are only belief-like thoughts – might be expedient in some sense, being psychologically useful or otherwise useful, while yet not being the sort of thing capable of truth or falsity. Perhaps we can shunt religion and metaphysics off onto such a siding. Such an account is subject to all the usual (and apparently insuperable) difficulties in adequately characterizing proper verification. Moreover, it makes it difficult to accept that scientific theories can ever be true, since, unlike particular facts, they can never be verified beyond reasonable doubt. One might be willing to accept that, however, taking good theories to be expedient even if incapable of truth. Yet it seems to be an expedience which is directly linked with truth, which is the link they denied in the absence of verification. Dewey incurs yet further problems, as he spoke (1938) of truth as being something which happened to a proposition *when* it became verified, as if it had not been true prior to that time. In this, Dewey has found few supporters. One is inclined to think that there is a reality which is as it is and about which we can hope to discover truths previously unknown – truths which were true before we verified them. Moreover, this seems to violate the law of excluded middle, leaving gaps where neither one thing nor its negation can be verified. I shall say a few more words on this issue in connection with Dummett, in chapter 9.

Peirce and Dewey over-reacted, I believe, and became too restrictive in the face of James's tolerance, but I think they did right to suspect his too ready equation of truth with even long-term expedience. I wish to suggest that – unless we become more selective about what sort of even long-term expedience we have in mind – truth does not always determine expedience, and expedience does not necessarily define truth. James of course denied the possibility that a belief could be expedient in the long run, and so pragmatically 'true', even though false in actual fact. His line of reply is always that actual fact will, or at least would, sooner or later make a decisive impact on our awareness and so on our expedience. But could it not be that actual fact might, no matter what we did, make no impact (or only a very minimal one) on our awareness? To take a fanciful example, did Lucy's mother see Lucy's father the day she (the mother) died? 'Lucy', as she came to be called, was an *Australopithecus afarensis* (pre-human) female who died in Africa somewhere around three million years ago, leaving a skeleton discovered much more recently. Though it seems unlikely that we could ever find out what, something must be true about what Lucy's mother saw that day. In his reply to this line of objection James makes one very good point, one well worth retaining, but I believe that he is ultimately unable to overcome the difficulty.

James (1909a: chapter 15) concedes that there is a truth about antediluvian events. At the same time, he insists – quite correctly, I believe – that, though reality is what it is, there can be no truth without a thinking being to conceive of it. Truths no more than meanings float in the abstract, nor do they exist on their own, embedded in the bedrock of reality. Truth is a matter of meaning in relationship to external reality, but while reality is out there, whatever is true or false of it has meaning only in someone's cognitive scheme. So, whatever may have happened involving Lucy's mother, anything which is true of that can only be true dependently on a cognitive scheme. Before Lucy's bones were discovered, the bones were there, and whatever happened in the past happened. Even so, between when Lucy and her family were forgotten about and when her bones were discovered there were no truths about them, though it is true that certain things would have been true had anyone thought of them. I think that James is quite correct in maintaining that there can be no true statements (or other truth-bearers) without there being someone able to conceive of them.

However, he goes on to claim that

> The truth of an event, past, present, or future, is for me only another name for the fact that *if* the event ever *does* get known, the nature of the knowledge is already to some degree predetermined. The truth which precedes actual knowledge of a fact means only what any possible knower of the fact will eventually find himself necessitated to believe about it.
>
> (ibid.: 294)

Here I think he is starting to slide off the rails. We must certainly grant that what would be known by someone who knew is the truth – but I think we ought not to *define* truth in terms of potential knowledge. In some cases there may be no potential knowledge. It is true that Lucy's mother saw the father that day, or else it is false, even if no one could ever possibly know. Any belief, conjecture, statement, etc., has meaning only with respect to someone's cognitive scheme, certainly, but it need not be knowably true or false. James appears to take a different point of view:

> . . . if truth and knowledge are terms correlative and interdependent, as I maintain they are, then wherever knowledge is conceivable truth is conceivable, wherever knowledge is possible truth is possible, wherever knowledge is actual truth is actual . . . and truth *conceivable* certainly exists, for, abstractly taken, there is nothing in the nature of antediluvian

events that should make the application of knowledge to them inconceivable.

(ibid.: 296–7)

This, I think, evades the issue. While knowledge presupposes truth, the relevant question is whether truth presupposes even possible knowledge. Some events that far in the past may be unknowable *in principle*, due to the accumulation of intervening quantum indeterminacies or other factors obscuring the causal record. Whether or not that is so is not a matter to be decided by *a priori* fiat. It seems to me that a conjecture about Lucy's mother can be meaningful, and true or false, even though I have no idea what difference its truth would make in practice, and even though I do not know whether it could make a practical difference under any circumstances whatsoever. I believe, therefore, that truth is not to be defined as even the long-term expedient.

While the truth is not necessarily expedient in some way, we should also note that the expedient, even the long-term expedient, is not necessarily true. For various reasons I might find it expedient to believe one thing or another about what Lucy's mother saw that day. (Perhaps I find it emotionally satisfying, or perhaps it fits in with some pet theory of mine.) My belief may be expedient for me whether or not false. In fact, it might be so expedient for me to believe it that I find it expedient to explain away rather than recognize some slight bit of scientific evidence that my belief is false. The evidence might be far from overwhelming, and I might easily find it more convenient to discount the evidence than to come to terms with it properly. People have often found it expedient to ignore evidence or blatant fact which was far more pressing. What, then, of truth? As Russell observed (e.g. at 1910: 95) – and here I basically agree with him – there are quite different ways in which a belief may work out well. It might be psychologically congenial or otherwise contributory to our well-being. Or, which is a matter only contingently related, it might work out well in a more truth-related sense. As Russell characterized it, the belief may work out well in a theoretical sense in so far as it yields verifiable propositions all of which are true (whether the belief suits us well or not). Though I doubt very much that reality is always so co-operative as to yield verifiable consequences for *all* truths, it seems quite plausible that some forms of expediency stem from a thing's being really true, while other forms stem from other factors. These are different *ways* of being expedient, which are not the same even when they coincide. If I truly win the lottery, my belief that I have is expedient in a factual sense which does not depend on my psychological satisfaction, though that is also present. We must ask what sort(s) of expedience are relevant to truth.

Failure to recognize that there are relevant differences in forms of expedience led James to drift into suggesting that truth is not just relative to a cognitive scheme, but factually dependent on the needs of the conceiver. Thus:

> . . . in any concrete account of what is denoted by 'truth' in human life, the word can only be used relatively to some particular trower. Thus, I may hold it true that Shakespe[a]re wrote the plays that bear his name, and may express my opinion to a critic. If the critic be both a pragmatist and a baconian, he will in his capacity of pragmatist see plainly that the workings of my opinion, I being what I am, make it perfectly *true for me*, while in his capacity of baconian he still believes that Shakespe[a]re never wrote the plays in question. But most anti-pragmatists take the word truth as something absolute. . . .
>
> (1909a: 274, italics added)

While truth, so far as I can entertain it, must be relative to my cognitive scheme, its suiting me to believe something, even if it suits me in the long run, is not what makes a truth true.

Not all expediency is wedded to truth, even if it be long-term expediency. But may we not equate truth with that sort of expediency (however it is to be characterized) which *is* wedded to truth? I doubt that it could be that simple. To start with, it may not be possible to characterize the sort of experience which is wedded to truth without in some way characterizing it in terms of truth. What makes a belief expedient in the relevant sense is that it has consequences which, unlike psychological satisfaction, are *evidence*. To say the least, it is not at all clear that we can distinguish evidence from other consequences except in terms of the obtaining of that for which it is evidence. If truth-relevant expedience can only be characterized in some such way, then proclaiming that the true is the expedient would amount only to saying that the true is the true. It need not be so bald, however. Perhaps the sort of expedience which is relevant to truth could be characterized in terms of something else (perhaps correspondence of some sort, or coherence, or whatever), something which could serve as a definition of truth in its own right. It would be lovely if we could find the right characterization. The fact remains that a useful characterization of truth-relevant expedience has not been given.

For my part, I am inclined to doubt whether anything which could reasonably be characterized as expedience could serve as the definition of truth. I doubt it because I suspect that some truths have little or nothing to do with expedience and may even be forever unknowable. There may be a modicum of indeterminate evidence, or perhaps none at all, but I would think that there can be a particular truth even where there is no definite indication. Moreover, if I can even coherently conceive that a truth might be forever unknowable, that in itself suggests to me that truth is not to be defined in terms of its consequences for us.

The conclusion I come to is that the pragmatic conception of truth is not adequate. This is not to say that the pragmatists confused the criterion of truth with the nature of truth, as they, like the coherentists, were accused of doing. They consciously identified the two. The identification, though, I have argued, is incorrect. Expediency of any sort is, I believe, only an indication of truth. None the less, I believe that there are things of value to the pragmatist's conception of truth which we would do well to remember. Certainly they did well to insist that we must come to terms both with the brute fact of the real world and with the relativities inherent in truth being tied to, and fitting in with, our cognitive scheme. Here it seems they were trying to combine the best of the coherentist insights with the insistence on alogically given fact characteristic of the correspondence theorists. The pragmatists were correct in holding that truth is not something which exists independently and in the abstract. Reality is independent and truth is tied to it, but what is true has being and meaning only in the context of someone's cognitive scheme. We with our cognitive scheme, and background interests and knowledge, form some thought, and reality determines whether that thought is true. It is a matter of *that* thought – as thought. Everything which we consider as true or false, the pragmatists point out, has its own particular meaning in terms of how it fits into our scheme of things, with our purposes and criteria for successful application, and therefore each has its own particular conditions which must be satisfied in order for it, as meant, to be true. This is a point which has been too often neglected by those who treat truth and meaning in the abstract.

As we shall see, this last point is one which can profitably be salvaged (with some modification) from the pragmatist's conception of truth. For now, let us consider another alternative point of view on truth, one which ties truth even more closely to particular propositions, doing so to the point of dismissing truth as a distinct consideration.

THE REDUNDANCY THEORY OF TRUTH

To Ramsey in 1927, truth theory – largely on the part of coherentists and correspondence theorists – seemed to be tangled in hopeless muddles about various problematic entities, linguistic and otherwise, joined in bizarre relationships, all of which created confused answers to confused problems. He attempted (1927) to cut the Gordian knot with what became known, with moderate accuracy, as *the redundancy theory of truth*. Consider: it is clearly true that Caesar was murdered if, and only if, Caesar was murdered. Looking at it that way, one is led to Ramsey's theory that 'p is true' and 'it is true that p' each means only the same as 'p', and that 'so-and-so believes (hopes, doubts, etc.) that p is true' means only that 'so-and-so believes (etc.) that p'. A parallel account is given of falsity. Similarly, 'It is a fact that p' comes only to 'p', and so on. Indeed, 'It is true that' and 'It is a fact that' are not only similarly redundant in terms of meaning, they are also used to convey much the same verbal emphasis. On this account, when 'true', 'fact', or any of their verbal derivatives are linked to a sentence (or independent clause), the latter means just what it meant before. No meanings are added or taken away. The problem of truth, then, evaporates without philosophical residue. An added bonus is that we no longer have to worry about the question of what things are truth-bearers. Instead, we can get back to the business of working out what is true. Yet one wonders if it is really all that simple. Though 'It is true that p' and 'p' are truth-functionally equivalent – and it is hardly surprising that they should be *truth*-functionally equivalent – is there no way in which the 'is true' part of it contributes to the meaning? Certainly it *seems* to add something.

Before going on to consider what, if anything, truth assertions might add to bare assertions, I would like to raise a point about truth-functional equivalence. As Austin pointed out (1950: 26n), we must beware of exceptions to accustomed inferences in the case of such an extraordinary concept as truth. I should think that we must particularly beware of assuming that two statements must have the same meaning (be 'logically' equivalent) when they are true or false together, especially when making the assumption appears to be on the brink, at the very least, of begging the question. That two assertions are true or false under the same conditions does not automatically entail that they mean the same thing. 'There is white smoke issuing from the Vatican chimney' and 'A new pope has been selected' are said to be true or false together, yet they do not have the same meaning. Even if infallibly true that one entails the other, only one is about smoke in terms of its direct meaning, and only one is about a pope in terms of its direct meaning. These statements are only contingently correlated, but one can make a similar point about statements which are true or false together as a matter of logical necessity. 'F is a trilateral', 'F is a triangle', and 'F is a polygon whose internal angles are equal to two right angles' are, in Euclidean geometry, true or false together, depending on whether F is that way. Yet it is not clear that they convey the same meaning. When it comes to 'p is true' and 'p', the former does not necessarily mean the same thing as the latter, even if it is true when, and only when, the latter is true. *Of course* they are true or false together, since the former is saying that the latter is true. Similarly, any other reformulation removing the offending words 'is true' would not necessarily have to amount to the same thing just because it never differs in truth or falsity. There is no bar here to rejecting Ramsey's account, should there be reason to do so. Is there reason to do so?

Ramsey's account faces a crucial problem with what has become known as the 'blind use' of 'true'. A stock sort of example of that would be 'What Paul said is true', which one might believe even though one did not know what it was Paul said. We might have considerable faith in Paul. We cannot eliminate the 'is true' in this case, as 'What Paul said' is not equivalent to 'What Paul said is true'. This seems to indicate that the 'is true' does add something, which suggests that truth is meaningfully being predicated of what Paul said. Ramsey recognized (1927: 158) that in such cases 'we get statements from which we cannot in ordinary language eliminate the words "true" and "false" '. He maintained, however, that formal logic can rid us of the difficulty. An analysis of the form 'For all p, if he asserts p, then p' is proposed (ibid.). Normally, we would say 'What Paul said is true', in ignorance of what he said, on the strength of our faith in Paul's consistent reliability. The proposed formula appears to be at least a more or less plausible rendering of

'What Paul says is [always] true', when we are speaking in general about things Paul says (though we might worry because the idiomatic use of English would insist on 'For all p, if Paul says p, then p is true', which hardly solves the problem). Yet what if we were *not* making a claim about Paul's invariable veracity? Perhaps we believe, for some reason, and in spite of Paul's being a habitual liar, that what he said on a particular occasion was true, even though we do not know what it was he said. Perhaps because he had that special light of truth in his eyes, or because someone was holding a gun to his head. Again, perhaps, though he was speaking a language we do not understand, he had a very convincing manner. To handle such cases, Ramsey's formula would then have to be revised to 'For all p [specified in some more complex way, allowing it to refer to only that particular, though unknown p] , if Paul says p, then p'. To be sure, such an analysis has managed to eliminate the words 'is true', but it is certainly starting to show the strain.

More to the point than mere strain, if the redundancy theory is to hold, it must reduce what appears to be a proposition about a proposition – saying that it is true – to some form of the putatively true proposition itself. Mere elimination of the words 'is true' is not enough. *Any* theory of truth can do that ('What Paul said corresponds to the facts', 'What Paul said coheres with the Absolute', . . .). Ramsey's elaborated formula evidently does not amount to a straightforward assertion of whatever it was Paul said on that occasion, and our revised version fares even worse. Both versions veer in the direction of telling *why* we have faith in what Paul said (then), which is another matter. Certainly they seem to be saying *something* about what Paul says. The conclusion I come to is that Ramsey's account is incorrect, since it cannot adequately handle the problems raised by 'blind' ascriptions of truth. I believe, then, that to say that p is true is something other than just to say that p.

In due course, I shall attempt to show how predicating truth of a statement does indeed say something about the statement, about its truth, something beyond what the core statement says and which is not captured by a reformulation in the style of Ramsey. Some would prefer not to go so far, though they agree that there is more to it than Ramsey allowed. Attempts have been made by Strawson and some others to develop a somewhat Ramseyan theory wherein, while it is conceded that to say that a statement is true does add something, it is held that what is added is not another statement. Let us now consider Strawson's revised version of Ramsey's account.

Certain other accounts of truth, in some part derived from that of Ramsey and also seeking to eliminate the truth-predicate, will be discussed in chapter 9.

THE PERFORMATIVE THEORY OF TRUTH

A concept important in much twentieth century philosophy is that of the *performative utterance*. A performative utterance does not just say something. Rather, it actually *performs* something. An example would be 'I promise that . . .', which does not merely describe a promise but actually performs the act of promising. 'I do' uttered in a marriage ceremony, and 'I move that . . .' uttered, when in order, at a formal meeting also constitute performative utterances. We should bear in mind that performative utterances and utterances which actually state something do not necessarily belong to mutually exclusive sorts. A given utterance may be used both to perform and to state, as 'You are hereby notified that . . .', or 'I'm *warning* you, . . .'. These manage to do both. With language, we very often do more than one thing at a time.

It was Austin who first employed the analysis of performatives and related speech-acts as a major conceptual tool. Certainly this is something which has very real value as part of the philosophical tool kit, in connection, for example, with the moral or other analysis of questions of intent. His paper, 'Other minds' (1946), together with his lectures at Oxford and his other writings, did a great deal to spread through the English-speaking philosophical world the idea of the philosophical significance of performative utterances. At one time (from the late 1940s into the 1960s), the concept enjoyed a great vogue, with philosophers applying it to all manner of cases – in some instances much more successfully than in others. It was not surprising, then, that someone would develop (what has become known as) a *performative theory of truth*.

According to Strawson's account (1949), saying that a statement is true says nothing more than the original statement said, full stop. Yet it does have a different force. Strawson emphasizes that using language is not just a matter of conveying information. What we say and how we say it, and what we manage to accomplish in so doing, depend on the linguistic tasks we are trying to perform and are responsive to the occasion on which we speak. Conveying information is only one of many things we might be doing. He suggests that attributing truth to a proposition fulfils a performative rather than a statement-making function (though he has some reluctance to adopt Austin's term). He analogizes between 'yes', 'ditto', and 'that is true', holding that they all require a statement serving as a linguistic occasion for their use, and that using one of them does not make a statement about the statement which serves as the occasion for its use. Such utterances are not used to make any statement whatsoever. They are performative utterances, serving to express agreement with the statements which occasion them. So, to say that a statement is true is to endorse it, not to say something about it. (The exact nature of the performative force, Strawson says, will vary considerably, depending on both the nature of the linguistic occasion and our response to it.) By extension, 'is false' must be taken to be a suitably occasioned expression of disagreement.

Strawson's performative theory of truth amounts to an adaptation of Ramsey's redundancy theory, with the addition of a performative element to explain the function of truth-statements. In that way, it satisfies our inclination to believe that 'is true' adds *something* to the original statement. Certainly it must be allowed, whatever else one might conclude about this theory, that Strawson does well to recognize that what we say is best understood in the light of the circumstances in which we say it. Moreover, it is well to ask what we are doing when we say it. Now that he draws it to our attention, it certainly does seem correct that statements using the words 'is true' (and the like) at least often do more than straightforwardly convey information. No doubt a performative element is, at least often, present. Your saying that it is true that Perth is west of Sydney does seem to perform the act of endorsing my statement that Perth is west of Sydney. Yet the question remains, is the performative theory an adequate theory of truth?

In addition to the act of endorsing it, does saying that a statement is true make a statement about that statement? After all, as Austin pointed out (1950) with reference to Strawson's theory, one statement could well serve both functions. To be sure, stating that it is true that Perth is west of Sydney does not say anything more about Perth or Sydney than would be said by the statement that Perth is west of Sydney. Even so, we might be saying something *about the statement* that Perth is west of Sydney, doing so at the same time that we are endorsing the statement. Indeed, that we think the statement true would seem a very good ground for endorsing it. Our question remains: is the endorsement the only thing added to the statement said to be true?

Strawson's theory is better able to face criticism than was the redundancy theory, but it still has difficulties. There remains a problem with the blind use. Saying 'What Paul says is true', without knowing what he said, is now understood as performing an act of endorsement (even though we cannot be endorsing Paul's statement by re-issuing it). That gives the utterance something to do. While it is possible, it does seem strange that one might endorse a statement without suggesting that there is something about what is said which merits endorsement. Are we perhaps doing something in addition to making the endorsement – perhaps something which does carry such a suggestion? Warnock (1964) argues that using the words 'is true' certainly involves more than simple endorsement. After all, we can endorse decisions, wishes, value judgements, and various other things, yet 'is true' cannot be used to make such endorsements. The use of such terminology is tied to statements. Warnock concludes that, in addition to its function of endorsing, the use of 'is true' makes a statement about a statement. If so, Strawson's account is radically incomplete and in need of an account of what it is that we state about a statement when we state that it is true. Warnock substantially adopted Austin's account of truth, which we shall consider later. Here we must ask what reply Strawson can make to this line of objection.

Strawson quite agreed that the use of 'is true' is tied to statements. Moreover, he came to concede that he had overemphasized the performative element and underemphasized the importance of the occasion on which we use such words. He came to accept as 'the undisputed thesis' the thesis 'that someone who says that a certain statement is true thereby makes a statement about a statement' – though with the proviso that what is said about the statement is not that it is true (1964: 68). He takes as his example 'A's statement, that X is eligible, is true'. He does not render this simply as 'X is eligible', which would be to follow Ramsey's line much too simplistically and to fail to take into account the occasion of use. Instead, he renders it as 'As A stated, X is eligible' (ibid.: 78). This is still Ramseyan in so far as the 'is true' part of it disappears. Moreover, something is being said about the statement that X is eligible. It is said to have been stated by A. In cases where we do not know what that statement is, we use something like '. . . things are always [or on this particular occasion?] like the Pope says they are' (ibid.: 79). That, too, says something about the statements in question. Again, perhaps no one has said anything: 'As may be urged/objected/ . . .

etc., *p*' (ibid.: 81). As well as to standard cases, then, these forms apply to the blind use, where we have no idea what was said, and even to cases where nothing was said at all. Even so, the use of 'is true' looks to at least the hypothetical making of a statement, and endorses the statement. In a way, something is said about the statement. The statement is referred to at least hypothetically as having been made – that much being said about it – but it is not the subject of further predication (ibid.: 78–81). So, we have recognized the performative aspect, and 'is true' has been analysed out of the account. Does this solve the problem?

In the assessment of such an account, the central issue may not be one of whether something is stated about a statement. Indeed, according to Williams' analysis (1976) which is in some ways similar, the statement is not even said to have been made, but is *presupposed* to have been made. By his account, 'What Percy says is true' amounts to (paraphrasing from the Polish notation) 'Percy made exactly one statement [this is presupposed], and for all *p*, if Percy says *p*, *p*' (ibid.: 73). In his version, as well as in Strawson's, the word 'true' is eliminated, while the statement said to be true is in some way referred to and reasserted. Yet the question remains, do such paraphrases as theirs capture the meaning of the originals, which seem to be attributing a property, truth, to a statement. O'Connor argues that:

> The question then arises: in virtue of what supposed properties do we endorse or reject statements? We may no longer say that it is because they seem to us true (or false) for these terms have been assigned other duties. . . . Whatever labels of acceptability or its opposite we applied to beliefs and statements, we would still have to defend our assignment of these labels by reference to some rational criteria.
>
> (1975: 127)

Certainly we do accept or reject statements on the basis of appropriate criteria. That X is eligible would be accepted relative to the prevailing eligibility rules. But on what *grounds* do we decide whether what the Pope (or Percy) says is to be endorsed or rejected if we do not know what is said? Is it not because their statements have an important characteristic? This is not an issue which we can eliminate by eliminating the word 'true'.

P.T. Geach (1965) and A.R. White (1970) have suggested some cases which would be very difficult to deal with in the manner of

Ramsey and Strawson (or Williams). 'If that's true, you had better give up' (White 1970: 101) seems to me to provide a persuasive counter-example. Suppose the occasion for that statement, S, is the suggestion (statement, conjecture, or whatever), C, that the match is rigged. S seems to come to something more than simply 'If the match is rigged, you had better give up', and the difference seems not just to be one of some act of agreement (doubt, warning, or the like). A Strawsonian-style 'If, as has been suggested [stated, or . . .], the match is rigged, you had better give up' seems closer to the mark, as it does not fail to take the occasioning suggestion, C, into account. Yet such a reformulation seems to lose some of the point of the original. While the consequent presumably does follow if the match is rigged, the force, the *point* of S appears to be that it follows if C is true. C is true if the match is rigged, but it seems evident to me that the *primary* thrust of the hypothetical, S, is that you had best give up if the antecedent suggestion has a certain highly significant property, and only by implication that you had best give up if the match has a certain unfortunate feature. Such considerations persuade me that truth is indeed a property of statements or propositions.

Where, then, do we go from here? Certainly we can all, whatever else we might think, agree with Strawson that 'A's statement is true' involves 'Things are as A says they are'. Whether or not that is all of the story, it must be part of the story. Strawson recommends that we let it go at that, and turn our attention from truth (in general) to the more profitable pursuit of various truths of various sorts. Truth theory itself can lapse into the more productive branches of philosophy (Strawson 1964: 84):

> Better, perhaps, let the theory of truth become, as it has shown so pronounced a historical tendency to become, part of some other theory: that of knowledge; or of mind; or of meaning.

Tarski, too, concluded that it would be wise to abandon the attempt to develop a general account of truth. Rather, he proposes that we should turn our attention to systematically understanding, in a language, the truth-conditions for individual statements in their variety. His approach, with which Strawson by no means agreed, is discussed in chapter 5. Whatever approach we take, we must accept that just what is involved in a statement's being true will vary widely among widely varying statements. This is a point stressed by the pragmatists (who should have been more widely heeded). It is a point which forced itself on Wittgenstein and one which, in their different ways, both Tarski and Strawson accepted. Even so, I am persuaded, as above, that to say that A's statement is true is to predicate truth of it and thereby to say something – however minimal – about A's statement as well as about whatever A's statement is about. Whether we must, with Warnock, adopt Austin's account is another matter. That account has problems of its own. These topics will be discussed in further chapters, as will later theories of truth. First, some other issues must be developed.

5

THE SEMANTIC CONCEPTION OF TRUTH

I attempt to present, explicate, and criticize Tarski's semantic conception of truth. While it is a technical achievement of the first magnitude, it does not offer us an adequate account of truth. The most it can do is extensionally to offer us a frozen cross-section of language in a particular application. It cannot come to terms with the inflexibility and imprecision so important to the actual use and effectiveness of a natural language. Rather, as Davidson shows, given a pre-analytic conception of truth, semantic analyses can be more useful in exploring the meaning-structure of a language. An adequate account of truth must take stock of the pragmatics of person, purpose, and circumstances.

Alfred Tarski's *semantic conception of truth* has in one way or another influenced virtually all subsequent truth theory, and indeed, is one of the great landmarks of twentieth-century philosophy.[1] Certainly it did much to fill the gap left by the decline of the *Tractatus*, particularly among those who desired to define truth with formal precision. Tarski attempted to formulate a definition of truth which was formally sound and theoretically fruitful, which did justice to the traditional conception of truth as agreement with reality, and which avoided those difficulties concerning entities and relationships that had plagued so many previous theories. He defined truth relative to a given language, and for his material he used only mathematical logic together with that language for which he defined truth. The theory which he developed attracted a large following by reason of its admirable theoretical parsimony, its avoidance of many theoretical dead-ends, its well developed formal rigour, and through being congenial to the presumption that truth is answerable to reality. It has proved to be of quite considerable value in that it offers us an approach by means of which we can usefully study the broad structure of a given language (natural or otherwise). For that reason it is of critical importance for much of the philosophy of language as currently pursued. Many substantial results have been achieved thereby. Among that of many others, the work of Donald Davidson immediately springs to mind in this connection. Tarski's conception of truth has thus been of significant instrumental value, and this will always be to its credit even if it does not prove adequate as an account of truth.

Not only has the semantic theory been widely employed, it has been variously interpreted, often in mutually inconsistent ways. Karl Popper, for instance, sees it as supporting a realist theory of science and a correspondence theory of truth, while others have interpreted it as a purely formal conception quite divorced from any implications about the relationship between our beliefs (even true ones) and reality. In the following, we shall primarily be concerned with Tarski's theory in its own right, and for its implications for truth theory, rather than for its wider applications. Even so, we must be careful not to make of the theory other than it is.

To avoid the identification problems attached to such entities as propositions and the like, and to focus on truth in its concrete manifestation, Tarski took the bearers of truth and falsity to be sentences. These he took to be 'not individual inscriptions, but classes of inscriptions of similar form' within the framework of a semantic system (1944: 370n). Truth, then, is to be ascribed not to sentence-tokens, as individual inscriptions are called, but to sentence-types. His attempt is to define truth for the sentence-types of a particular language. Given that 'semantics . . . deals with certain relations between expressions of a language and the objects (or "states of affairs") "referred to" by those expressions' (ibid.: 345), he proposed to take truth as a semantic conception and to build his definition of truth on the basis of other semantic notions. And what is it that we are to ask of a worthwhile definition of truth? He demands that an acceptable definition must meet two basic requirements: it must be materially adequate, and it must be formally correct.

MATERIAL ADEQUACY

To be materially adequate, our account of truth must agree with the facts. We must require, that is, that the sentence 'Snow is white' be true if and only if snow is white and, in general, for all sentences '*p*', that the sentence '*p*' be true if and only if . . . whatever '*p*' says. This seems little enough to ask. An account of truth would be no more than ridiculous if it allowed it to be false that snow is white when snow is white. However, Tarski wants to build this into an adequacy condition which is really very strong. He wants our definition of truth to be *fully* adequate, in the sense that truth or falsity is to be fully specified for every meaningful sentence in the language for which we are defining truth. Accordingly, his condition of material adequacy, his *requirement* (*T*), is not just that the consequences of the definition are to be consistent, but that our definition is to entail all sentences of the form

'*p*' is true if and only if *p*.

A definition of truth is to be recognized as materially adequate only if it meets requirement (T). It may not look like it at first glance, but this is really asking quite a lot. While (T)-sentences, as they are often called, are clearly truisms, it is by no means a trivial requirement that all meaningful (T)-sentences actually be entailed by our definition of truth. This is to require not only that the definition be in accordance with the facts, but that it specify the truth-conditions for every meaningful sentence in the language with which we are dealing. This may be an appropriate requirement for an artificially contrived formal language, but for an ordinary language in general use, it would be a very stiff requirement. But, then, Tarski is not primarily concerned with ordinary languages in general use, since they are insufficiently precise for his liking.

FORMAL CORRECTNESS

Not only must our definition of truth be materially adequate, it must be formally correct. We can get a formally correct definition only in a formal system, Tarski tells us, since 'the problem of the definition of truth obtains a precise meaning and can be solved in a rigorous way only for those languages whose structure has been exactly specified' (1944: 347). Neither English nor any other natural language has a precisely specified structure, so we must have recourse to a formal language – that is, a formal system serving as a language. Our formal language must be set up in such a way that it does not fall prey to the ills of our natural languages. Before we go on, however, I would remark that it seems to me that Tarski is too prone to equate precision with correctness, or to take it as a necessary condition for correctness.

To be sure, we must impose some demands on a formal system. As Tarski reminds us, one thing we must require of any formal system is that it avoid paradox. This is a genuine and serious problem, as many formal systems which were contrived with insufficient caution have indeed given rise to paradoxes. Set theory as it was originally practised, for instance, gave rise to the famous Russell's paradox which sent shock waves through philosophy for decades. Since we are trying to define truth, we must particularly take care to avoid paradox having to do with the notion of truth. Certainly we must avoid any version of the liar paradox. Consider:

This sentence is not true.

The problem of course is that by requirement (T), 'This sentence is not true' is true if and only if it is not true, and vice versa. This is a sad state of affairs, and a fatal flaw in any formal language. There are any number of versions of this, the liar paradox (e.g. 'I am now telling a lie', and the like). How, then, are we to contrive our formal language so as to preserve it from paradox?

As part of his resolution of the problem, Tarski demands that the language for which we are defining truth be *semantically open* rather than closed. That is, it must exclude all names of its own expressions, and it must exclude all semantic terms, such as 'true', which refer to any of its sentences. All such expressions which we may wish to employ – and some of them will be very important – are to be included in a *meta-language* used for talking about the language, the *object-language*, for which we are defining truth. The key expressions reserved to the meta-language must not be interpretable in the object-language, else we would be led back into paradox. The basic idea is that paradox is, as it were, the savage bite of the vicious circle, and can be abolished only by abolishing circularity. The problem with 'This sentence is not true' is that it can be defined only in terms of itself, a situation wherein truth keeps circling back on falsity, and falsity on truth. In contrast, those sentences which come by their meaning honestly stay out of such trouble. To say that sentence S in object-language O is true or not true is to say something in the meta-language, which is permissible, but 'This sentence is not true' is a confused attempt to use an object-language sentence to make a meta-language statement. It is ruled out by the way in which Tarski specifies the structure of his object-language and the meta-language used for dealing with it.

Tarski's approach to dealing with paradox is recognizably similar to that used by Russell in dealing with those paradoxes which threatened set theory. Russell's paradox concerned the set of all sets which are not members of themselves. That set generates a paradox because it is a member of itself if, and only if, it is not a member of itself. This was quite upsetting to those who depended heavily on set theory. Russell proposed to solve the problem with his famous and still controversial *theory of types*, which defines set theory in a hierarchical fashion from the bottom up (Russell 1908). Sets (of the first order) can have only individuals as members. Second-order sets can have individuals and first-order sets as members, but not second-order sets. And so on up the line, with each level being defined only in terms of previous levels, and not in terms of the same or a higher level. (The set – on a given level – of all sets which are not members of themselves can be composed only of lower order sets. It cannot possibly be a member of itself, nor does its non-membership lead to paradox, so the problem is solved.) The *ramified theory of types* extends this to propositions. Again, there is a hierarchy, with propositions not being definable in terms of equally or more complex propositions. Propositions cannot say things about themselves, circularity is ruled out, and paradox avoided. This is roughly the approach which Tarski takes in trying to avoid the semantic paradoxes. We are given a hierarchy of languages, such that whatever the object-language may talk about it, it cannot talk about itself or any of its linguistic components. That is what the meta-language is for. And if we want to talk about *it*, we need a meta-meta-language. And so on.

There is some dispute over whether this is the right approach. There is question both about whether this approach works in all cases, and about whether it is too stringent, ruling out things which ought not to be ruled out. Before going on I shall take a very brief look at this matter, considering it only in connection with Tarski's account. Let us first take the question of whether this approach does work in all cases. Consider

1 Sentence number 2 is true.
2 Sentence number 1 is not true.

We clearly have another paradox here, one evidently related to the 'liar paradox' that Tarski was concerned about. Yet while these sentences say things about each other, it is not at all clear that they are defined in terms of one another. Nor is it clear that we can assign them levels in the hierarchy. Tarski would certainly not be prepared to concede that this version of paradox slips through his net. Sentence number 1 can only refer to lower order sentences, on his scheme, and can be referred to only by sentences of a higher order. If sentence number 1 can talk about sentence number 2, it cannot be talked about by sentence number 2. At least one (both?) of the sentences, therefore, is semantically malformed and so cannot be part of our formal system, whether in the object-language or in any of the meta-languages. If we take this approach, though, we may have to make a purely arbitrary decision about which one to declare illegitimate.

Not only does Tarski commit us to a language which is strictly hierarchical, he commits us to one which is quite firmly extensional as well. The meaning of each term, that is, is given by those things for which the term stands, and not by any concept we might have in mind. The meaning of 'snow' is snow, and the meaning of 'sentence number 2' is sentence number 2. I might have thought that sentence number 2 was the second item on the list, the one following the numeral '2', and that I could identify it and know what was said about it without knowing in more detail what it was. On Tarski's approach, I evidently cannot, nor can I even know that sentence 1 is a proper sentence until I check, in detail, what it is about. Again, as we pointed out in connection with the redundancy theory, it does not seem impossible or incoherent for me to say that what John said was true even when I do not know what he said. Do we really want to say that I cannot meaningfully make that claim, and that you cannot understand it if I do unless *you* know what it was which John said? It may be that we are willing to accept such results. Or it may be that we can weasel out of them some way. Dispute here is unresolved. Some, such as Kripke (1975), have suggested that we need an alternative approach to solving the problem of paradox, one which digs more deeply into the origins of paradox. Kripke suggests that paradox is often not a matter of logical form at all, but of how particular forms work out in their application. Their individual problems require more individualized solutions. This is not a question which it would be profitable to pursue further here, but we should note that there is not universal agreement that the approach of Tarski (and Russell) does succeed in solving the problem of paradox.[2]

Whether or not Tarski succeeds in avoiding paradox, there is the further question of whether he is paying too high a price in his attempt to do so. Even if we are prepared to go along with Tarski's hierarchical and purely extensional approach, there are further results which, to say the least, may seem less than fully plausible. Some sentences would be ruled out on Tarskian grounds because they are self-referential, and thus in breach of the hierarchical ordering, even though they seem, intuitively, to be quite in order. The following sentence, to quote a common example, appears to be unparadoxical, meaningful, and quite true:

This sentence is in English.

Again, authors frequently say in their book that in their book they are trying to do such-and-such. That information does not usually seem to be incoherent. Yet again, it seems quite true to say that I am doing the initial writing of this manuscript on a word processor, even though the 'this manuscript' is self-referential (and even quite indeterminate at this stage). Are we to agree that such sentences (or would-be sentences) are technically meaningless or malformed, even though they appear to be well formed and meaningful, to function properly, and, indeed, to be true? I just cannot buy that. It seems to me plausible that not all circles are vicious, and that we can hope to avoid paradox while employing some usages which Tarski and Russell would rule out. Strict hierarchical ordering with strict avoidance of self-reference may be neither necessary nor desirable. Personally, I would like to go along with those who maintain that we need a more finely tuned approach to paradox and, in general, a more flexible approach to the structure of language. Once again we have come to an area of active dispute.[3] To follow the dispute in detail, however, would lead us too far astray from our main purpose. Apart from that, there is some question about whether it is desirable to treat language on a purely extensional basis. Subsequently I shall explain why I believe that for purposes of truth theory it is not. For now I shall return to Tarski's exposition.

MORE ON FORMAL STRUCTURE

The problematic semantic terms, then, are to be restricted to the meta-language. It may perhaps be that our object-language is quite different from our meta-language. Using English as a meta-language we might, for instance, talk about Polish. The two languages need not be all that different, however. The object-language might just be a sub-portion of the meta-language, with all the semantic terms stripped out. We might well use English, with the semantic terms, as the meta-language for talking about English without the semantic terms. Indeed, that would usually be the most convenient way of proceeding. We just have to be careful not to get tangled up about what belongs on which semantic level.

Following Tarski, in formalizing the structure of our languages we are to employ set theory – in a suitably paradox-proofed version which keeps the different levels from getting tangled up – augmented with a version of the *Principia Mathematica* axioms.[4] This supplies the logical skeleton. Given that, we can then start about the business of specifying the structure and content of our object-language. This we do using names and predicates, e.g. 'snow', 'white', and 'is taller than', which are correlated with those actual things, e.g. snow, white things, and things which are taller than other things, which our object-language is used for talking about. On this basis we can create and deploy object-language sentences. We manipulate it all through our meta-language wherein we detail the structure and transact the semantic business of specifying which terms go with which objects in what way.

TOWARDS A DEFINITION OF TRUTH

While we have set up our language and given it solid structure as a formal system, we cannot just define being true in terms of being provable in that formal system. There are two good reasons for that. For one thing, not even all of the necessarily true sentences are provable in the formal system. A Gödel-style proof will establish that. (This is, in fact, a limitation common to all formal systems which are strong enough to say anything very interesting. That includes all those based on the *Principia Mathematica* axioms.) Moreover, there are the contingent sentences, such as 'Jill is taller than Jack'. Obviously, we cannot sort out whether Jack or Jill is the taller just by looking at the structure of some formal system. Rather, we have to look at Jack and Jill. Truth, then, must be defined some other way.

Again, it might be thought that we could define truth by generalizing requirement (T). Tarski tells us that

We can only say that every equivalence of the form (T) . . .

may be considered a partial definition of truth, which explains wherein the truth of this one individual sentence consists. The general definition has to be, in a certain sense, a logical conjunction of all these partial definitions.

(1944: 344)

Such a conjunctive definition might work for a language which was finite, but finite languages are not particularly interesting. Even if we did not wish to include the capacity to handle the natural numbers, which in itself would be enough to make the language infinite, a worthwhile language would still need the capacity to form infinitely many sentences. The capacity to form new combinations in response to novel situations is critical to the utility of a natural language. We need the flexibility to do so. Even if we start with a finite vocabulary (as one does even with the natural numbers), we still require an unlimited capacity to form new combinations. We cannot just piece together a conjunctive definition of truth by putting together, one after another, an infinitude of individual components. We could never complete the definition. But perhaps we could give the definition all at once, via the formal mechanism of universal generalization. That would give us something along the lines of

(p) ('p' is true if, and only if, p)

as our definition of truth (in language O).[5] Tarski rules out any such attempt on the formal grounds that we cannot quantify through quotation marks. This is not just a quibble based on arbitrary fastidiousness. After all, a sentence and its name are very different things, even though the quotation marks do not have a high level of visual impact, and we cannot just ignore the difference. Nor can we take the name as a straightforward function of the sentence it names. If we could, then it would be in order to quantify through quotation marks, but Tarski derives another paradox from the assumption that we can do this. His conclusion, then, is that we cannot properly quantify through quotation marks, and so that we need to develop some better definition of truth (1956: 162). Again, we have come to an area of disagreement. Some have maintained that other restrictions are the key to avoiding paradox, and that, with sufficient care and a properly contrived formal system, we could properly treat naming as being a type of function.[6] Perhaps, if we watched our step, we could in some way quantify through quotation marks under some conditions. Tarski did not attempt such a procedure, however, and it would take us too far afield to try to follow the debate on the complex issues here. In chapter 9, we shall look into quantificational matters somewhat further.

More relevantly here, let us ask what it would do for us if, some way, we could use the universally quantified formula suggested above, or something like it, as our definition of truth. That would just tell us that 'p' is true if, and only if, p, no matter what sentence of our object-language 'p' is. That ought to look quite familiar. Ramsey's redundancy theory told us that to assert that a given sentence is true is really, at bottom, to assert that sentence. The universally quantified formula, could we but use it here, would apply this fundamental idea in defining truth for our object-language in terms of every sentence in that language which obtains. Truth, that is, would be defined extensionally in terms of the set, no doubt an infinite set, of all sentences in our object-language which hold good. According to such a definition, true sentences are members of that set. To tell us that is not to tell us what makes a sentence hold good, or how we can know when it does – it would tell us nothing of how sentences came to be in the favoured set – but, then, perhaps that would be too much to ask of a definition of truth. Still, we would need some means of knowing, or specifying, which sentences of our language do hold good. Tarski, in fact, does attempt to offer such a means for us. Of course he does *not* accept the universalized formula as a definition, since he regards it as bogus. Even so, remember that Tarski tells us (above) that each of the (T)-sentences is a partial definition of truth, with the general definition being, in some sense, their logical conjunction. To build toward his general definition, Tarski does address himself to the task of specifying just which sentences of the object-language do hold good.

THE SEMANTIC DEFINITION OF TRUTH

When a formula has one or more unbound variables, it is said to be a *sentential function*, and is neither true nor false. It is a sentence, and true or false, only if all variables are bound. For instance, 'x is taller than y' and 'x is white' are sentential functions, while '$(x)(x$ is snow » x is white)' and 'snow is white' are sentences. The idea is that sentential functions are to become sentences when we fill in the blanks in such a way as to make them actually say something. Tarski goes on to define the concept of *satisfaction*. Intuitively, the idea is that certain objects are said to satisfy a given sentential function if the latter becomes a true sentence when its unbound variables are replaced by the names of those objects. The sentential function '*x* is taller than *y*' is satisfied, amongst other combinations, by Mt Everest and me, in that order, since it is taller than I am. The sentential function '*x* is white' is satisfied by snow, among other things, as the sentence 'snow is white' is true. While that is the basic idea, we cannot formally define satisfaction in terms of truth, since our objective is to define truth in terms of satisfaction. Instead, Tarski constructs a formal definition of satisfaction. We start by specifying which ordered classes, or '*sequences*' of objects satisfy the logically simplest sentential functions. Provided of course that we can do that, we then specify those sequences which satisfy sentential functions compounded from those simplest sentential functions. Progressively, we specify satisfying sequences for everything which can be meaningfully said in the language with which we are concerned.

To take up the examples introduced above, '*x* is taller than *y*', is satisfied by a large number of sequences. To start with, *any* sequence whose first two members were Mt Everest and me would satisfy that sentential function. The third term of the sequence might be a microbe, or Mars, or Montana. That would not matter, since the third and subsequent terms do not actually get used in filling in the blanks. So why bother with more than two terms? For formal reasons, Tarski finds it convenient to define satisfaction in terms of infinite sequences. That way, he can offer a general definition of satisfaction, rather than giving a definition for one-place sequences satisfying one-place sentential functions, and then another definition for two-place sequences and functions, and so on for three places on up. He uses infinite sequences as an alternative to an infinity of definitions. However, the long tail-end of a sequence does not really matter so far as satisfying a sentential function is concerned. As for '*x* is taller than *y*', it is satisfied not only by any sequence whose first two members are Mt Everest and me (in that order, obviously), but also by any other sequence whose first member is taller than its second member. Unless we were dealing with a very impoverished language, there would be quite a lot of sequences satisfying the sentential function, since a great many things are taller than a great many other things. Again, the function

93

'x is white' is satisfied by any sequence whose first member is snow, or milk, or anything else which is white, and is not satisfied by any sequence whose first member is not white. This is because we formulate our satisfaction specifications accordingly.

Whether a given sequence satisfies a given sentential function, then, is a matter of whether the unbound variables of the function can satisfactorily be replaced by the names of the first that-many members of the sequence. There is a special class of sentential functions, beloved by semanticists and logicians, which are satisfied by all sequences of objects, and another class of functions which are satisfied by no objects. Examples of these would be, respectively, 'x is white or is not white', which is satisfied by any x, and 'x is white and is not white', which is satisfied by nothing at all. For logical or formal reasons, it really does not matter one way or the other what gets plugged-in in place of the variables. The remaining sentential functions, such as 'x is white', are satisfied by some sequences and not by others, and thus have far more interesting careers in a world of contingent fact. In any case, the question is one of whether the unbound variables of a sentential function are satisfied by the first so-many objects of a sequence.

Let us return to 'x is taller than y'. As we mentioned, this sentential function is satisfied by any sequence whose first two members are, in order, Mt Everest and me, and it is also satisfied by any sequence whose first two members are the Eiffel Tower and me, or some Jack and some Jill, or that Jack and me, or various other combinations. Accordingly, 'x is taller than me' (this particular me) is satisfied by any sequence whose first member is Jack or Mt Everest or the Eiffel Tower, or anything else which could have paired with me to start a sequence satisfying 'x is taller than y'. It follows from the previous specifications that 'Jack is taller than me' is satisfied by all sequences, while 'I am taller than Jack' is satisfied by none. With no slots left to fill, the membership of the sequence does not matter. When the number of unbound variables dwindles to zero, then, a sentential function is a proper sentence and is true or false, being true if it is satisfied by all sequences, and false if by no sequence. 'Snow is white', for another example, would be satisfied by all sequences, as it would have *already* have been specified that all sequences beginning with snow satisfy 'x is white'. The actual membership of a sequence is then irrelevant, for every one of the objects in any sequence is then supernumerary. The question of truth and falsity has already been settled by the specification of the

94

satisfying sequences for the sentential function of which the sentence is an instance.[7] Accordingly, Tarski defines truth as follows:

> A sentence is true if it is satisfied by all [sequences of] objects, and false otherwise.
>
> (1944: 353)

This definition of truth is materially adequate, according to Tarski's requirement (T). All instances of the (T)-schema follow from it by virtue of the satisfaction-specifications which we have built into our object-language. Moreover, it is formally correct, without technical fault, and is beyond doubt one of the greatest achievements of formal semantics. From his definitions of satisfaction and truth we can obtain the laws of non-contradiction and excluded middle (in their semantic version) and, in general, lay the foundations of a substantial and useful system of formal semantics. Yet, we must ask, is it an adequate definition of truth? What ought we, and ought we not, to conclude from it – and what can we use it for? These questions are not really separable. I shall turn first to the former question, and in so doing I shall try to shed some light on further issues.

IS IT AN ADEQUATE THEORY? OBJECTIONS AND LIMITATIONS

Whether Tarski's definition provides an adequate theory of truth – and, indeed, whether any theory of truth *can* be adequate – will depend on what we take as our criterion of adequacy. Tarski observes that 'the very possibility of a consistent use of the expression "true sentence" which is in harmony with the laws of logic and the spirit of everyday language seems to be very questionable' (1956: 165). He remarks that there are doubtlessly several popular conceptions of truth, of varying degrees of imprecision, and that there is no one central account of truth which could possibly do justice to them all (1944: 355–67). Max Black (1948: 61) adds that if we are 'searching for a general property of the designata of true object-language sentences . . . the semantic definition of truth makes no contribution'. But, then, Tarski is not attempting to contribute to that search, which he considers to be quite hopeless. Rather, we should concern ourselves with truth as a technical concept in formal languages, which we might then be able to apply, for various purposes, to some aspects of natural languages.

As I shall eventually argue, I do believe that it is possible to give an account of truth, though a very minimal account, which is correct, general, and in basic accordance with ordinary usage. I also believe that Tarski is essentially correct in his opinion that no very strong general definition of truth is possible, since there are a great many differing sorts of discourse and types of proposition, upon which we make varying demands. Truth theory has too often been obfuscated by rickety theoretical superstructures which do not apply to all, if to any, cases. Let us, then, see how far we can get with Tarski's approach.

One line of objection to Tarski's whole approach concerns its relevance to actual fact and our linguistic dealings with fact. O'Connor argues that since satisfaction is defined for sentential functions, and since the factual make-up of any sequence is irrelevant to the question of a sentence's truth, satisfaction thus applies only vacuously to sentences, the actual bearers of truth or falsity. He then concludes that the semantic conception of truth 'has no relevance to the problem of empirical truth in everyday natural languages' (1975: 111), as that must certainly be a matter of factual relevance. This is too simplistic. While true sentences are satisfied by all sequences, irrespective of the content of those sequences, satisfaction and the factual content of the world is of central importance to the definition of truth. The sentence 'Snow is white' is satisfied by all sequences precisely *because* the sentential function '*x* is white' is specified as being satisfied by any sequence starting with snow (as well as by any other sequence starting with anything else which is white). In the course of specifying those sequences which satisfy simple and complex sentential functions, we have in effect specified the facts we are dealing with. Truth is then, in effect, defined in accordance with that factual relevance. While truth is not claimed to be a matter of correspondence, in any traditional sense, between what is true and a fact, Tarski's conception of truth is certainly a matter of a relationship between a sentence and something independent of the sentence which makes it true.

Even so, something may seem unsatisfactory here. Tarski's approach seems to make every meaningful sentence true or false by definition. If I want to know whether there really are any ghosts, or intelligent life in the Andromeda Galaxy, or whether the 'Big Bang' theory is correct, or whether John is a secret drinker, I cannot solve the problem by looking up the satisfaction-conditions of the relevant terms as specified in our semantic handbook. More likely, if we find out about the Big Bang, *then* we would know what semantic specifications to make. The semantic definition of truth does not give us a criterion of truth, and it is not intended to. In a sense, we might say that it does not even give us a definition of truth. Rather, *we* give it a definition of truth, which we build in to the satisfaction-specifications. We specify that '*x* is white' is satisfied by sequences starting with snow and not those starting with coal, because snow is white and coal is not. This is *not* to say that we presuppose some definition of truth on the basis of which we find that 'Snow is white' is true. Instead, Ramsey-like, we depend on our knowledge of snow and coal, which includes knowing that one is white and the other is not. It is out of such bits that we construct our definition of truth. As we have noted, Tarski remarked that

> . . . every equivalence of the form (T) . . . may be considered a partial definition of truth, which explains wherein the truth of this one individual sentence consists. The general definition has to be, in a certain sense, a logical conjunction of all these partial definitions.

> (1944: 344)

We define truth extensionally, building up one step at a time from the simple to the complex, in effect incorporating the specified truth-conditions for individual sentences into a structured body of truth-conditions for a given language. But *which* language? It is not a definition of truth for our natural language (e.g. English) at large. That is too fluid and ill-defined. Rather, we have a definition of truth for a formalized mock-up of our language. That is by no means to dismiss it as trivial or irrelevant. Just as a mathematical mock-up of a physical system can be a very great help in understanding and dealing with the physical system, so a formal system of semantics can be a very great help in understanding and dealing with our natural languages. Developments in linguistics in recent years have shown that conclusively. Still, the mathematical system is not the physical system, and the latter will have features not captured by mathematics. So too, the semantic system is not the natural language, and the latter is not entirely captured by the former. In giving an extensional definition of truth in our semantic system we are not giving even an extensional definition of truth in our natural language. Much less are we giving the essential meaning of truth. Nor are we giving an explanation of the use of the word 'true' in our natural language. Rather, by specifying things which satisfy certain sentential functions, we record a number of sentences which, as it happens, are true. From simple structures we can build to complex ones, and in so doing we can build a useful working model of a language, but we cannot go beyond the limits of what we have specified into our semantic system to start with.

Tarski's may seem like a very limited conception of truth. But, then, whether it is *too* limited will depend on whether there is anything beyond the limit which is worthwhile and achievable. An attempt to give the essential meaning of truth would not be in order, according to Tarski, because there are a great many divergent meanings of truth, and they tend to be impossibly vague. Again, we cannot give an extensional specification for truth in natural languages, because that would be too vast a project and because, in any case, what is true is constantly changing. It is better, he suggests, to settle for the possible.

TRUTH AND LANGUAGE-RELATIVITY

Tarski's proposal to extensionally specify truth for a formal system, while relatively modest, still attracts considerable criticism. O'Connor (1975: 104–6), Strawson (1949: 262–4), and others have urged against it the objection that it is incorrect to take truth as a property of sentences. In this connection, Strawson opposes the claim that to say that a sentence is true is to make a meta-language statement about an object-language sentence, arguing against it on the grounds that the translation of an 'is true' sentence from one language to another does not contain a quoted and untranslated sentence. If we were still making the same truth claim about one particular sentence, presumably *that* sentence, rather than another sentence in another object-language, should be the one quoted and deemed true. It depends on what we are talking about. Sometimes we actually are talking about one particular sentence. It is quite possible, for instance, that Germans might wish to discuss the truth-conditions of an English sentence, in which case they might say ' "Snow is white" ist wahr wenn und nur wenn der Schnee ist weiss', leaving the English sentence quoted and untranslated. Normally, though, we are not talking about a particular sentence in a particular language, but about whatever the sentence is about. The German translation of 'It's true that some swans are black' would not use any English words, quoted or otherwise, since what is being talked about is swans rather than English sentences. Seemingly, this instance supports Strawson's contention that 'is true' is not used to make a statement about a sentence. At least it seems to lend support to the contention that 'is true' is not (normally) used to say something about a sentence. Let us inquire further concerning what it is to be a proper translation.

According to a Tarskian point of view, one sentence in one language is a translation of another sentence in another language if they have the same truth-conditions (more precisely, when their subsidiary sentential functions are satisfied by the same things). If we translate an 'is true' sentence into German, we translate it into an 'ist wahr' sentence which has the same truth-conditions. While it is sentences which are true or false, it is not sentences *per se* which are true or false, but sentences in some language or another, sentences with their attendant semantic roles and particular truth-conditions. To say 'It's true that some swans are black' is to assert, in English, something about swans. In the 'that-clause' we use a sentence to state which conditions are fulfilled, and in another language we would use an equivalent sentence to state the same thing. A translation requires us only to say the same thing about whatever it is we are talking about. If we are talking about a sentence (a particular form of words), saying that its truth-conditions are fulfilled, we must quote it in translation. If instead, by saying that the sentence, as used in the 'that-clause', is true we are talking about those conditions – using the sentence to say what they are – then the translation would take us to a different sentence (in another language) saying the same thing about those conditions which would render that sentence and its translation true. The point of a translation is to produce an equivalent statement using another means of statement.

In considerable part, Strawson's misgivings centre on the troubling concept of truth in a language. Tarski defines the truth of a sentence in terms of the satisfaction-conditions of its particular object-language, whereas one might naturally assume that whether what is said is true is independent of any particular language. This difficulty, as we can see now, is more apparent than real. Certainly a *particular* sentence is true if it meets the satisfaction-conditions of the language in which it occurs. Still, any equivalent sentence in any other language would have to meet the satisfaction-conditions of its own language in order to be true, else it would not be equivalent. The nature of truth is not held to be fragmented into separate bits for separate languages. Truth is defined with respect to particular languages, to be sure, but that Tarski can apply his method to languages in general is because he has a general conception of truth in terms of sentences meeting the satisfaction-conditions of their own particular languages, whatever languages they may be. It is presumed that truth is expressed in some language, and the truth of a given sentence is defined with respect to its language, but truth is tied only to languages, not to any one language. Thus, while we might say, as some would put it, that 'Snow is white' is true in English, that should not be taken to mean that there is some such thing as truth-in-English, which is fundamentally different from truth-in-German or truth-in-Polish. There is such a thing as being true, which 'Snow is white', as a sentence in English, is. (To be sure, there is a sense, I think a trivial sense, in which we might say that each sentence has its own particular truth definition in terms of its own particular satisfaction-conditions. But something of the sort is true for *any* theory of truth. Any truth-bearer has its particular correspondence to its appropriate fact, or its own particular way of being useful or of cohering with the Absolute, or whatever.)

This goes some ways toward meeting Strawson's objections concerning truth in a language, but there are more fundamental issues to be faced. Tarski's theory, he argues (1949: 262–7), confuses questions of meaning with questions of truth. Indeed, Strawson would make a similar charge with respect to any theory which attempted to analyse truth in terms of some relationship said to hold between language and the world. He maintains that something like '*S* is true if and only if such-and-such' does not determine or define what 'true' means, nor does it even explain what it is for sentence *s* to be true. Rather, instead of '*S* is true *if and only if* such-and-such' giving us the meaning of truth, or of the truth of sentence *S*, '*S* is *true if and only if* such-and-such' gives us, if correct, the meaning of sentence *S*. The formula gives us the extensional truth-conditions of *S*, and so gives us its extensional meaning. The phrase 'is true if and only if', according to Strawson, is a synonym for 'means that', and it is only as a component of such a phrase that 'is true' can be used to say something about a sentence. An 'is true if and only if'-formula gives us the extensional rather than the intensional meaning of *S*. 'Unicorns exist' is true if and only if centaurs exist, since neither exists, yet that does not give us the intensional meaning of 'Unicorns exist'. Neither can such a formula give us the intensional meaning of truth, or of anything else. Still, there is room for an extensional definition of truth, in the event that we go along with

Tarski and accept a fully specified language. Then, we can just say – in the meta-meta-language, of course – that '*S* is true' is true if and only if *S* is on the master list of true sentences (which it is if and only if it is satisfied by all sequences). That would give us the meaning of '*S* is true', given that 'means that' and 'is true if and only if' are synonyms. Of course, this expedient would only give us an extensional definition of truth for a fully specified language in the Tarskian mould, which Strawson would not be willing to accept as a proper definition of truth (whatever its advantages for formal semantics).

Strawson, we must be clear, ruled out any sort of definition of truth in terms of a relation between language and the world, all of which share the same shortcoming. Any such definition must make use of a formula of the form '*S* is true if and only if (it corresponds, it coheres, it is useful, it . . .)', yet any such formula would, were it viable at all, give us only the meaning of *S*. It could not serve as a definition of truth as a property of sentences or statements, because truth is not a property. Rather, the word 'true' has, he claims, a very different linguistic role, as was discussed in the previous chapter. We saw there, though, that his account is questionable. Let us then inquire further just why Strawson equated 'is true if and only if' and 'means that'. Consider, with him, the following:

> 'The monarch is deceased' is true if and only if the king is dead.

or, as he says, more strictly,

> 'The monarch is deceased' is true in English if and only if the king is dead.

In such cases, he tells us, we

> make use of the phrase '*is true if and only if*' as a synonym for '*means that*'. It is only *as a part of the former phrase* that the expression '*is true*' is used, in such statements, to talk about sentences.

> (1949: 266)

A degenerate case of the above is

> 'The monarch is deceased' is true if and only if the monarch is deceased,

which can serve as a model for any (T)-sentence. He continues,

101

To read the degenerate cases, then, as specification, or parts, of some ideal defining formula for the phrase 'is true' is to separate the phrase from the context which alone confers meta-linguistic use upon it, and to regard the result as a model for the general use of 'is true'. It is to be committed to the mistake of supposing that the phrase 'is true' is normally (or strictly) used as a meta-linguistic defining predicate.

(ibid.)

However, this is to assume the very point with which we are concerned. Strawson claims that 'is true' has another linguistic role, and only that role. Yet, if we do not accept his claims about what 'is true' does do, why should we accept his claims about what it does *not* do? Why must we agree that it has no meta-linguistic use, that it has use only as a part of 'is true if and only if' used as a synonym for 'means that'? May it not be that 'is true' does have meaning in its own right – a meaning which, in fact, lends itself to the formation of the other expression? We have no sufficient reason here not to think so. (As we shall see in chapter 7, he later gives another reason for rejecting such definitions, that being that there is no synonym for 'is true' with which all who use the term would agree. That also turns out to be a bad reason.) Let us assume, then, that Tarski's account can be considered as a definition of truth. Let us ask how we are to interpret the definition, and whether it is a good one.

IS IT CORRESPONDENCE?

Truth, while tied to language, is not tied to any particular language, natural or contrived. Nor are things true or false just because we define them to be so. Would it be correct, then, to say that true sentences are true because they conform to an independent reality? Karl Popper comes to this conclusion, claiming that Tarski

rehabilitated the correspondence theory of absolute or objective truth which had become suspect. He vindicated the free use of the intuitive idea of truth as correspondence to the facts. . . .

Thanks to Tarski's work, the idea of objective or absolute truth – that is truth as correspondence to the facts – appears to be accepted today with confidence by all who understand it.

(1963: 223–5)

In his contention that the correspondence theory has been rehabilitated, Popper (1979: 367) claims the support of Tarski himself, when the latter says

> I would only mention that throughout this work I shall be concerned exclusively with grasping the intentions which are contained in the so-called *classical* conception of truth ('true – correspondence with reality') in contrast, for example, with the *utilitarian* conception ('true – in a certain respect useful').
>
> (1956: 153)

However, one can attempt to grasp those intentions without advocating a correspondence theory. Elsewhere (1944: 342–3), Tarski says quite explicitly that while he would like to do justice to the intuitions which adhere to the correspondence theory, it cannot be considered a satisfactory definition of truth.

According to Popper's interpretation, the main problem with previous correspondence theories was the difficulty in giving an account spanning the thing said to be true on the one hand and the fact to which it is supposed to correspond on the other. The difficulty is to somehow get beyond words to the factual correspondent. Tarski's semantic scheme, using object-language and meta-language in tandem, is supposed to overcome this difficulty. On this interpretation, a (T)-sentence, such as

'Snow is white' is true if, and only if, snow is white.

tells us in the meta-language, on the right-hand side, what the fact is to which the object-language sentence must, if true, correspond. It corresponds with fact when its particular specified fact obtains. Given a vantage point outside of the object-language it is now possible, and not even very difficult, to explain what a statement's correspondence with fact consists of. 'Once the need for a (semantical) metalanguage is realized', he tells us (1963: 224), 'everything becomes clear'.

Popper misinterprets Tarski's achievement. In noting how that is so, I hope to better explain what the semantic conception does and does not amount to. First, we must recall that requirement (T) is *not* a definition of truth. It is an adequacy condition which must be met by *any* theory of truth with a claim to be taken seriously. Bradley and Blanshard could have accepted the condition just as well as Popper. That requirement (T), and the semantic conception of truth in general, are epistemologically neutral was stressed by Tarski himself (1944: 362). Moreover, he explicitly repudiated a critic's claim that ' "Snow is white" is taken to be semantically true if snow is *in fact* white'. Tarski replied that

> . . . the words *'in fact,'* . . . do not occur in the original formulation and . . . are misleading even if they do not affect the content. For these words convey the impression that the semantic conception of truth is intended to establish the conditions under which we are warranted in asserting any given sentence, and in particular any empirical sentence. . . . this impression is merely an illusion . . .
>
> (ibid.: 361)

Requirement (T) does not offer a definition of truth, whether in terms of correspondence or anything else. At most, a single (T)-sentence is one small part of an extensional definition. Moreover, there is no claim, explicit or implicit, on Tarski's part that (T)-sentences hold or do not hold by virtue of meeting any correspondence standard. Popper notes that object-language sentences are true when things are as they are said to be by that object-language sentence. We assess a (T)-sentence, when we are able to do so, by checking its object-language sentence and noting in the meta-language whether what it says is so. We could all agree to that much. He then goes on to recommend (1979: 326ff) that we think of (T)-sentences on the model of

> 'Snow is white' corresponds with the facts if and only if snow is white.

However, a coherentist could accept requirement (T) and assess (T)-sentences according to whether or not the object-language sentence meets the coherence criterion. We would check the object-language sentence by noting in the meta-language whether what it says is so (is coherent). Accordingly, the coherentist could proclaim (T)-sentences on the model of

> 'Snow is white' coheres with the Absolute if and only if snow is white.

Whatever our definition of truth, we could proclaim something of the sort. As Haack (1976: 325) points out, it is conceivable that someone might accept such (T)-sentences as

> 'Snow is white' is asserted by the Pope *ex cathedra* if and only if snow is white.

Requirement (T) is a very minimal requirement and cannot be spun into a substantive theory of truth, be it a correspondence theory or be it otherwise. Instead of giving us a definition of truth in terms of correspondence, Popper, in effect, takes it as a definition of correspondence, telling us that an object-language sentence corresponds with the facts if and only if what it says is so. That makes just about anyone an adherent of the correspondence theory.

There is another factor which leads Popper to characterize Tarski's theory as a correspondence theory. He takes it to be 'absolute' and 'objective', as opposed, as he uses the terms, to 'subjective'. It is not subjective in so far as it does not define truth in terms either of our knowledge or of the meeting of some criterion. A statement is true if things are as they are said to be, quite independently of the state of our knowledge or the meeting of any criteria. Pragmatic and coherentist theories, in contrast, are held not to be absolute or objective. Popper considers it to be a desirable feature of Tarski's theory that truth should be defined independently of criteria. He is a fallibilist, holding that we can be wrong about things no matter how good the evidence. An independent objective truth offers something for us to aim at, and permits us to think that one conjecture might be nearer to or further from the truth than another conjecture. This is very important to Popper, since the concept of *verisimilitude* plays such a central role in his realist philosophy (see Popper 1963, 1979). This, I believe, takes us to the heart of his interpretation of Tarski's theory as a correspondence theory. His basic idea is evidently that a theory of truth is a correspondence theory if it maintains that true statements are true because of an independent reality. Popper, I think, misconstrues Tarski's theory and misconstrues correspondence theories as well. It is a misconstrual of Tarski's theory because it is, as Tarski stated (1944: 362), independent of any epistemological attitude, including that of realism. While truth is not defined in terms of our awareness, it is not necessarily independent of it. It could conceivably be that snow is white just because we think it is. While Tarski's theory is compatible with Popperian realism, it does not demand it.

It should also be noted that correspondence theories do not necessarily demand an independent reality. Correspondence theories claim only that statements, when true, are true because of their relationship to something else. Perhaps they fit or conform to that something else, as Russell and the early Wittgenstein maintained, or perhaps it is some other sort of relationship with the something else, as was evidently the case with Moore's unanalysable truth relationship. Even so, the something else which makes the statement true is not necessarily independent of the statement and the knower. So long as there are two things, one of which makes the other true, they can still be connected in some way. Correspondence theories are no more committed to Popperian realism than is Tarski's theory.

There remains a sense, quite a weak sense, in which the semantic conception of truth properly could be described as a correspondence theory. Sentences, when true, are true because certain sentential functions are (specified to be) satisfied by certain things. However, this is correspondence in a very trivial and attenuated sense. In a full-bodied correspondence theory, true statements are true *because* things are the way they are. We find out by checking the facts. In the semantic conception, true sentences are true because they are specified to be so. We find out by checking the rule-book. Why was the rule-book written one way rather than another, making snow white instead of black? The semantic conception of truth offers us no criterion of truth. Nor does it even say anything about what it is we are trying to capture when we develop our own criteria for specifying one thing rather than another as satisfying a sentential function. Do we do so because snow rather than coal is white? Because it *is* true that snow is white (whatever that means)? The semantic conception of truth tells us nothing here. Perhaps there is nothing to be told. While we might, perhaps naively, hope for an *intensional* account, it may be that we must settle for an extensional account which specifies which things are true in our system of formal semantics. Tarski claims that we can hope for no more. What he does offer is considerable, being a formally sound tool with useful application for certain purposes. We may ask, though, whether there is any carry-over from formal systems to natural language so that Tarski's theory can tell us something worthwhile about truth there. We may also wonder whether we really must settle for an extensional account.

EXTENSIONAL SEMANTICS

That truth is defined extensionally, based on the specified satisfaction-conditions of particular sentential functions, and thus sentences, would appear to me to be both a strength and a weakness of the semantic conception of truth. It is a strength that, given a basic set of rules and specifications, it is determinate whether a meaningful sentence in the system is true or false. Moreover, a semantic system can be consistently extended to cover new subject-matters or peculiar cases. In principle, if we extend enough, doing so well enough, we can get a model which – extensionally – reflects what is true or false in some given sample of a natural language as used. If, for example, in that sample I said truthfully that Jim is at the door, I can specify for a model of that given sample that 'x is at the door' is satisfied by sequences beginning with Jim, and perhaps those beginning with a few other things, such as the doormat. The whole thing is quite *ad hoc*.

What is more difficult is to provide a model which captures the actual working dynamics of a substantial part of a natural language. This would be a very significant accomplishment, and we might well be willing to accept a touch of the *ad hoc* with it. This is still very much unfinished business. Donald Davidson and various others have worked with considerable success towards developing systems whose object-languages approximate more and more closely to natural languages, coming much closer than anything developed by Tarski. Substantial progress has been made towards semantically accommodating comparatives, performatives, adverbials, various sorts of nouns, and other important features of natural language (Davidson 1973). Of particular importance has been progress concerning indexical statements, those tied to particular times, places, or language-users. (After all, we can hardly get far with language until we are able to take account of the fact that such sentences as 'I had eggs there for breakfast this morning' can be used to make many different statements, some true and some not.) These models, resting on the semantic conception, give us valuable tools for the investigation of the syntax and meaning-structure of a language. They are not primarily intended to tell us about truth – nor, as I shall argue, do they do so.

If we are to model a natural language properly, we must take account of the fact that we can use one to do many new and different things. An outstanding feature of our understanding of a natural language is that we are able, even those among us who are dull, to understand and evaluate the truth-conditions of a large if not infinite number of sentences, the great bulk of which we have never before encountered. Accordingly, a virtue of the semanticist's approach is that they are able, in intention if not yet in execution, to provide semantic machinery by means of which we are able to generate and evaluate an infinite number of sentences on the basis of a finite number of rules and satisfaction-conditions. In general, the attempt is to account for as much of a natural language as possible by means of a basic and finite semantic structure, then to find *ad hoc* ways to reduce the remaining anomalous sentences to those more amenable to such treatment (Davidson 1973: 320). Admittedly, this programme is by no means accomplished, but I think that one would not be on safe ground to attack the semantic conception of truth, particularly in its more modern guises, merely on the grounds of the perhaps only present incompleteness of the programme attempting to model natural languages. If the programme were to be completed, as well it might be, it would be a very important and very worthwhile achievement. As I shall argue, though, it would still not explain the term 'true' because it could not deal adequately with our *use* of language.

That truth is defined extensionally on the basis of specified satisfaction-conditions is a strength of the semantic conception of truth, in that the truth it defines is at least highly determinate, and in that such a theory can be developed with a finite base for an infinite language. That appears to me to be also the source of its greatest weakness. In common with the *Tractatus* theory and most other correspondence theories, Tarski's conception of truth has a degree of rigidity which, while useful for formal semantics, is out of keeping with our actual use of language. Not only do we produce new sentences, we often use our language in novel ways. The semantic conception of truth has great difficulty in coping with this sort of novelty. (Davidson recognizes this problem and tries, not quite successfully, I think, to deal with it.) Whereas many correspondence theories have tried to fit unit-propositions, simple or complex, to unit-facts, Tarski's theory ties specifically defined sentential functions to specifically satisfying sequences of objects. Either way, we cannot properly accommodate that fuzziness around the edges of our concepts which is not only characteristic of but absolutely vital for effective general communication. For technical and other purposes we may try to reduce that fuzziness, at least so far as it hinders rather than aids our purposes, but we must not forget, as logicians and other formalists are prone to do, that it is there. This fuzziness of natural language is a direct result of the fact that in real life we often need the flexibility to serve purposes and express meanings which have not arisen before in quite that form.

When we do not have previously established patterns available and precisely suitable, we adapt patterns to suit our own needs and purposes (interests, etc.). To be sure, a well constructed semantic system will permit us to form (or analyse) sentences with which we have had no previous experience, as articulations of a basic structure, but our communicational needs and purposes cannot be prespecified into a semantic system. So, we must employ our sentences to serve our needs and purposes as suits the occasion. The truth of a sentence is then a matter of whether things are as we say they are – relative to the standard implicit in *that* specific use of language. This is commonly not a matter of meeting a precise standard, but of falling sufficiently within a suitable range. To take an Austinian sort of example, whether it is true that France is six-sided will depend on what we mean by 'six-sided' on that particular occasion. From a rigorously geometrical point of view, France is certainly not a hexagon. Yet in a more general sense, enabling us to readily identify it on a map of Europe, France could quite properly be said to be six-sided. Whether it is so depends on what meaning we are trying to get over and on what our communicational purposes are on that occasion.

Mere ambiguity is something with which a well-constructed semantic system can cope, as it can offer us two or more alternative analyses for an ambiguous sentence. (Indeed, I would believe that for some sentences it might offer a denumerably infinite number of analyses: 'China has a lot of people'. How many people qualify as a lot?) However, it is not just a matter of there being some number of alternative senses of 'six-sided', a strict sense and one or more looser senses. We can tailor our own sense of the term to suit the subject we wish to describe and the manner in which we wish to describe it. There may be any number of standards of six-sidedness which we might employ, for any number of communicational purposes. Concerning the shape of France, for instance, we might adopt a combination of standards of straightness, relative length, contrast with the borders of nearby countries, and the like. There could be a non-denumerable infinity of possible standards, with whether a thing is as it is said to be depending on what we take to be important in the business at hand. Here and in general, it is not just a matter of there being different factors, with different possible weights assigned to them, it is also a matter of there being different ways in which standards may be set, and variable degrees of precision which may be required. Language is not the poorer but the richer that this variability and imprecision (to be distinguished from inaccuracy) is

109

available for our use. It permits us to vary the use of a term to suit the occasion, instead of requiring us continually to explicitly define new terms. Doing the latter may be very difficult – or even impossible in the face of genuine novelty, if we have to achieve new aims with old mechanisms. Truth is a matter of what we use language to do in the situation at hand, and that is something which cannot entirely be pre-specified into the structure of a language.

To be sure, post-Tarskian semantic theories can take more account of our variable use of language. As mentioned, Davidson advocates the development of a semantic theory of truth which can accommodate the indexical features of a natural language (1969, 1970, 1973). Some sentences are true in some instances and not true in others, depending on time, place, speaker, and spoken to. Clearly, our semantic machinery must take indexical features into account if it is to provide a foundation for anything even approaching a natural language. While this is clearly a necessary condition, however, I would still maintain that much more is required to account for our actual use of language. I maintain that no semantic system and no 'theory of truth' – as semanticists rather confusingly refer to the specification of the truth-conditions for an object-language – can be made adequate. While such theories can no doubt be successfully indexed for time, place, speaker and audience, it is asking more of indices than indices can give to ask that a semantic theory be indexed to a particular language-user's particular *ad hoc* use of language. We may be able to handle 'He moved it' with an indexical theory, but we cannot so handle something like 'The top of the mountain is covered with snow'. While we may well be able to indexically specify which mountain is being referred to under particular circumstances, we cannot pre-specify what is to count as top, covered, or snow, all of which are very imprecise and flexible concepts which are used according to the language-user's intents and purposes in the situation at hand. Words do not and cannot mean in isolation from a language-user. Beyond semantics, then, in order to understand our use of language we must have recourse to what has been called pragmatics. Whereas syntax deals only with the formal structure of a language, on the basis of which semantics deals with specified extensionality, pragmatics takes into account the language-user with his or her intents and purposes in the given situation. Whether our primary concern be with meaning or with truth, we must take language-user and situation into account if we are to adequately account for our use of language.

110

CONCERNING INTENSIONALITY

Semantics can contrive an account, of sorts, of intensionality, though a limited one. We can give an extensional account of intensional meaning, and even take account of the fact that terms can have differing intensional meaning while having the same extension. For instance, while 'the Prime Minister of Australia' and 'the husband of Hazel Hawke' are at this writing satisfied by the same object and thus have the same extensional meaning, their semantic definitions will vary markedly, reflecting their different intensional meanings. Being Prime Minister will be defined in terms of certain constitutional procedures, while being the husband of Hazel Hawke will be defined in terms of other procedures, all of which can be defined extensionally. Thus, while 'x is Prime Minister of Australia' and 'x is the husband of Hazel Hawke' are, as it currently happens, satisfied by exactly the same sequences, their semantic analyses will differ and will permit them to be specified to be satisfied by different sequences in the future.

This way of extensionally defining a difference in intensional meaning, while very useful, only goes so far. While we can take account of some systematic differences in intensional meaning, such a method cannot fully take account of differing user-intentions on different occasions of linguistic use. At the furthest extreme, the very most we could do would be to 'freeze' the action at a particular instant, specifying satisfaction-conditions with respect to the intentions of a particular language-user on a given occasion. Thus, if someone says that something is six-sided or covered with snow, we might specify on an *ad hoc* basis the truth-conditions of that sentence as used by that person (intentions and all) at that time and in those circumstances. This goes rather beyond what semanticists call for in analyses of natural languages and would, I believe, be impossible in principle as well as in practice. Even were such a specification possible it would not provide us with an adequate account of truth in even that slice of language. To start with, it would not be possible to give a precise specification because sometimes we do not mean anything precise. In the case of 'The top of the mountain is covered with snow', the language-user might not mean anything precise by 'top', 'mountain', or 'snow'. These terms might be used with enough precision that we know *as nearly as matters* to anyone what is being said, but it is quite unlikely that a language-user would have such a precise criterion that it could be used to distinguish snow from everything which is too icy or full of mud to count as snow. Similarly, there would be no precise dividing line between tops and middles, or mountains and hills. So, even were we to succeed in specifying the satisfaction-conditions as faithfully as possible to the intentions of the language-user for the purposes of that occasion, we would still not have a *determinate* semantic theory for even the slice of language used. On the contrary, there would be any number of possible semantic theories consistent with the language-user's intentions on that particular occasion – no one of which would have a claim to represent the user's intentions, nor even, necessarily, those of the average (standard, etc.) language-user. For some things x, 'x is snow' will be true with respect to some of these semantic theories, and false with respect to others. That poses no difficulties for the language-user who has met his or her communicational goal. The plain fact of the matter is that people focus their meanings enough to serve their communicational purposes, not to serve the more precise requirements of systems of formal semantics. An *ad hoc* specification of the use of language by a particular person on a particular occasion, then, even if successful, would not necessarily provide a precise account of either meaning or truth in even that restricted slice of the language-user's language.

To continue, let us suppose the improbable, that we had a fully precise extensional specification of a language-user's use of language on a given occasion. If we had such an account, would even that give an adequate account of meaning and truth for even that slice of language (which may be only one sentence)? Perhaps surprisingly, the answer must be in the negative.[8] To start with meaning, we should note that having an extensional specification of the truth-conditions of a sentence does not give its meaning. After all, 'Bachelors are unmarried' is true if and only if all cats are feline. Neither is the meaning revealed merely through the technical expedient of developing a canonical proof, from our basic axioms, of the truth-conditions of the sentence. The meaning is not revealed even if we have the truth-conditions, together with proofs, of every sentence in the language. As Davidson points out, we might have all that paraphernalia and still not know in what way it is attached to reality. Just as we can understand a mathematical system without knowing how it applies to substantive reality – and it may have many quite divergent interpretations – so we may understand the formal workings of a language without knowing what it is used to do. According to Davidson, what is needed in order for us to interpret (and, *a fortiori*, to understand the meaning of) the sentences of some language is that the totality of truth-conditions should 'optimally fit evidence about sentences held true by native speakers' (1973: 325–6). While we need to know the conditions under which sentences are true, we must also, to get the meaning, be able to recognize evidence for the T-sentences – used as statements of truth-conditions – for sentences in that language. Davidson concedes that in order to do this, we must have a pre-analytic notion of what truth is. The scheme, then, is that a pre-analytic notion of truth, plus a recognition of evidence for T-sentences, and a subsequent knowledge of T-sentences, will yield (or at least are necessary for) a subsequent theory of meaning. He takes a similar stance, further elaborated, in his 'The structure and content of truth' (Davidson 1990). A complicating factor is that there may happen to be more than one possible specification of satisfaction-conditions for a language, in which case we are to seek for meaning as that which is invariant between different workable accounts. The point remains, though, that no matter how precise a specification of satisfaction-conditions we are able to arrive at, we must somehow 'get the drift' of what is being said.

What we seem to come to is that it is highly unlikely that we could arrive at a precise extensional specification of satisfaction-conditions for any worthwhile slice of natural language, and that even if we could, that would not tell us what the terms mean and it would not tell us the role of the notion of truth. Rather, we need to have some idea of truth in order to arrive at a specification of satisfaction-conditions, or to arrive at an understanding of someone else's satisfaction-conditions. I conclude, then, that semantics cannot offer us a general definition of truth. Tarski arrives at the same conclusion, though he does so on the basis of very different reasons. He proves that in a language with an unlimited number of semantic levels – which apparently would be required in order to simulate a natural language – attempting to define truth in terms of the material which he allows himself results in the production of sentences which violate requirement (T). (Interestingly, he also shows that if we introduce the undefined term 'true sentence' into the meta-language, doing so in the proper way, all the (T)-sentences in the language, as specified, would be derivable. Also derivable would be the semantic version of the law of excluded middle, and other such desirable features. So, even if we cannot define truth – and we

113

certainly cannot on strictly Tarskian grounds – it might still be useful as an undefined concept.) Davidson, too, came to abandon the attempt to develop a semantic definition of truth, though at one time he had thought that it would be possible to do so by taking an approach somewhat different from that of Tarski. We have already seen some of the factors which led him to change his mind, yet it would be worth our while to take a closer look.

DAVIDSON AND TRUTH THEORY

Davidson, in his 'True to the facts', tells us that

> A true statement is a statement that is true to the facts. . . . I shall take the licence of calling any view of this kind a *correspondence theory* of truth. . . . The chief difficulty is in finding a notion of fact that explains anything . . . I defend a version of the correspondence theory. I think truth can be explained by appeal to a relation between language and the world, and that analysis of that relation yields insight into how, by uttering sentences, we sometimes manage to say what is true. The semantic concept of truth . . . will play a crucial role . . .
>
> (1969: 37–8)

He rejects the formula

(p)(the statement that p is true if and only if p)

on the grounds that quantifying over such variables is to take 'p' as standing for sentences in the abstract. Sentences in a natural language do not happen in the abstract. 'Truth (in a given natural language) is not a property of sentences; it is a relation between sentences, speakers, and dates' (ibid.: 43). What we need, then, to define truth (in English), is to define

> 'sentence s is true (as English) for speaker u at time t'
>
> (ibid.: 44)

or, if we prefer to deal with statements,

> 'the statement expressed by sentence s (as English) by speaker u at time t is true'.
>
> (ibid.)

114

This leads us to the following schema, each instance of which will be true:

'Sentence s is true (as English) for speaker u at time t if and only if p',

(ibid.: 45)

where 'p' stands for a sentence which gives the truth-conditions for s. (The sentence giving the truth-conditions must involve reference to speaker u and time t if s is indexical.) The schema plays much the same role as Tarski's requirement (T), and like that requirement, it does not itself provide a definition of truth. How, then, are we to define truth?

In the past, he notes correctly, correspondence theories of truth have repeatedly failed because they have been based on a defective account of facts. Correspondence theorists have tried to take facts both as that which makes true statements true and as what true statements state, a dual role which is beyond the capacity of one sort of entity to play as I shall elaborate on in the next chapter. A correspondence theory based on the relation of satisfaction is preferable, in that it bypasses such difficulties. It would still be a correspondence theory, he held, in that it would define truth in terms of a relationship between what is true and something else.

Another difficulty which he escapes, though he does not explicitly so claim, is one raised by Tarski, the difficulty being that the attempt to provide a formal definition of truth for a language with an unlimited number of levels leads to anomaly. Davidson escapes this because on his scheme we have only a finite number of levels. Whatever the level of complexity of a language-user's sentence or statement, if it has meaning at all it must have been constructed in a finite number of steps from some linguistic base, and it is to be understood and analysed accordingly. Instead of attempting to define truth for a language with unlimited levels, we are to define it for the complex but finite utterances of real language-users. That his approach *is* geared to language-users in actual instances is a major departure from Tarski.

In place of a fully articulated theory, Tarski offers us a programme. We have to work out in detail the linguistic structure on the basis of which sentences or statements have truth-conditions. While, as he reminds us, encouraging progress has been made, Davidson concedes that this is still very much a matter of unfinished business. Indeed, it was in 1969 and it is now. He notes a further difficulty. On his approach, since truth is to be defined relative to sentence/statement, time, and speaker, there is a difficulty with anything like

'Peter's statement that Paul is hirsute is true.'

Peter makes a statement and speaker u backs him up by confirming or endorsing the statement. This has to be analysed in terms of a statement about a statement, which involves two speakers and two times. The above statement comes to

'Paul is hirsute. That is true, and Peter said (stated) it.'

Both speakers, then, say the same thing, that Paul is hirsute, though they use different sentences at different times and may even use different languages. To cope with that we need to develop a workable notion of *samesaying*, and a workable scheme of *translation*. Indeed, the notion is needed not just for the overt two-speaker cases. A notion of translation is inherently presupposed by his formula

'Sentence s is true (as English) for speaker u at time t if and only if p',

wherein we are interpreting speaker u's remarks. Moreover, it was presupposed by Tarski's requirement (T), inasmuch as an object-language sentence is being interpreted in every (T)-sentence. Davidson came to the conclusion that:

> We can get away from what seems to be talk of the (absolute) truth of timeless statements if we accept truth as relativized to occasions of speech, and a strong notion of translation. The switch may create more problems than it solves. But they are, I think, the right problems: providing a detailed account of the semantics of natural language, and devising a theory of translation that does not depend upon, but rather founds, whatever there is to the concept of meaning.
>
> (1969: 53)

He went on to note Strawson's characterization of Austin's theory of truth as one which holds 'that to say that a statement is true is to say that a speech-episode is related in a certain conventional way to something in the world exclusive of itself' (Strawson 1950: 32). Unlike Strawson, who rejects such theories root and branch, Davidson thought that it might be possible to elaborate a theory on such a basis. Austin, as we shall see in chapter 7, tried to define truth in terms of reference and description relative to speaker and time, an approach which Davidson thought was fundamentally sound. So, why did Davidson come to abandon his attempt to develop a definition of truth?

One difficulty for Davidson concerns this difficult notion of translation. In 1969, Davidson was suggesting that we understand truth and meaning on the basis of a workable notion of translation. A few years later (Davidson 1973), he came to the conclusion that we must presuppose a notion of truth, whether or not explicitly defined, in order to develop a scheme of translation. This is the line which he continued to develop in later years:

> It is a mistake to look for . . . any . . . explicit definition or outright reduction of the concept of truth. Truth is one of the clearest and most basic concepts we have, so it is fruitless to dream of eliminating it in favor of something simpler or more fundamental. Our procedure is rather this: we have asked what the formal properties of the concept are . . . Tarski's work provides the inspiration. It remains to indicate how a theory of truth can be applied to particular speakers or groups of speakers.

> (1990: 314)

Truth is the more fundamental notion. Even if we had a perfect knowledge of the structure of someone's language, we would not know how it attached to reality, nor how to translate it into our own language, unless we already had a conception of truth and assumed that it was a major consideration in the language-user's use of language. We could not even begin to make sense of people's use of language unless we assume that there is something for their making sense to be. Since meaning must be understood on the basis of translation, and that on the basis of truth, Davidson concludes that we therefore cannot define truth on the basis of either. We shall take a closer look at certain of these issues in the next chapter. Let us here take a brief look at the direction which Davidson came to take with meaning theory, and consider what, if anything, it has to do with truth theory.

MEANING, DAVIDSON, AND TRUTH

Davidson rejects what he calls 'the building block method', often resorted to during the early days of semantics, according to which the meaning of sentences is supposedly built out of the meanings of words. He rejects this on the grounds that words must be understood according to the roles which they play in sentences (1977a: 253). The meaning and reference of words must be explained, if at all, in terms of the sentential roles which words play, rather than their roles in terms of some antecedent meaning or reference. Indeed, there may be more than one way to specify satisfaction-conditions for the component terms in our language. Hence, Davidson concludes, we must abandon the building block method in favour of a more holistic approach to meaning. He moves away from the too mechanistic approach and toward an approach which centres on the sentence as the fundamental unit of communication. Certainly I would applaud the taking of a more holistic approach, and I would urge that we must be concerned not just with sentences, but with sentences as employed within a whole communicational and factual context. We cannot rest with the sentence/utterance *per se* (can there be a *per se*?), but must take into account the sentence/utterance as used then and there by some language-user with that language-user's intentions and purposes. Presumably Davidson would wish to take that sort of thing into account with the evidence concerning the speaker. My point remains that when we use language we employ various intensional criteria, and what we say is to be assessed in terms of those criteria. We must rely on intensional criteria in order to frame the extensional specifications for a use of the language. To rely on an extensional account of the meeting of intensional criteria is to reverse the natural order of things. Objects are in the extension of a term if they meet an intensional standard; they do not meet an intensional standard because they just happen to be in the extension of a term for some unknown reason. As children, we may learn to use the term 'dog' through ostensive definition, but we eventually come to learn that Spot is not a dog because she is a member of the class of dogs, but is a member of the class of dogs because she is a dog. While dogness can no doubt be defined in terms of simpler qualities, sooner or later we must come to an intensional standard serving as the basis for our extensional specifications.

There is more to the story than just that we must take intensionality into account. Let us suppose that we could capture the intensionality of the matter on a given occasion. We would know within what range of meaning the language-user was using language on that particular occasion. (Actually, I doubt that we ever know *entirely* what another person means, though most of the time we know enough to achieve our communicational objectives.) Supposing we had that, would that give us an account of meaning for the language? The most it could do would be to give an account of meaning for the portion of the language then used, as used then. One cannot give a complete meaning-structure for a language because a language has no such thing. There is only a skeletal framework upon which language-users hang meaning. In some areas the framework is more complete than in others, but it could never be entirely complete. A language is not a definite thing at all, but an indefinite and more or less flexible system of usages serving as bases for uses varying from one moment to another. What we hear or read must always be interpreted in terms of the language-user's own particular use, and particular intentions, on that particular occasion in those particular circumstances. Obviously, the skeletal framework is critically important, and to develop a successful account of it would be an achievement of immense significance – but it is still only the skeleton. For an adequate account of meaning and truth, the skeleton would have to be fleshed out to take account of intensionality, occasion, and the imprecision and flexibility of actual application. It is a matter of how we use it. That is not a matter which can be extensionally specified into a semantic system.

Davidson himself largely grants this and, indeed, semanticists almost universally no longer see themselves as offering, or even building toward, a definition of truth. Rather, they quite correctly see themselves as elaborating the skeletal meaning-structure for languages. According to Davidson,

> a theory of truth[9] for a natural language (as I conceive it) differs widely in both aim and interest from Tarski's truth definitions. . . . Tarski could take translation [between object-language and meta-language] as syntactically specified, and go on to define truth. But in application to a natural language it makes more sense to assume a partial understanding of truth, and use the theory to throw light on meaning, interpretation, and translation. . . . What a theory of truth does for a natural language is reveal structure.
>
> (1977b: 204–5)

Elsewhere, he states that

> . . . I have assumed that the speakers of a language can effectively determine the meaning or meanings of an arbitrary

expression (if it has a meaning), and that it is the central task of a theory of meaning to show how this is possible.

(1967: 35)

In effect, Davidson is suggesting that we read T-sentences in the *opposite* direction. Instead of proclaiming that such-and-such is true *if* so-and-so, we try to determine what follows about the language if such-and-such is true. As he says

> A theory of truth for a speaker is a theory of meaning in this sense, that explicit knowledge of the theory would suffice for understanding the utterances of that speaker. It accomplishes this by describing the critical core of the speaker's potential and actual linguistic behavior, in effect, how the speaker intends his utterances . . .

(1990: 312)

Granted that speakers of a (natural) language can work out (well enough) what expressions mean, and have a workable intuitive conception of truth, the problem is to determine, as closely as we can, the meaning-structure on the basis of which this is done. That is a very important and very interesting project, but determining the meaning-structure of some language is not to give an account of truth. So, what *are* we to say about truth?

WHAT, THEN, OF TRUTH?

Semantics, I conclude, cannot give us an adequate general definition of truth, as it cannot account for the actual use of language. Tarski and Davidson, for their own reasons, agree that semantics cannot offer a general definition of truth. Does that mean that we must give up on truth theory? Or that we must accept something as tedious and unsatisfying as a contrived extensional specification for a dead and frozen slice of language, detached from living use – or else settle for something as trivial as the platitude that a sentence is true if what it says is so? No, I think that we are not forced all the way back to square one, and that our consideration of the semantic conception of truth does offer us some useful pointers. Certainly I think Tarski is correct in rejecting any grandiose overall unitary conception of truth. Instead, we must consider what differing things are involved in the being true or false of widely differing statements. Semantics can shed some light on that, since truth rests, to some degree, on an underlying meaning-structure. Yet truth also involves things which cannot be extensionally specified for. Broadly, a statement is true when its own particular truth-conditions, of whatever sort, are satisfied. We must be careful how we proceed from there, however. We cannot go anywhere but in a circle if we define truth in terms of truth-conditions when truth-conditions presuppose a notion of truth. We must find another way forward.

Austin, I think, does offer a way forward, one which Davidson did not take. As well as attempting to define truth for statements relative to particular instances of language-use, Austin was also attempting to define truth otherwise than in terms of what must be true for the statement to be true. Instead, he attempted to define truth without presupposing a notion of truth, doing so in terms of something's being as described – an attempt which would, if successful, remove the element of circularity.

Later, we shall briefly consider a few more points concerning semantic conceptions of truth, but let us take it that we cannot adequately define or otherwise give an account of truth on such a basis. There are other matters to be considered. Certainly the Austinian account requires consideration. In the next chapter, however, let us clear the decks somewhat by taking a closer look at the nature of truth-bearers, and also at the nature of facts. Difficulties concerning such things – if things they are – have long complicated truth theory. Sharpening the focus on them will help us to sharpen the focus on truth.

6

INTERMEZZO

Before we go on to investigate other theories of truth, inquiry is made into the nature of truth-bearers and facts. Truth-bearers are not sentences per se, *nor are they propositional entities of any sort. Rather, I take truth-bearers to be statements, sentences as used by language-users on particular occasions for particular purposes in saying something about something. I explicate this, and discuss how they are to be identified and equated. Facts are not entities of any sort. An alternative account of 'fact'-language is presented.*

All of the various theories which we have discussed take something-or-other to be true, but, thus far, we have not directly tackled the question of what truth-bearers are. Just what is it, be it proposition, sentence, judgement, statement, or whatever, which is said to be true? For that matter, what, if they are part of the story, are facts? Many of the theories tell us that what we say is true if . . . something-or-other having to do with facts. Perhaps what we say is true if it is a fact, or if it corresponds to the facts, or to *a* fact, or if it coheres with other facts or with the great fact-Absolute, or what-ever. But what are truth-bearers and facts? So far, not to obscure other issues, and discretion being the better part of valour, we have not tackled these questions head-on, but only in passing, in connec-tion with our consideration of various theories of truth. I think that it would be useful now to inquire more directly concerning just what they are and, while we are at it, to investigate some closely related matters of importance to our inquiry. Let us start with truth-bearers.

If I say, truly, that the cat is on the mat, what is it which is true? To be sure, what is true is that the cat is on the mat. But what is going on there? In criticism of the redundancy and performative theories, we came to the conclusion that to say that a truth-bearer is true is to say something about the truth-bearer as well as to say something about whatever the truth-bearer is about. Until now we have been primarily concerned with that which is then being said about the truth-bearer. Now, though, we ask what the truth-bearer is, the thing about which something is being said. Perhaps a satisfactory answer to that will help us to determine what is being said about it when it is said to be true. The usual answers, though, all have their difficulties.

TRUTH-BEARERS AS SENTENCES

Evidently – as seems to have emerged from our previous discussions – the precise nature of what is true or false is determined by the particular use of language on the particular occasion. Perhaps we ought to take that as our clue, and decide that truth-bearers are the particular sentences used (then, and in that way). This would be to attempt to take a line which is closely addressed to actual instances. Doing so would not give a proper account of what truth-bearers are, but would only sketch a general shape for an account to take. We cannot just conclude that truth-bearers are sentences used, and let it go at that. To see why, let us take a closer look at sentences as truth-bearers.

To start with, just what is to count as a particular sentence? In one sense, it is evidently true that

'The cat is on the mat.'

is the same sentence as

'The cat is on the mat.'

Alternatively, we might say that, while highly similar, they are two different sentences appearing in two different locations. There is no real choice here, it is only a matter of *type* and *token*. There are two tokens here of the same type. Conceivably, this passage might be printed several times, but there would still be one sentence-type involving the cat and the mat, though there might be a great number of sentence-tokens. Both sentence-types and sentence-tokens are things which might plausibly be said to be true or false. If the cat is on the mat, then I say something true if I say so, writing or speaking a particular, presumably true, sentence-token. We might all decide to comment on the cat/mat situation, each of us saying 'The cat is

123

on the mat'. We would each be uttering something true – each utterance being a token of a sentence-type which might also be said to be a true sentence. There are still problems in taking the sentence-type to be the truth-bearer. Suppose the cat walks away from the mat. Does this mean that the sentence-type, which used to be true, is no longer true? There are various responses we might make here. We might decide that what is false now is not what was true before, that under the changed circumstances the same words are a different sentence-type. On another occasion, those words might be saying something else about a different cat and mat. This would mean that the identity of the truth-bearer is determined not just by the words, but by the surrounding context in which the words are employed. Again, we might decide that it is still the same sentence-type when the cat leaves, that what the changing circumstances determine is not the identity of the sentence-type, but its truth-value. Yet suppose I say, falsely, that the cat is on the mat, while simultaneously you say, truly, with reference to a different cat and mat, that the cat is on the mat. Unless we want to say that the same sentence-type is both true and false at the same time, the conclusion we must come to is that what is true or false is not the sentence-type *per se*, but the sentence-type in the context in which it is employed. Either way, whether or not the sentence-type has a different identity in a different context, if the truth-bearer is a sentence-type at all, it must be the sentence-type cum context of use.

Could it be that the truth-bearer is not the sentence-type at all, but the individual sentence-token? Perhaps individual tokens of 'The cat is on the mat' are true or false, according to whether the cat and mat in question are so arranged. (If there were no cat and mat in question, we would have to decide on whether such tokens were false or meaningless.) Instead of having to worry about identity-conditions for sentence-types, we just take the truth-bearer to be the individual utterance, then and there. Still, we cannot just let it go at that, for the 'then and there' part of it carries more weight than is immediately apparent. Suppose that a sign on the notice-board informs me: 'Seminar, 7 p.m. today: *Shakespeare's Use of Imagery*'. Often I am puzzled, since such notices occasionally get left up for several days. Perhaps it will turn out that the notice went up yesterday morning, and the seminar has already happened. Is the notice a different token today than it was yesterday? Or did the same token change its truth-value overnight? Either way, if the truth-bearer is a sentence-token at all, it must be a sentence-token identified in terms of its context of use. Whether truth-bearers are seen as centring on the type or the token, or on either, then, the context in which it is employed is critical to the identity of what is true or false.

In the preceding I have not played quite fairly, as I have been doing what Wittgenstein warned against, offering a one-sided diet of examples. My examples have all been *indexicals*, which are truth-bearers whose identity is dependent on person, time, place, or circumstance. If a sentence is an indexical, just knowing the language is not good enough. In addition, we have to understand what terms like 'I', 'you', 'here', 'now', and the like, are connected with. It is an indexical if we are talking about *this* thing, *that* thing, *the* thing, the thing *now*, or if we use a proper name. With the doubtful exception of those involving proper names, context is critical to the identity of indexical truth-bearers, and we might say that it is critical to the precise identity of – to the meaning of – a particular sentence-type or sentence-token. (In which case it would be part of the identity of the seminar-notice that it was posted on a given day, though that might not be visible to the eye.) The question I want to raise is that of whether context of utterance is part of the identity not just of indexicals, but of *all* truth-bearers.

Let us consider sentences, -type or -token, which are not indexicals. Certainly it is not always apparent what is context-dependent. It turned out that the identity of 'Swans are white' was context-dependent. What Europeans had in past times noted to be true was really a matter of 'Swans (around here) are white', not taking into account the black swans of Australia. However, it may seem less likely that the identity of 'Snow is white' is context-dependent, the case being quite different. Seemingly, snow is a physical substance which does not change its nature so strikingly from one place to the next. Snow is snow. Or is it? Snow can be dirty, and it can have red algae growing in it. Is that grey or red snow? Or is it white snow with grey or red stuff mixed in with it? Again, snow can have a slightly bluish cast, depending on light conditions and the condition of the snow. Can the term 'white' be stretched to cover slightly bluish snow? Or is it that the snow is not really bluish but just looks that way? There are any number of answers one might give to these questions, but it would be quite absurd to try to dictate what 'Snow is white' must necessarily mean. Rather, it is, at least in large part, a matter of how we, then and there, use our terms. To start with, we may use the terms 'snow' and 'white' in very broad or very narrow

125

senses. It is more complex than that, though. It is not just that we may use the terms with more or less latitude, but that a particular language-user may employ any of a great many differing patterns of use, differing in different ways, as suits the occasion and the person's convenience. Perhaps we distinguish very sharply between snow and that compacted snow which is almost ice, yet are fairly tolerant about impurities. Or perhaps we are strict about impurities, but not about the snow-ice distinction. Or perhaps we employ criteria drawn along quite different lines. The inference must be that the identity of the truth-bearer 'Snow is white' is context-dependent, even though it is not indexical, in that just what is being asserted depends, at least in large part, on the way in which the language-user is then using language.

Whether or not we are dealing with indexicals, then, if truth-bearers are sentences, truth-bearing sentences, be they -type or -token, must be true or false as used in particular instances. There are various issues to be considered here. For one thing, to be explicit, is what is true (or false)

1 The sentence itself, which might have a different truth-value elsewhere (or under changed conditions)?

Or, is it

2 The sentence-in-context (-type or -token), which cannot be just anywhere?

Either way, there are difficulties. It is a problem for the first alternative that it allows a truth-bearer, a particular sentence, to have two different truth-values at one and the same time, accordingly as it is employed in one context or another. Even non-indexical sentences can be given quite different meanings in different contexts of use. 'Snow is white' might be true as used by you and false as used by me. This, I think, is enough to rule out the first alternative, since the truth-bearer must be what is true or false. It is quite absurd that one might, as that alternative allows, know the identity of a truth-bearer and even know that it is true (somewhere) and yet not know what is true. If we know the truth-bearer and know that it is true, we must know what is true.

The second alternative seems preferable but also has its problems. For one thing, we will still have to determine whether it is sentence (-tokens)-in-context which are truth-bearers, or whether it is sentence (-types)-in-context which have that role. That truth is tied to context seems much easier to accept in the case of sentence-tokens than in the case of sentence-types. The former, after all, are particular items with particular occurrences in particular contexts, while the latter may show up anywhere. Tokens, for that reason, are much more readily identifiable in terms of a particular use. However, it may seem a strength of sentence-types as truth-bearers that they can have multiple occurrence. Even so, we will have to find some way to establish equivalence (as truth-bearers) between different sentences-in-context, be they -types or -tokens. After all, we must recognize the palpable fact that two people do often express the same (equivalent) truth. Certainly they do not employ the self-same sentence token, and they may well use different sentence-types.

Let us start with equivalence, first considering sentence-types. Suppose that I say 'The Queen is well-spoken' while listening to her speak on television, and on another occasion you say 'The Queen is well-spoken' while discussing the traits of famous people. These are different tokens of the same sentence-type expressed in different contexts. Certainly it seems that we have expressed one and the same truth via one and the same sentence-type. Perhaps we could claim that what is true (or false) is the sentence (-type)-in-(a relevantly similar type of) context – the context being of a relevantly similar type in terms of how we are using language on the particular occasion. We can if we like say one sentence-type is the same truth-bearer as the other, so long as the contexts are sufficiently (and relevantly) similar to allow for that. We have a problem, though, in determining what contexts do allow for that. Are they equivalent if, therein, the sentence-type says (is used to say) the same thing in the two occurrences? That is uselessly circular unless we can find an independent characterization of saying the same thing. In any case, taking the line would not be sufficient, as we often express the same truth with quite different sentence-types – as with 'He did it' and 'John broke the vase'. Then, to take the truth-bearer as the sentence-type we would have to form an equivalence class from different sentence-types in different contexts. We would then have to be concerned with what that occurrence of the sentence-type in that context was being used to say. Taking that line would really be to take the truth-bearer to be the sentence (-*token*)-in-(its own particular) context. Quite a lot of explaining would still be required. How are we to equate, as truth-bearers, such sentences-in-context? Are they equivalent when they (are used to) say the same thing? That seems to take us in the same circle as before. If we are to take truth-bearers as sentences-in-context, we must somehow break the circle.

One possible way out would be to maintain that sentences, -type or -token, are to be put into the same equivalence class as truth-bearers when they (are used to) express the same proposition or make the same statement. We must then explain what propositions or statements are, and how we are to identify them and to know when different sentences (are used to) express or make the same one. If we could somehow do that successfully, we would be in a position to form equivalence classes of sentences-in-context as truth-bearers. If we could do that, though, we might just as well entirely bypass sentences, -type and -token, as truth-bearers (as primary ones, at any rate), taking our truth-bearers to be propositions or statements themselves. This has often been advocated and has its attractions. It would allow us to maintain that a given truth is one thing, conveyed by different sentences, rather than being a matter of an equivalence class of different things. Seemingly, that they have the same content is the only plausible or relevant reason for equating quite different sentence-tokens or -types in quite different contexts. Let us then consider propositions and statements as truth-bearers. Through doing so we will, I believe, be led back to taking truth-bearers as sentence (-tokens)-in-context – having then a better understanding of what they are and how they are to be equated and distinguished.

TRUTH-BEARERS AS PROPOSITIONS

Let us begin with propositions, frequently proposed – particularly by correspondence theorists – as being those things which are true or false. To explain what propositions are, it is usual to distinguish them from sentences – taking them as being, in some way, the *content*, or part of the content, of sentences. If I say 'The cat is on the mat' and an Italian, commenting on the same reclining feline, says 'Il gatto è sul tappeto', we have used different sentences to say the same thing. The claim is that the two different sentences have been used to express the same proposition. Not only may two different sentence-types or -tokens express the same proposition, two different propositions may be expressed, on different occasions, by the same sentence-type – e.g. 'The milk is cold', used different times with reference to different milk. (It is even arguable that a given sentence-token of a relatively enduring nature, such as an 'Open for Business Today' sign, might express a number of different propositions on different occasions.) It is as if propositions were things of quite a different sort from sentences, somehow employing them as vehicles, yet by no means to be identified with them, and transcending their worldly entanglements of words, time, place, and circumstance. Moreover, propositions are said to serve as the contents not only of assertions, but also of beliefs, doubts, conjectures, etc., and even of questions. The proposition is true or false even so, though what we say or think may be neither. It will be clear, then, that propositions are not simply to be equated with declarative sentences, or with sentences of any other sort. In general, propositions and sentences follow different careers. What, then, *are* propositions, and how are they related to sentences?

While propositions are not the same as sentences, it is not at all easy to separate them. For one thing, if propositions are held to be entities of some sort, conveyed by sentences yet different from them, one can easily fall into metaphysical quagmires in attempting to explain what they are. Yet, seemingly, all we can ever really know about propositions lies in their involvement with what we say or think. Whether we let it go at that, though, or whether we dabble in metaphysics, there remains the question of what propositions have to do with the sentences which convey them. This has particularly been a problem for correspondence theorists. They tell us that what we say is true if it fits with reality, yet this is to be explained in terms of the mutual fit of propositions and facts which seem to have been tailor-made for each other. That leaves us with the problem of explaining what propositions have to do with our thoughts, utterances, or sentences and, for that matter, of explaining what facts, at the other end of the correspondence relation, have to do with reality.

There are further problems with accepting propositions as truth-bearers. Not only is it difficult to explain what propositions have to do with sentences, and difficult to explain how they differ, there is also a problem in relating propositions to our use of language. Propositions are often presented, particularly by correspondence theorists, as precise and rigid units abstracted not only from the language used but from the language-user. Actually, as Wittgenstein was finally forced to accept, the identity of what we say – be it true, false, or otherwise – is a matter of how we use language and what we use it to do. This is something which is highly variable and subject to continuous gradation. To be sure, there may well be *more or less* definite definitions for our words adding up (when they do) to some more or less definite literal meaning for a sentence we use, but there is very often the additional factor of what we use those meanings to mean. That may well not be discoverable from a dictionary. In the opening scene of *Hamlet*, ' 'Tis bitter cold, and I am sick at heart' is used to mean more than the words mean. Given that the identity of what we say turns on the use we make of language, it is not at all easy to accommodate propositions as distinct entities separate from the sentences/utterances supposedly serving as their delivery vehicles. Granted, it is not logically absurd that there should be a continuous gradation of separate units in some way associated with the continuous diversity of language-use, but – to say the least – it seems considerably less than plausible. Propositions are much more at home with the conception, which we have rejected, of languages as being precise and rigid. Moreover, the only real reason for invoking propositions at all is the questionable assumption that there is some common content. If the identity of what is true or false varies continuously with our use of language, it seems much more believable that it should be something which is directly a matter of our use of language and not just something which is, somehow, conveyed by language.

We now have a twofold reason to consider the possibility that truth-bearers are not abstract propositions but statements – linguistic entities of some sort, involved in . . . well, . . . statement-making. What they are will obviously have to be explained. One advantage of taking truth-bearers to be statements would be that statements, more than discrete contents, presumably have the continuous flexibility required by our very flexible use of language in saying what is true or false. A second reason for opting for statements rather than propositional contents is that the latter can be identified (if at all) only in terms of that of which they are contents, so truth or falsity must in any case be identified in terms of that which has the content. That is what we can most readily identify and get a hold on. Accordingly, let us consider statements for the role of truth-bearer.

TRUTH-BEARERS AS STATEMENTS

Just as much as that of propositions, the nature of statements needs explication. The term 'statement' is certainly an ambiguous one, as it can refer both to the act of stating and to what is stated. While the act might perhaps be truthful, it is what is stated which is true or false. Even so, we cannot just dismiss the act of stating as being irrelevant, or even as being separable. Whatever is stated is stated through one or more particular acts of stating, acts performed on particular occasions, using language in particular ways. Those particulars are often critical in identifying what is stated. But in what way are we to identify that which is stated in a particular act of stating? Is *everything* involved in the act part of the identity of the truth-bearer? How is it that through *different* particular acts of stating the same or equivalent thing can be stated? (What is it which makes it the *same* thing being said – or which makes the two things equivalent? Or what is it that makes them relevantly different?) In answering these questions it would be convenient if we could point to something readily identifiable and say that *that* is what is being conveyed through these acts of stating – but, as we have just noted, in attempting such an approach we run the risk of losing contact with the nuances of actual usage. Moreover, we cannot go beyond words to give a characterization of what our words do or, as it were, convey. Any characterization must be in words. The idea now, in looking to statements as truth-bearers, is to look for the truth-bearer as what we say, not as something else somehow conveyed by what we say. The primary difficulty is to elucidate this without lapsing into triviality or circularity. Circularity it would be, were we to attempt to explain this in terms of the content of what we say – unless we could develop an independent characterization of that. Yet most of the time we can tell well enough what other people are saying. We do not need to know what statements are in order to understand one, or to recognize that one differs from another, or sometimes to know that they amount to the same thing. That might be our clue. Instead of trying to characterize what is said from the outside, as it were, let us accept that we can often know what is being said, and consider the question of what is involved in stating.

Not just any use of words (in context etc.) amounts to statement-making. A question does not make a statement and neither does an interjection nor various other things, though they might be involved with statements in a number of different ways. They might even presuppose that certain things are true or false. Unlike them, though, a statement actually asserts or denies something. It has a subject-matter and it says something about that subject-matter. In a quite broad sense we can say that, as opposed to questions or other things, a statement says something-or-other about something-or-other. There may be – as in the case of 'There are no pink swans' – no particular referent serving as an object of description. Yet we are saying something, and saying something about some subject-matter, be it pink swans, or swans, or the biosphere. We need not be talking about any *particular* thing in order to be talking meaning-fully and saying something true-or-false. I suggest that it would be possible and profitable to maintain that a statement is made on a *particular* occasion, using words then, there, and in that way, to say something-or-other about something-or-other, and to maintain that the statement is the truth-bearer. That comes back to taking a truth-bearer to be a sentence (-token)-in-context. Not just any sentence-token in any context, but a sentence-token *used* in context to say something about something.

We still have the problem of equating truth-bearers. It seems now that we cannot look for one truth-bearer to span a number of different instances. Propositions were posited to play such roles, but positing them is useless and should seem unsatisfactory, since the only way to identify them, and the only reason for believing there are any, rests on the assumption that they are there to play the role. Nor can we cast statements in such a role. If we took 'He did it' and 'John broke the vase' to be equivalent by virtue of making the very same statement, that would be to cast statements in the sterile role of propositions, abstracting them as contents from actual statement-making. What we still have to do is to develop a way of equating the two different sentences-in-context as truth-bearers. It may seem counter-intuitive that truth-bearers are so individual, and so spatio-temporally localized, but we must recognize the distinction between identity and equivalence. Different people on different occasions do not make the *identical* statement, as something is identical only with itself, but they may well make *equivalent* statements. What they say is not identical but it is the same – relative to whatever our purposes and standards are in terms of which we are assessing whether they are the same. If two people make statements which are, in this sense, the same, what they say will be relevantly equivalent by virtue of saying the same thing about the same thing. What they say will have the same meaning and will be true or false together. So long as we can equate or distinguish between different statements, truth theory has no need for truth-bearers being absol-utely identical in different sentences used. If we can give an ade-quate account of how we identify, distinguish, and equate what is true or false, in a way which cuts with good effect across the boundary lines of utterances and sentences (-type or -token), we will have given an account of truth-bearers which bids fair to serve us adequately for the purposes of truth theory.

EQUATING TRUTH-BEARERS

What would it be for two sentences or utterances to (be used to) make equivalent statements, or, as we can properly put it, to (be used to) express the 'same' statement? What is it to say the same thing about the same thing? Perhaps, as is often suggested (e.g. by Davidson, among many others), we can say that this is so when one sentence or utterance (as uttered, then and there) can properly be translated into the other, as with 'Il gatto è sul tappeto' and 'The cat is on the mat'. This is not to claim that they each convey some propositional entity, but only that the latter coming from me amounts to the same thing as does the former coming from the Italian (when we are both concerned with the same cat and mat). We can also make translations within the same language. But what makes a correct translation correct? However we put it, we still have to work out what it is for the two to say the same thing about the same thing. We have already noted the suggestion that two sentences or utterances can be equated when they have the same truth-conditions – which we might take to mean that they express the same proposition, make the same statement, or, if one likes, have the same meaning. We have also noted that this approach has some problems. One problem is that 'All bachelors are unmarried' and 'All cats are felines', for instance, have the same truth-conditions – being true under all conditions – though they are apparently quite different truths. Of course it is possible to take account of the different meanings involved by equating on the basis of the satisfaction-conditions of the sentential functions which contribute to the finished product. Clearly, 'x is unmarried' and 'x is a feline' have quite different satisfaction-conditions. Accordingly, while the finished sentences have the same truth-conditions, they have different semantic analyses and so could be said to have different meanings, and thus could be said to express different propositions or make different statements. Even so, we have to take into account the fact that words are used in different ways by different people at different times. As we noted in the previous chapter, it is possible, to a point, to take account of this variation by specifying satisfaction-conditions for particular uses. We can then work out rules for determining when two sentences have the same truth-conditions. According to Rudolf Carnap (1947: 59), two sentences are equivalent when there is an 'intensional isomorphism' between the two, defined in terms of the satisfaction-conditions for *that* use of the words. One sentence, then, used a particular way, could be said to be 'reducible' to the other, or to be a translation of it.

It comes very close to being a truism, though it may not be entirely a truism, to say that truth-bearers are equivalent, saying the same thing about the same thing, if the analyses of their truth-conditions in terms of the satisfaction-conditions of their underlying sentential functions, *to the extent that it is possible to give them*, are the same. But the difficulty is that language is used by language-users, and what they do with it is not something which can be pre-specified into the structure of our language. Formal semantics can no more provide an account of the truth-conditional equivalence of statements as they arise in actual use than it can provide an account of truth. The most it can offer is a frozen sample. Davidson had a more promising suggestion when he proposed to find a scheme of translation which did not depend on the notion of meaning but could serve as a foundation for an explication of meaning. If we knew how to translate properly from one sentence to another, whether in the same or a different language, that could serve as the basis of an account of both meaning and truth. As was noted in the previous chapter, Davidson came to the conclusion that this sort of approach tacitly presupposed an intuitive concept of truth, and so could not without circularity do the job required of it. Even so, I believe that we can find things of benefit to our inquiry by taking a closer look at Davidson's views concerning translation.

Suppose that we are trying to learn another language from scratch, without benefit of being taught by someone who knows how to translate from that language to one which we already know. We start by noticing as much as we can about what words native speakers use, in what sorts of combinations, and in what circumstances. To make sense of it all, we proceed on certain basic general assumptions. We must assume that there is some sort of a rationale to the language, and that the people who are using it are not just making random noises but are more or less sensible people trying to say more or less sensible things about what they are talking about. Indeed, if we do not make such assumptions as that we are not recognizing what is going on as being the use of a language. Getting it all to add up will be neither straightforward nor purely mechanical. As Davidson points out:

> Not all the evidence can be expected to point the same way. There will be differences from speaker to speaker, and from time to time for the same speaker, with respect to the circumstances under which a sentence is held true. The general policy, however, is to choose truth conditions that do as well as possible in making speakers hold sentences true when (according to the theory and the theory builder's view of the facts) those sentences are true. That is the general policy, to be modified in a host of obvious ways.
>
> (1974: 152)

In so proceeding we are employing what has become known as the *principle of charity*, which is not merely an option but is a necessity if we are to make sense of things. We assume not just that what native speakers say generally comes out true when they are in a position to know the truth, but that it generally makes sense in terms of the available evidence and the surrounding circumstances. Anomalies are bound to occur, and success can only be a matter of degree, but by pursuing an understanding along these lines we can hope to get the best possible (for us) understanding of the language. Not only is that how we might learn a foreign language, it is how we all learned our native language. Even within our own language it is how we are able to work out one another's meanings, since we all use language somewhat differently.

It is essential to this programme that in developing our understanding of the language we, as nearly as possible, make come out true those things which ought to come out true. We must do that, for no matter how well we comprehend the internal workings of the language, we could not otherwise know how it attaches to reality nor know how to translate from that language to our own. Therein, we recall, Davidson found the rub. We must start with a pre-analytical understanding of truth, and only from there can we go on to understand truth-conditions and their satisfaction, and it is on that basis that we can develop a scheme of interpretation, meaning, and all that goes with that. As Davidson and others have demonstrated, we can thereby discover quite a lot about the meaning-structure of a language and about how it is attached to reality. As far as truth is concerned, Davidson is prepared to let it go at that. Given that we can understand quite a lot about language and our use of it, doing so on the basis of a pre-analytical understanding of truth, however, I maintain that we can go on to develop a useful characterization of what truth is. To do so would be no more circular than for a zoologist to investigate a lot of things already known to be birds in order to go on to develop a characterization of what birds are.

In pursuing our project, I propose to identify truth-bearers as sentence-tokens (used)-in-context, ones which are used to say something about some subject-matter, equating them if they say the same thing about the same subject-matter. I shall use the term 'statement' to refer to truth-bearers. While statements may be very different in many ways, they are to be equated in so far as they do say the same thing about the same thing, properly serving as translations of each other. Thus, 'Der Schnee ist weiss' and 'Snow is white' can be equated (if indeed they are being used to say the same thing about the same thing). There may of course be somewhat different conceptions of snow and white involved, which might make a difference in certain cases. In working out our translations, it should be noted, we cannot always proceed just on a word-for-word basis. In the example quoted we can pretty well equate '(der) Schnee' and 'snow', 'weiss' and 'white', and 'ist' and 'is', but things are not always that simple. 'The flesh is willing but the spirit is weak' must be understood in terms of what it is used to say. The words individually have to be understood in terms of the statement, not vice versa. A word-for-word translation of that saying into a foreign language would produce hilarious results (perhaps something like 'The meat is agreeable but the liquor is of low alcoholic content'). The point in translation is not to equate words with words but what is said with what is said.

Translation requires a sufficient grasp not only of the relevant portions of the relevant languages, but also of the way in which the statement-makers are then using them. Translation does not just concern languages – as if it were a matter of semantics alone – but language-users as well, their intents and purposes, their cognitive frames of reference, and the situations in which they use language. To some degree, high or low, this will require us to rely on intensional considerations concerning what the language-user intends. That is always involved to some extent in understanding human communication. A consequence of this, which may seem unpalatable at first, is that we can never quite know exactly what another person has in mind, and we cannot exactly equate truth-bearers. Not only do we not have identity, we do not have full equivalence. What you mean by 'Snow is white' no doubt is not quite what I mean by it, and neither of us can ever quite know what the other has in mind. That is just another fact about human communication. Nevertheless, we can communicate. To understand, we need not understand every nuance of meaning nor be able to follow the exact boundaries of vagueness. Communication and understanding are matters of degree. The example used in the last chapter, 'The top of the mountain is covered with snow', illustrates that point. Hearing that, one can understand the core of what is said even though what is understood may not coincide exactly with what is intended. The statement concerning the particular case may correctly be assessed and agreed to be true or false, even though speaker and hearer may be unable exactly to fix the boundaries of applicability of the terms and might not agree on their applicability in other cases. I shall say more about this in chapter 8.

In identifying the truth-bearer as I have, I have tried to retain the best insights of the different points of view we have considered. Certainly the coherentists had something of merit in their emphasis on system. By their nature and role, truth-bearers cannot stand alone or in the abstract. We have to consider them in their role in the language-user's cognitive frame of reference, and we have to consider them as judgements whereby the language-user attributes something to something. The correspondence theorists stress, I believe correctly, the latter part of that, that statements are about something. Truth-bearers need not actually be articulated, but what is believed, doubted, conjectured, just thought of, or whatever, has, for its truth or falsity, to be considered as at least a possible statement. As the pragmatists correctly stressed, a statement has to be understood in terms of the role we assign it in particular situations for particular purposes. I shall have more to say on these matters in subsequent chapters. Now, though, as I have raised the matter of the use and meaning of a term, I would like to take time to say some things concerning meaning.

IN PASSING: THE THEORY OF MEANING

This century has seen a great deal of philosophizing about *meaning*, much of it being, in some connection, associated with truth theory. The pragmatist's theories of meaning, for instance, were associated with pragmatic theories of truth, and the idealists had their own ideas about meaning, involving internal relations and their meta-physics, which affected the coherence theory. Analogous remarks can be made concerning various versions of correspondence and other theories. I have mentioned some of these connections in passing. Still, while truth theory and theory of meaning have gone hand in hand to a considerable extent, and have exerted much influence on one another, it would not be correct to say that they are two sides of the same coin. That is, it is not the case that for each theory of meaning there is a particular theory of truth, or vice versa. Moreover, they are separate inquiries in that a number of consider-ations are important to one of the two but not to the other. While our own discussion of truth theory has led us up to some very tricky issues concerning the theory of meaning, I shall continue to try to avoid getting us unnecessarily entangled, discussing theory of meaning only as relevant to our own inquiry.

That being said, though, I do think it relevant to discuss briefly certain salient points concerning the theory of meaning. While I am not presupposing any particular theory of meaning, firmly intend-ing not to do so, I do take the position that meaning, for truth theory, must be understood not just in semantic but in pragmatic terms. That is, we must take into account language-users, with their interests and purposes in the contextual circumstances. In this connection it is appropriate to mention the 'speaker-meaning' theory of meaning and the controversy surrounding it. That theory, which is very much a pragmatic theory of meaning, is, to put it roughly and without qualification, the view that words and sen-tences mean what people use them to mean. In slogan form: 'Words don't mean. People mean.' Not only is intensionality central, the intentions of the language-user are central. It was Grice (1957) who made this theory prominent. Certainly it does seem plausible that words have no meaning, are not even words, except in so far as they are used, and that if we had used a given word in a very different way then it would have had a very different meaning. Moreover, we can and do give them different uses on different occasions. Those who take this approach give various analyses in terms of what the speaker intends, what the hearer is intended to think, how the latter is intended to respond, and so on. There is considerable debate about the details of the analyses, debate which need not concern us here. More to the point for our purposes is the objection that if we take this line far enough, Humpty Dumpty could use any word to mean anything at all. Whatever we do with it, we must rest on the meaning-structure of the language we are using, which is not an infinitely plastic putty in our hands.

The contention is, as we might say, that pragmatic meaning must rest on semantic meaning. Certainly I would not doubt that effective communication does, in general, have to rely on some core of established linguistic usage. On the one hand there is the fact that *we* use language, and on the other is the fact that we *use* language. Language-use is something we engage in collectively, within the general usage of our linguistic community. Yet language-use takes place in particular instances with particular language-users using language in particular ways for particular purposes. Evidently there is some no doubt rather fluid balance between meaning as shaped by the usage of the linguistic community and meaning as tailored by individual language-users to suit the needs of specific occasions. There are any number of theories in the field here: theories about semantic meaning, theories about pragmatic meaning, and theories about how they fit together. I shall not attempt to defend or present any theory as being correct.

Without endorsing any particular theory, I do suggest that the differences between the semantics and the pragmatics of language are matters of degree rather than of kind. Perhaps we could think of language as being something which has a rigid core but, gradually and progressively, becomes more flexible toward the periphery. It is the periphery which we shape to the needs of particular applications, though as shaped and supported by the more inflexible interior. Metaphor aside, language is a matter of use. Partly it is a matter of the usage of our linguistic community, which offers us a range of options and a certain amount of flexibility, and partly it is a matter of our own use of language on and for the occasion. The relative importance of these factors would be difficult to assess and would undoubtedly vary from one case to another. It may not be possible to assess them separately at all. In any case, we need not make such an assessment. What is important is that the truth-bearer has meaning as used on the occasion, regardless of how much or how little of that meaning is contributed then by the language-user.

A MATTER OF FACT

I have argued that truth-bearers, statements, say something about something, being used by language-users to do so, and I have offered an account of what they are. There remain a number of questions concerning what it is statements have to do with the world, and concerning what it is that statements have (or fail to have) to do with whatever they are about which makes some of them true and some of them not true. For now, what are statements about? Among the things they are about, seemingly, are various things and events in the world, and their properties and inter-relationships. Also, facts[1] are often said to have something to do with the story, in some way or another. Facts have a way of intruding into truth theory as well as into practical affairs, and in each case we must come to terms with them. Even so, I believe that while a practical concern for the facts is usually of benefit, truth theory has very often suffered as a result of a preoccupation with facts. This is because truth theorists have too often taken facts as if they were entities of some sort. Rather, I maintain, 'fact'-language is a means we have for talking about things, with facts being merely linguistic substantives. They are not entities of any sort, not even propositional entities. (There are no propositional entities.) The word 'fact' ought to be retained in our vocabulary as it has its uses, but we should not try to erect a theory of truth on the very infirm foundation of facts taken as entities of a sort. Those theories of truth which have tried to do so – correspondence theories, most notably – have always foundered. Always, a major problem has been that of what fact-entities have to do with the world. A related problem is that of what they have to do with statements.

At this point I think it would be in order for me to make clear why I conclude that facts are not entities, and to explain what I believe 'fact'-language is used to do. While the subject of facts and 'fact'-language is one worthy of our consideration for its own sake, I shall not pursue it for its own sake. I shall pursue it for the sake of helping free us from entanglements in bogus issues about bogus entities. That would be of considerable advantage in dealing, for one thing, with Austin's theory of truth.

'Fact'-language is very complex, following a number of related but different patterns. I shall argue that we can, at least normally, identify a performative-like factor, wherein our use of the term 'fact' serves to express certification of the adequacy of the evidence for some directly verifiable empirical statement. Beyond that, we can point to broad patterns of the use of 'fact'-language, patterns which are quite different, and which are worth noting in connection with our inquiry into truth. No account of facts as entities, worldly or otherwise, will allow them to fill all the roles facts are called upon to play. When we employ 'fact'-language we are talking about some portion of the world, employing various useful linguistic patterns for talking about properties and interrelationships of things and events in the world, and conveying, I believe, the performative-like force just mentioned; but to attempt to distil entities from these linguistic patterns is not justifiable.

FACTS AND THEIR ROLES

As any account of facts must also account for the roles they are assigned to perform, I shall start with an investigation of some of these roles and their associated patterns of linguistic usage. Of these, many shed little if any light on what facts actually are or are not. However, there are two quite common (and central) roles assigned to facts by linguistic usage which do make (incompatible) suggestions about the nature of facts. On the one hand, we are said to state facts, and to state as a fact *that* so-and-so. Note likewise that where we may say 'It's a fact that so-and-so', we may also say 'It's true that so-and-so', and similarly with 'That so-and-so is a fact' and 'That so-and-so is true'. All of this suggests that what is a fact and what is true are the same thing. This 'soft role' is linguistically oriented and tends to centre on 'fact that'. Yet while this suggests that facts are true statements of some sort, or are linguistic entities of some related sort, they are evidently still closely tied to the non-linguistic world.

On the other hand, facts are taken to be hard brute features of the world. They are spoken of as if they were independent of language, and as if they had effect in the world. ('His defeat was due to the following facts:. . . .') We are said to notice or observe them, and we must accommodate ourselves to them. We discover new facts, or attempt to, and we try to be true to the facts. This 'hard role' suggests facts as entities of some sort which are independent of language, and has served as an inspiration of correspondence theories of truth.

If facts were themselves truth-bearers, or linguistic accusatives of propositional acts, or anything else along such lines, then we could in no way accommodate the hardness and bruteness of facts in their hard role. Normally we would allow that there were facts which are unknown, perhaps never known, and, for that matter, unstated – though they might possibly become both known and stated. While

141

knowledge and (some) truth-bearers may be made for facts, so to speak, facts – hard facts, at any rate – evidently are not made for (true) propositions or statements, as Strawson contended (1950: 37–8), but are in some ways independent of knowledge and statements. While our statements, to be true, and we, to survive, must take account of facts, brute facts evidently are independent of language.

In either role, facts are also seen as that in virtue of which true statements, or at least some true statements, are true. These hard and soft roles and associated patterns of linguistic usage lend themselves to opposing theories of truth as well as to opposing theories about facts. For example they provide, as we shall see, considerable ammunition for Strawsonian and Austinian style theories, respectively, concerning facts and truth. Philosophical parallax then leads us to stress those accounts of facts or patterns of usage which most suit our philosophical perspective.

If we try to treat facts as things (entities) of any sort, the divergent demands of the divergent roles facts are called upon to play make it impossible in principle to give an account of facts which will meet all of those demands. These polar fact-roles threaten us with the horns of a dilemma. On the one hand, in addition to difficulties in defending any specific account of language-independent thing-in-the-world facts, we are forced to recognize their linguistic dimension. On the other hand, if we attempt to take facts as language-dependent entities (as being members of some class of true propositions or statements, or something of that general sort), then we become impaled on the other horn, for we lose their bruteness and independence. In principle, no entity can fill both of these polar roles. Any successful account of facts must therefore treat them in some fashion other than as entities of any sort, while yet meeting the legitimate demands made upon fact theory by these roles. We must ask not what facts are, but what 'fact'-language is used to do.

'FACT'-LANGUAGE AND TRUTH-RELATED DISCOURSE

I shall turn briefly to the broader matter of truth-related discourse, and go on to make a suggestion about how 'fact'-language fits into it. Recall that Strawson claimed that to attribute truth to some statement is to perform the act of agreeing with or endorsing that statement. As he himself came to admit, there is more to the story than that. Yet he performed a signal service in calling our attention to the surrounding linguistic situation, which involves questions of when, why, and to accomplish what, is truth-related discourse employed. After all, it does not take place in a vacuum – nor do we just blurt out 'It's true that the cat is on the mat' unprovoked. While it would be strange to just announce 'It's true that so-and-so' or 'It's a fact that so-and-so' apropos of nothing, if a given statement is disputed (for example), one might well say the former, and, in the case of a certain class of statement, we might well say the latter.

It is important to note that 'fact'-language is not used for talking about just any sort of statement, nor is it used for talking about just any sort of true statement. There are many instances wherein it would be quite in order to say 'It's true that so-and-so' or 'That so-and-so is true', but not 'It's a fact that so-and-so' or 'That so-and-so is a fact'. Examples may be found in law (or other statements of rule), in expressions of right or wrong, good or bad, taste, attitude, etc. Analytic truths are examples, and perhaps examples are to be found in formal logic or mathematics, or in theoretical science or philosophy. To give two examples: while true, to say that it is a *fact* that all bachelors are unmarried would have a very odd ring to it. It conjures up pictures of someone going out with a clipboard and taking an exhaustive survey. Again, it might be true that the stew tastes very good, but it would be strange indeed to call it a fact. (To be sure, there are certain special uses according to which we may extend the range of the term 'fact', as 'The fact that the stew tastes good does not mean that . . .', but that is another matter, which we shall get to in due course.) Evidently, 'fact'-language is most at home with directly verifiable (or falsifiable) empirical statements. Stipulatively, I shall refer to such statements as *factual statements*. Factual statements may be true or false, and their expression might not contain the term 'fact' or any similar term. (Thus, 'The cat is on the mat' expresses a factual statement even if the cat is elsewhere, while 'Bob is a twit' does not express a factual statement even if he is a twit.) When I speak of evidence in the following, I shall be referring to evidence appropriate to such statements.

Austin (1950: 24n) and Strawson (1950: 38) both held that 'It's true that . . .' and 'It's a fact that . . .' have the same applicability, and here they miss much of significance. The use of these formulations is coextensive only with respect to factual statements, and I would claim that even here they do different jobs. Austin, who was primarily concerned with factual statements when he formulated his account of truth, suggested that statements of other types should not be thought of as being true or false. This suggestion does violence to our normal patterns of usage – a strange thing for Austin! – and serves only to detract from the investigation into truth. I suspect that this was due to his being too anxious to involve facts, as he understood them, as parts of the truth-relation he was attempting to elaborate. By coming to terms here with 'fact'-language, I hope to clear the way for a discussion of the more fundamental issues of truth theory – particularly as they bear on Austin's own account.

THE FORCE OF 'FACT'-LANGUAGE

Strawson was no doubt correct in thinking that a performative element is, at least often, involved when we attribute truth to a statement. For reasons which we have already reviewed, though, there must be more to it than that. There must be something about a true statement which makes it properly to be endorsed. Gertrude Ezorsky (1967) took up this point, in effect, when she tried to combine the best features of Strawson's account with those of the pragmatic theories of truth. Rightly, she stresses that there is an important distinction between truth claims and other forms of agreement. She took up the pragmatist's emphasis on evidence, and maintained that to call a statement true amounts to a performance of agreement in the implied context of (adequate) evidence. A truth-endorsement, according to this conception, is in order only if there is sufficient reason to believe the statement true. This seems, in a way, an advance on Strawson's position, but it still faces the difficulties facing the pragmatist's theories. Truth does not necessarily go hand in hand with evidence. Recall the example about Lucy's mother and what she might have seen the day she died. Something is true there, though it could never bear Dewey's stamp of warranted assertability, as she requires. It is true that Lucy's mother saw Lucy's father that day, or else it is true that she did not, though both are unverifiable.

To talk about truth is not to say anything about evidence, nor is it to entail or otherwise necessarily indicate anything about evidence. At best it might inconclusively *suggest* something about evidence. Granted that truth claims are at least customarily made in certain linguistic contexts and, among other things, perform the function of expressing agreement, there is still the task of giving an account of truth. Nevertheless, evidence and presuppositions about evidence are relevant to certain aspects of truth-related discourse. It is highly relevant to our use of 'fact'-language with respect to factual statements. It is worth noting that it seems quite out of order to claim either that it is a fact that Lucy's mother saw Lucy's father the day she died, or it is a fact that she did not.

'Fact'-language, I suggest, has the primary linguistic force of expressing certification of the adequacy of the evidence for a factual statement, or of endorsing a factual statement in the context of evidence held to be adequate. To be sure, 'fact'-language has a complexity of usages, but this feature certainly seems to tie together quite a lot of it. This performative, or performative-like, factor is non-descriptive, though it is closely tied to the descriptive elements in language and is used to build on them. When we use 'fact'-language we do something which is more than just saying something. Uses of the term 'fact' and the term 'true', while both truth-related, are inherently different, doing different jobs, even where they have the same applicability, as they have for true factual statements. That their range overlaps is because verifiability implies truth. Even so, implication is not identity. (Note, too, that saying that someone is truthful amounts to something different from saying that he or she is factual.)

That 'fact'-language has this performative-like force, distinct from any performative-like force that might be attached to ascriptions of truth, is illustrated by the following hypothetical example:

George: That twit, Bob, bet me ten dollars that Reno, Nevada, is further west than Santa Barbara. Where does he think Reno is, anyway, out in the Pacific Ocean somewhere?
Edward: I wouldn't have made that bet if I were you. It's true that Reno's further west. As I recall, the coast turns far to the east, south of Point Conception.

The statement that 'Reno is further west than Santa Barbara' is a factual statement if ever there was one, but if I were Edward I would not go so far as to say *'It's a fact that* Reno is further west than Santa Barbara' until I had checked the map. Santa Barbara might be somewhat closer to the bend than I think it is. I do not want to stick my neck out too far and make twice the fool of myself. To claim that it is a fact seems to imply that I have certifiably adequate evidence, that I am *surer* than if I merely say that it is true. This is so, whatever conclusion we might come to about whether there are fact-entities of some sort.

As a further indication of this performative-like force, consider a case where someone states that such-and-such is a fact. Later it turns out that such-and-such was indeed true, but that the person had made the assertion without evidence. He or she had been 'whistling in the dark'. We would feel that the person's remark had been out of order, much more so than if he or she had merely asserted that it was true. I would suggest that this was because the performative-like act was, in Austin's term, 'infelicitously' performed, that she or he was acting to certify the adequacy of the evidence when there was none to be certified. (Compare knowing something, and knowing something for a fact.) We should bear in mind that what is required for evidence to be taken as adequate depends on the case at hand. Accordingly, just what it takes to know something for a fact depends on what is riding on it. I may know for a fact that a gun I am about to 'dry fire' at a target is empty, but before I put the muzzle to my temple and pulled the trigger, I would want to re-check.

It is also significant that we do not use 'fact'-language for future-tense statements, no matter how good the evidence might be. If I drop an egg off the top of a tall building, even while the egg is falling I cannot properly say that it is a fact that the egg will break, though it obviously will. Evidently, factual statements must be directly verifiable in a way which excludes the future tense, no matter how well-founded the claim might otherwise be. Indeed, there may, or may often, be a suggestion that the proposition is verified. (There also seems to be a reluctance to use 'fact'-language for hypotheticals, I think for similar reasons, though patterns of usage there seem less definite.) These points seem to underline 'fact'-language's more-than-truth-stating role.

FACTS AND 'FACT'-LANGUAGE

If we view 'fact'-language in this light, we can find a way to give an account which meets the legitimate demands of the divergent fact-roles and which does not invoke fact-entities. It appears that true statements are sometimes referred to as facts – as if they were fact-entities, taken according to their soft role. To refer to them as facts invokes this performative-like force of certifying the adequacy of the evidence for the statement. (If I claim that it is a fact that there is a bottle of beer in the refrigerator, I thereby certify the statement that there is a bottle of beer in the refrigerator, indicating – whether or not reliably – that I am doing so on the basis of adequate evidence.) Here the use of 'fact'-language, as if there were fact-entities, does its job without the necessity of there being fact-entities.

When we speak of facts, taken according to their hard role, the performative-like force of our use of language is still central to the linguistic job being done. The use of the term 'fact' as a grammatical substantive allows us to manipulate factual statements with linguistic convenience, thereby aiding us to describe independent reality. If facts are spoken of as if they had purchase in the world ('His defeat was due to a number of different facts'), their purchase is thereby attributed to the material things of the world, concerning which we are able to make statements of a properly certifiable character. (If one of the factors in his defeat was the fact that so-and-so, then the statement that so-and-so is an evidentially certifiable one, and whatever it is about materially contributed to the event.)

It is worth noting that if we have a proposition cast in a form which ostensibly refers to facts in the hard role, we can translate it into one which ostensibly refers to facts (that so-and-so) in the soft role while (otherwise) saying the same thing about the world. For example, 'Though the lurid light gave the scene a dreamlike quality, it was a terrifying fact that the volcano erupted/ . . . quality, the volcano's eruption was a terrifying fact'. While we can translate from a sentence in a pattern associated with the hard role to one in a pattern associated with the soft role, or vice versa, neither hard nor soft facts can fill the bill all the way around. Neither statements nor linguistic entities of any other sort are hard enough, nor can hard independent entities fit well as linguistic accusatives. That the different formulations are equivalent would indicate that neither is about fact-entities of either a hard or a soft sort. Thus, that such patterns are intertranslatable seems to indicate that this performative-like function of 'fact'-language is basic rather than derivative, expressing itself in a number of linguistic forms of convenience. This is the Ariadne's thread running through these and others of the various divergent patterns of usage of 'fact'-language, though there is more to it, in the various patterns, than just that performative-like factor. There are many strands to be taken into account when discussing the patterns of 'fact'-language, and clearly they have something in common, but it is not some *thing*. Certainly we cannot, with any hope of success, build a truth theory around fact-entities. Rather, what we should be doing is looking into the nature of linguistic functions and the activities we engage in when employing them in truth-related discourse.

To be sure, there are many patterns of usage of 'fact'-language, not all of which fit neatly into the patterns which I have discussed. It might be profitable to discuss a few of them, particularly as some of them might appear to undermine the account which I have given. To start with, note that we sometimes speak of facts which are not specified ('He refuses to face the facts'). It might be a worry that we are not here certifying the evidence for any statement, as none is being brought forward, and therefore that the performative-like feature cannot be the unifying element of 'fact'-language. Still, when we speak of unspecified facts we speak of matters which may be described – whether they are or not – by factual statements. As distinct from statements of other sorts, they would be appropriate for such performative-like certification. In the example given, the person is said to be refusing to face truths for which the speaker indicates there is certifiably adequate evidence. Again, in a related pattern, it is not unnatural to speak of discovering (previously unknown) facts, but this is not to speak of discovering previously undiscovered entities. It is to speak of discovery. We discover that certain factual statements are true, we discover certifiably adequate evidence for them, and, very importantly, we often discover *how* to formulate productive but previously unthought of factual statements. Such are the discoveries of scientists and historians. In this way we can accept the independence of facts without conceding any entityhood. (Compare: 'There are great paintings yet to be painted'.)

Other variations are of some interest. For instance, while it would be quite peculiar to say 'It's a fact that the painting is beautiful', no matter how beautiful it is, it would be quite unexceptionable to say 'The fact that the painting is beautiful does not mean that I'd be willing to pay five thousand dollars for it'. That its being a beautiful painting should be a fact in one case but not in the other would be a mystery beyond adequate explanation, were we to attempt to elucidate the matter in terms of fact-entities. Yet when we turn our attention to what we are using language to do, the case admits of a reasonable explanation. The latter, non-anomalous, statement would typically arise in a case where we have already agreed that the painting is beautiful, and are continuing the discussion on that basis. While we have not established a fact in so doing, for our purposes the painting's beauty is no longer an open question. When we use 'fact'-language in this way we are not certifying the adequacy of any evidence for the painting's beauty. Rather, we are using this form to take account of the fact that the point has already been accepted as established (in this case by agreement); it is this quite factual matter, of its having been appropriately established, which is being recalled and taken for granted as a basis for further comment. Once again, the performative-like factor is being used as a basis for description. In general, such a pattern is often used to concede a particular point of agreement, perhaps in order to define the bounds of disagreement or uncertainty. A related pattern, where we also rely on the fact of a particular point's having been established, would be that wherein an examiner might say 'Judging by your answers, you are evidently unaware of the fact that negative numbers have imaginary roots', though one might well be reluctant to say 'It's a fact that negative numbers have imaginary roots'.

It would be fair to say that what is to be taken as a factual truth turns on the nature of the frame of reference within which we are operating – and that truths of any sort will be factual if we define truth in terms of a factual (empirically verifiable) criterion. We might say that it is a fact that negative numbers have imaginary roots or that certain arithmetical questions are undecidable, if we mean that proofs of a particular sort come out a certain way. This is a factual matter, just as it is a factual matter that certain laws are in the statute books – though we may or may not take this as meaning that certain acts are wrong. For that matter, given Beckmesser's frame of reference, in *Die Meistersinger*, it was undoubtedly a fact – quite empirically verifiable – that Walther's song was a poor one.

A point for further consideration: what I have characterized as the hard and soft roles, which facts are called upon by 'fact'-language to play, do not always keep properly to themselves. In an earlier example, 'One of the factors in his defeat was the fact that so-and-so', we had a 'fact-that' contributing to a physical event – which requires a hard fact. This does not fit into any of the previously discussed patterns. Linguistic accusatives, 'facts-that', taken as true statements, or as some such linguistic thing, have no purchase in the world. They cannot cause events. Nor does this example fit the usual pattern for hard facts. Instead of trying to work out what sorts of things facts are supposed to be in this

149

instance – which would be impossible – it is better to recognize that our usage does not require them to be things at all. Here again, our use of the term 'fact' is a means for talking about other things. That which defeated him is something about which we have certifiably adequate evidence – or, perhaps, about which we have reached agreement – and the force of 'fact'-language allows us to use that as a base for further description.

The performative-like force of the use of 'fact'-language is closely tied to the descriptive use of language. To better see this, let us consider a related account. According to Frank Tillman, 'fact'-language is properly used only when one is 'in the authoritative position of knowing . . . it is an authority-giving device applicable to assertions' (1966: 128–9). The device is performative or performative-like, but he does not tell us what the 'authoritative position of knowing' amounts to. David Londey (1969: 75) noted some shortcomings in Tillman's account, as illustrated by the difference between 'He stated that Lund is in Sweden' and 'He stated the fact that Lund is in Sweden'. If Lund were not in Sweden, this would conflict with the latter but not with the former. This indicates that 'fact'-language here does a descriptive job and is not merely a matter of the performative-like force of certification, authorization, or endorsement. Tillman's account, centring on the 'authoritative position of knowing', is at least incomplete. On my account, in 'He stated the fact that Lund is in Sweden' we are ourselves certifying the adequacy of the evidence, endorsing his claim by stating it as a fact. It may be correct that he made the statement even if it is not true, but if it is not, it is incorrect of us to so certify it. In 'He stated *as a fact* that Lund is in Sweden', we do *not* certify it, but report only that he did so. Another example, 'Part of his statement was about the facts of the fall in butter consumption, 1967–1968; and part was about possible sources of action that we might take' is quoted by Londey (ibid.: 77) as being indicative that 'fact'-language does more than authorize or endorse (or otherwise convey performative-like force), that it is here descriptive of the treatment of subject-matter of a certain sort, as opposed to the subsequent non-factual discussion. On my account, the first clause of the quoted example indicates that part of the remarks being described dealt with factual matters – though whether those remarks were accurate is not indicated. The use of the term 'facts' serves a descriptive function here. If to say that something is a fact is to certify the adequacy of the evidence, then to say that a statement is about facts is to describe it as one for which there is at least possibly certifiable evidence, though we may not certify it.

ONWARDS

It could well be said that facts are important to truth theory – even though there are no such things. We still need to talk about those matters for discussing which the linguistic substantive 'fact' is a useful though not strictly necessary tool. After all, statements, other than analytical statements, are not true by virtue of themselves alone, but by virtue of the way things are out there. In pursuing truth theory it is appropriate to ask what relation that which is out there has to those statements which it makes true, and to ask what it is which it makes them when it makes them so. We could, without impropriety, speak of a statement as being or not being true to the facts. Talking about propositions also has its uses. There are no such things, and truth-bearers ought to be identified not as propositions, but as statements. Yet it is often the case that different statements, even statements made in different words, can properly be said to say the same thing. While it would be a mistake to take what they have in common as being an entity, let alone as being the truth-bearer – mistakes into which undue reliance on the word 'proposition' can lead us – the fact remains that different statements can say the same thing, and some times they are true because of what that which they say has to do with external reality. Truth theory must certainly address itself to these matters, for discussing which the word 'proposition' has often been a tool, sometimes a useful one. It is not improper, certainly, to speak of a proposition as being in accordance with the facts – but whether we use those words or whether we do not, the fundamental issues still remain to be dealt with. Certainly we cannot develop a worthwhile account by taking facts and propositions as things of whatever sorts in some way fitting together. However we relate them, they cannot offer us an account of truth on the level we need.

We have identified truth-bearers as statements, sentence-tokens as used in context to say something-or-other about something-or-other. That, of course suggests that a statement is true if the something-or-other is as it is said to be. That, I believe, is basically the correct view, though it will take considerable elaboration to raise it above the level of a truism. That largely defines the task before us: to explicate what it is that true statements have to do with the reality which makes them true, and along with that, to explicate what statements are when they are true. Our improved understanding of facts and truth-bearers gives us more manoeuvrability and flexibility in our pursuit of an adequate theory of truth. No longer need we fall into entangling involvements with bogus entities standing between what we say and whatever makes it true or false. Moreover, we can take proper account of the fact that neither the world nor what we say about it comes in discrete pre-delimited units. There are any number of ways, along any number of different lines, in which we can describe the world, and there are any number of different ways along different lines in which the world can be as described or fail to be so.

Having refused to accept facts and propositions as middle-men between what we say and what we say it about, and having given up on the idea of there being a structural isomorphism between truth-bearer and extra-linguistic reality, we have much less material with which to put together an impressive theory of truth. Still, impressive theories of truth have a way of coming unstuck. It might be advantageous to do what we can with sparser material. After all, as we have already concluded, to say that a statement is true is to say something about that statement, and not just about what the statement is about. We can still hope to give an account of what we say about a statement when we say that it is true, even – especially – if we give up pursuing truth by looking to bogus entities which are supposed to fit together in the middle in some way. In developing an adequate account of truth, we must consider what it is we use language to do in our dealings with the world. It is not just a matter of *use*, but of *our* use, for various purposes. We must ask what kind of a job (or jobs) it is we use language to do in truth-stating, and what it is for that to be done in such a way as to justify the application of the term 'true'. Let us continue by exploring the suggestion that statements say something-or-other about something-or-other, the true ones doing so correctly. Perhaps we could come to a better understanding of truth through an inquiry into the descriptive function of language, asking how it is that what we say describes things, and – very importantly – asking how what is described is to be identified. (The latter, as was suggested, has been seen as a major problem: if 'There are no pink swans' describes no particular thing, and if there is no fact to be described, what is being said about *what*?) In taking this line of approach there are pitfalls to be avoided, many of which, historically, have been fallen into. At the end of it, though, I believe, we can come to a viable account of truth. In the next chapter I shall discuss Austin's account of truth, which took this general line and went badly wrong, but which had some good points to be salvaged. In the subsequent chapter I shall offer, as viable, an account of truth which, while significantly different, is also along those general lines. In a later chapter I shall discuss some further alternatives, none of which, I believe, provide an adequate account of truth.

7

AUSTIN AND STRAWSON

The controversy concerning truth between J. L. Austin and P. F. Strawson is reviewed in the light of the material previously developed, concerning facts and truth-bearers. Austin's account of truth is presented, according to which statements refer to and describe some state of affairs, with true statements being those wherein the state of affairs is as described. Various objections and defences, on the part of Strawson, Austin, and others are considered. It is concluded that Austin goes badly wrong in taking the demonstrative correlates to be worldly entities of some sort. Moreover, contrary to Austin, the demonstrative and descriptive correlates must be seen as overlapping and tied to statements as actually made by the language-user, in context. Certain other adjustments must be made. Still, it is found that in Austin's approach there is something of merit which might be salvageable.

One of Austin's many significant contributions to twentieth-century philosophy, as we will recall, was his discussion of performative utterances. Another was his discussion of truth theory. His ideas about truth, and his controversy with Strawson on the subject, are of importance in their own right and through being productive of future developments. The account of truth which I shall eventually present is, at a considerable remove, based on that of Austin, and owes a great deal to Strawson as well. Accordingly, I shall discuss at some length the issues as they were developed in the controversy carried on by Austin, Strawson, and certain others.

Much of Austin's philosophizing, whether or not about truth, took an 'ordinary language' approach, seeking to find valuable clues to conceptual problems by paying careful attention to the usages and distinctions of ordinary language. It was to him that philosophy in the ordinary-language style owed much of its inspiration and practical guidance. The emphasis was on ordinary language not because its usages and distinctions are infallible but because, nevertheless, they do reflect centuries of thought and experience. Through something like natural selection, the features of a natural language have survived and developed because they are useful in a great variety of applications in our dealings with the real world. To ordinary language, then, we are to look for what is, if not the last word, at least the first word.

AUSTIN'S CONCEPTION OF TRUTH

Austin approached truth theory by asking how we use the word 'true', rather than by inquiring after truth in the abstract. What he takes to be true or false, at least in the first instance, are statements. These are not abstract and timeless truth-bearers, but are much more particular. As he explains it:

> A statement is made and its making is an historic event, the utterance by a certain speaker or writer of certain words (a sentence) to an audience with reference to an historic situation, event or what not. [In a footnote he adds that] 'Historic' does not, of course, mean that we cannot speak of future or possible statements. A 'certain' speaker need not be any definite speaker. 'Utterance' need not be a public utterance – the audience may be the speaker himself.
>
> (1950: 20)

Statements in this 'historic' sense are what are true or false, with the truth or falsity of beliefs, propositions, or whatever, to be understood in terms of real or envisaged statements. And what is it for a statement to be true? Basically, it is a matter of picking out and describing something, and doing so correctly. According to Austin, there are two sorts of linguistic conventions:

> *Descriptive* conventions correlating the words (= sentences) with the *types* of situation, thing, event, etc., to be found in the world.
> *Demonstrative* conventions correlating the words (= statements) with the *historic* situations, etc., to be found in the world.
>
> (ibid.: 22)

The demonstrative conventions involve statements, which of course are historical, because it is a matter of what in the world[1] is being talked about on *that* particular occasion. The descriptive conventions involve sentences because it is a matter of what in general that form of words is used to say about whatever is picked out for description by the demonstrative conventions. Given these two sets of conventions, we can now say what it is for a statement to be true:

> A statement is said to be true when the historic state of affairs to which it is correlated by the demonstrative conventions (the one to which it 'refers') is of a type with which the sentence used in making it is correlated by the descriptive conventions.
>
> (ibid.)

Speaking broadly, Austin is saying that meaningful statements say something about something, and that true statements are those wherein what is said about that something is so. This account could be described as being a correspondence theory, of a sort, in that things are true or false by virtue of independent fact, but the relationship said to be involved is not one of structural correspondence. Austin, I believe correctly, rules that out entirely. He tells us (ibid.: 24) that the correlation between 'words (= sentences) and the type of situation, event, etc. . . . is *absolutely and purely* conventional'. Any correspondence here is strictly conventional correspondence. Of course this is not to say that the truth of a given proposition is merely a matter of convention. Whether the situation (or whatever) is of a given type is a matter neither of convention nor of structural similarity, but of whether a conventional requirement is met. Though the linguistic correlations are conventional, it is not a matter of indifference which conventions we use. As Austin strongly and rightly insists (ibid.: 24–5), some linguistic structures are more flexible than others, and better able to handle complex or novel cases. Moreover, some subject-matters find certain sorts of language more congenial than others – which is why *1984*'s Big Brother was so concerned with linguistic reform. (Perhaps, too, as Chomsky later suggested, some linguistic structures stem from inherent features of the human mentality.) Even so, while our choice of conventions may be subject to various constraints, our linguistic correlations are still conventional.

In conclusion, Austin added a paragraph (ibid.: 30–1) which criticized Strawson's performative theory of truth, arguing along lines discussed above in connection with that theory. In turn,

Strawson (1950) subjected Austin's views to severe criticism. This was the start of a controversy which lasted several years, attracted considerable attention, and yielded some philosophical gains.

STRAWSON'S INITIAL OBJECTIONS

Before we investigate Strawson's more detailed criticisms of Austin's account of truth, let us first consider a very general objection he raises which would apply to any theory along those lines. Indeed, some version of the objection would apply to most theories of truth. Strawson claims that Austin is guilty of a fundamental confusion between

(a) the semantic conditions which must be satisfied for the statement that a certain statement is true to be itself true; and

(b) what is asserted when a certain statement is stated to be true.

(1950: 43)

He argues, that under Austin's theory, in saying that a statement is true we are either

(a) talking about the meanings of the words used by the speaker . . .; or,

(b) saying that the speaker has used correctly the words he did use.

(ibid.: 44)

Yet we do neither of these things, Strawson argues, in saying that a statement is true. While those conditions may have to be fulfilled in order for a statement to be true, saying that it is true is not to say that they are fulfilled. He maintains that Austin has at best given an elucidation of empirically informative discourse, rather than an elucidation of the use of the word 'true' in such discourse (ibid.: 44, 53). It is providing the latter which Strawson regards as the philosophical problem of truth.

Austin no less than Strawson took the task at hand to be the elucidation of the use of the word 'true'. Their differences concern what it is to do that. According to Strawson, we must tell 'what is asserted when a given statement is stated to be true'. On his Ramsey-based account, all that is asserted is the given statement.[2] What 'is true' does is merely to serve as a means for the performative act of endorsement. He also points out, as above, that people who say that a statement is true do not generally conceive of themselves as asserting that Austinian conditions are fulfilled. That is undoubtedly the case. In effect, however, Strawson is demanding that an adequate account of the use of the word 'true' must provide a synonymous rendering with which all who make truth claims would agree. Of course there is no such thing and undoubtedly never will be. Those who make truth claims do not generally conceive of themselves as claiming that the statement fulfils Austinian conditions, nor that it corresponds with the facts, coheres with the Absolute, works out well in practice, or meets Tarskian satisfaction conditions. The only statement they would agree on is the statement they claim is true. Such a requirement automatically pre-empts the field for some version of the redundancy theory. By that standard, though, can we ever elucidate the use of any term? We may agree that the cat is on the mat, or at least think that we know what it means, but there is no elucidation of 'cat', 'mat', or 'on' with which we would all agree. For that matter, by that standard, Strawson would have to abandon his own account, for not all who make truth claims would agree that they are performing an act of endorsement. The conclusion I draw is that correctly elucidating the use of a term does not require us to provide a synonymous translation with which all who use the term would agree. What is required is a correct account of what term-users, know it or not, are doing. To explain how those who use the term 'true' use it, it is not necessary to get them, when they use the word, to intend what is involved in the explanation.

On to more specific criticisms. With what do the demonstrative conventions correlate the statement? With what, for instance, is 'The cat is on the mat' correlated? The cat? If we take the correlates to be those things which the statement is about, we have problems, for some statements are not about anything in particular. There are no particular items which negative statements, universal statements, or existential statements are about. ('There is no one at the door.' Who is it that is not at the door?) This was, as we recall, a problem for the *Tractatus*, and Strawson raised the same point against Austin, concluding that his formulation applies, if at all, only to affirmative subject–predicate statements (1950: 50–2). However, while Strawson's objections were well taken on the assumption that the demonstrative conventions were supposed to correlate statements with particular items, Austin, as Strawson came to accept

(1965: 290), took the correlates to be not particular items, but states of affairs. Thus, 'The cat is on the mat' is correlated not with the cat, but with some sort of a cat/mat state of affairs. Austin's account thereby avoids one blunder, but is it only at the price of another blunder at least as bad? What sort of a thing is a state of affairs, and how is it, as is required of demonstrative correlates, 'to be found in the world'? It is a worry that Austin might be trying to overcome real problems through an appeal to bogus entities. Most of the considerable controversy surrounding Austin's account of truth centred on these states of affairs (also known as facts or situations).

SITUATIONS/STATES OF AFFAIRS

As the correlates of the demonstrative conventions, states of affairs are referred to and taken as the subjects of description. Moreover, they are said by Austin to be that which makes true statements true, by being as described via the descriptive conventions. This leads us into danger areas. One of the dangers is that in attempting to join words and world we do so by using a broad heading, 'state of affairs', to conflate worldly things/events, which are a certain way, together with the state of affairs *that* they are this way. That would be to join words and world via states of affairs which simultaneously, and illicitly, are features of the material world and verbal entities as well. Strawson warns us against this sort of thing, maintaining that:

> The only plausible candidate for the position of what (in the world) makes the statement true is the fact it states; but the fact it states is not something in the world. . . . the fact to which the statement 'corresponds' is the *pseudo*material correlate of the statement as a whole. . . .
>
> 'Fact,' like 'true,' 'states,' and 'statement' is wedded to 'that'-clauses; . . . Facts are what statements (when true) state; they are not what statements are about.
>
> (1950: 37–8)

According to Strawson, then, facts (states of affairs, etc.) are purely linguistic accusatives. True statements are true because of what is in the world. The world contains worldly things, but there are no worldly states of affairs/facts to make true statements true.

Austin, in 'Unfair to facts' (1954), denies that facts are linguistic accusatives tied to 'that'-clauses. Rather, he defends them as things

in the world which make true statements true. The worldly correlate which makes, for example, 'The cat has mange' true, when it is
true, is not the cat, as Strawson initially supposed, but the cat's
condition. The cat's condition, according to Austin (ibid.: 104), is
something in the world, and is a fact in the world. Perhaps we might
deem this fact the cat state of affairs. In arguing that facts can indeed
be worldly things, he treats us to a virtuoso discussion of etymology
and the fine points of English usage. Unfortunately, he does not
make it all clear *what* sort of worldly thing they are supposed to be,
and accordingly, it is not at all clear just what we are to make of his
account of truth. Austin's ideas on these matters have been subject
to multiple interpretation – by no means all of it accurate – in the
controversy which has continued since his premature death in 1959.
I shall try to develop the fundamental issues concerning Austin's
account of truth without getting us bogged down in distracting
discussions about what facts are – concerning which I have already
presented my own views. In the end, I shall argue that taking the
line which Austin did, concerning facts or states of affairs, was a
major blunder which undermined what otherwise might have been
quite a good theory of truth.

Warnock, Austin's philosophical disciple, and posthumous
defender and explicator, undertook (1962, 1964) to clarify some of
these points. Concerning the demonstrative correlates, he tells us
that Austin had presented his own position somewhat inaccurately,
and offered to rectify what he regarded as a 'slip':

> . . . he says that 'demonstrative' conventions correlate 'the
> words (= statements) with the historic situations, etc., to be
> found in the world.' But again, on his own view, that a
> particular *statement* relates to a particular 'historic' situation is
> a matter not of convention, nor in this case of fact, but of
> logic: for he implies earlier that a statement is identified, in
> part, by reference to the situation to which it refers. What
> 'demonstrative conventions' in part determine is not how
> statements are related to the world, but what statement is
> made by the utterance of certain words on a particular
> occasion.
>
> (1964: 67n)

Accordingly, he reformulated Austin's formula so that the demonstrative conventions correlate 'words as uttered on particular occasions' (ibid.: 55) with sentences. In Strawson's estimation, expressed

in a subsequent paper (1965), this approach raises some problems. If we take it to be a matter of logic that a statement relates to a particular situation, Austin's account tends very much in the direction of triviality. Indeed, worse than being trivial, it seems to imply that all statements which are meaningful must therefore be true:

> . . . presumably it must be possible in principle in every case to specify this situation. . . . suppose our statement is: 'This inkwell has no ink in it'. Then one might think that the particular historical situation in question is simply the situation of this particular inkwell's being inkless at the time at which the statement is made . . . But this style of answer won't do at all. For we are trying to specify the particular historical situation which it is a matter of the statement's *identity* that it refers to, and we must be able to do this in such a way as not to settle in advance the question of the statement's truth-value and, moreover, settle it in favour of the statement's truth.
>
> (1965: 295)

Such a result would be utterly objectionable, as there most assuredly are meaningful statements which are false. Strawson considers possible ways of getting around the difficulty, and dismisses them all as unworkable. However, instead of considering the possibility that there is something amiss with this account of situations and statement-identity, he draws for us the conclusion that Austin's account of truth must be rejected. It would, I think, repay us to have a closer look at the issues concerning the nature of situations, referred to by statements.

What, Strawson asks (ibid.: 295–8), is the situation referred to by 'The cat is on the mat' – supposing that it is not the situation *that* the cat is on the mat – and is that situation the same as that referred to by 'The cat is eating the mat'? Could the situation referred to by the former statement be that of the cat's either-being-or-not-being on that particular mat (at that particular time)? Does the other statement refer to the cat's either-being-or-not-being engaged in eating said mat? Strawson rejects that suggestion:

> It seems unlikely, however, that Austin would wish to pass off either of *these* phrases as a genuine specification of a distinct historical item to be found in the world, viz. a situation which could, without prejudice to its identity, be of one of two

incompatible types. Not that these forms of words are unintelligible. . . . Each might perhaps be taken to refer to a
question . . .

(ibid.: 296)

If situations, as referential correlates, are taken to be things in the
world, then it certainly does seem unlikely that the cat's either-
being-or-not-being on the mat could be a situation. The same
applies to the cat's *having some merely spatial relation or other* to
the mat, the next suggestion Strawson rejects. He remarks (ibid.)
that it 'seems scarcely intelligible unless taken as alluding . . . to the
question *what* situation actually obtains or obtained . . .' I agree
with Strawson that situations of that stripe will not do at all. To
anticipate, however, though I shall not elaborate until later, I
suggest that we can find here some of the clues to how we can
salvage something from Austin's account. To start with, I am
inclined to agree that we ought to give up on the idea of the referent
of the demonstrative conventions being a thing in the world. Also,
the suggestion tying situations to questions is worth bearing in
mind. Perhaps they serve as loci for differing possible descriptions,
to be supplied by the descriptive conventions.

To continue, Strawson also considers the possibility that 'The cat
is on the mat' and 'The cat is eating the mat' both refer to the same
situation (ibid.: 297), '*the* situation with respect to that cat and that
mat at that moment; . . . [situations being] identified or defined by
. . . the sum or combination of all the identifying . . . references . . .
by whatever means these references may be made'. The situation
would be subject to further description in terms of being on, or of
eating. This seems like the most promising alternative so far considered. Strawson, however, rejects this principle of statement
identification as leading to anomalous results:

> we should have to say that . . . 'Jack dined with Jill one day
> last month' and 'Jack played tennis with Jill one day last
> month' [same month, same people] . . . both referred to one
> and the same situation; and we should also have to say that
> two statements made . . . within different months, referred to
> two different situations. Moreover, we should have to say
> these things even if the two made within the same month were
> separated by weeks and were verified by engagements separ-
> ated by weeks . . .

(ibid.: 297)

Strawson does not explicitly say why he finds this anomalous, but he considers that the anomaly arises from Austin's taking the situation to be a worldly thing, 'an actual historical item' (ibid.: 298). The idea seems to be that it would be very strange indeed were the two statements somehow to refer to the same worldly item when they are about, and made true by, two totally different events at two quite different times and, one would presume, two separate places. For the same reasons, he thinks it too odd that 'There was a general election in the U.K. last year' should refer to the identical situation as 'There was a dry summer in the U.K. last year'. I quite agree that it would be difficult, I should think impossible, to deal with these examples on the basis of the given assumptions. Instead of abandoning the basic account of truth, however, I suggest that we reconsider those assumptions. I suggest that we need a much better account of demonstrative correlates.

Strawson is quite correct in pointing out that it would be just ridiculous to take the demonstrative correlate of a statement to be the situation *that* what the statement says is so. Doing this would be to require all meaningful statements to be true, and so to trivialize truth. Neither Austin nor Warnock suggests any such thing, however. A major error which they did make was to tell us that the demonstrative correlates are things in the world. Strawson's examples weigh heavily against that particular claim. Also, I suggest that it would be well to reconsider the assumption, implicit in the Austin–Warnock account, that a statement has only *one* referential correlate. If statements do have exactly one (at most one?) referential correlate, then certainly it might seem odd that the two Jack and Jill statements about two totally different events would refer to the same correlate. Perhaps, though, we see them as both referring to the/a Jack–Jill situation. But why not one to the/a tennis situation and the other to the/a dining situation? If the referential correlate were not a worldly thing after all, it would seem more plausible that we might be talking about a number of different situations, saying something about all of those different things: of Jack that he did such-and-such, of tennis that it was played together by so-and-so, and the like. But is the term 'tennis' in the reference or in the description? It seems to migrate back and forth according to what we are supposedly talking about. Yet on the Austin–Warnock account, the demonstrative and descriptive conventions are given as quite rigidly distinct, correlated with different linguistic correlates. But are they really that distinct? In another passage, Strawson cast doubt on that. Before we explore these points, however, there are some other matters in the historical debate concerning situations which need to be considered.

SITUATIONS: SOME ADDITIONAL POINTS

Warnock (1962) attempted to explicate and defend Austin's account of situations/states of affairs as demonstrative correlates. To clear the air somewhat, he proposed that we *not* formulate our account of truth in terms of facts. He agreed with Strawson that facts are identified by statements and are what true statements state, so they cannot explain *why* a true statement is true. Situations or states of affairs, in contrast, are independent and can make a statement true or false. The statement that the corn is green refers to the situation in a particular corn field, and the actual situation there renders the statement true or false. 'But situations are not, like facts, stated; they may be, like tables, described. . . . [unlike "the fact that . . ."] "the situation that . . ." is not admissible English' (ibid.: 14). He reminds us that 'situation' and 'state of affairs' were Austin's original terms. Even so, Austin certainly came to allow the term 'fact' to play a prominent role. Instead of writing 'Unfair to facts' (1954), perhaps Austin should have written 'What situations are'.

What indeed are situations – and are they in the world? Warnock:

> A state of affairs, no doubt, is not an object, and does not have a neatly bounded place in the world *just as* an object typically does; but is this the only sense in which anything can be said to be in the world? Suppose I were to say that one-party dictatorships are sometimes very popular; would it not be quite proper for a skeptical interlocutor to ask where in the world such a state of affairs is to be found? And might I not answer quite properly, even truly perhaps, 'In Cuba, for instance'? There does not appear to me to be any better reason for denying that situations, say, can be found in the world than there would be for denying that reflections, say, can be in mirrors.
>
> (1962: 12–13)

As Warnock then points out (ibid.: 14–15), there is no choice between talking about things and talking about situations. We can talk about the corn *and* about the corn situation. Talking about the latter is often how we go about talking about the former. That could well be true even if situations are not to be found in the world. Unlike Warnock, I am not inclined to grant that reflections are in mirrors, except in a figurative sense. That it is a highly useful figure of speech makes it none the less figurative. Could it be that talking about situations is only a useful means for talking about what really is in the world?

So what? Perhaps which terminology we use is a matter of indifference. Does it really matter whether a situation is in the world in the rather lame sense in which a reflection is in a mirror, or whether it is in the world in the rather more robust sense in which the glass is in the mirror? I think that it does matter. Wherever we say reflections are, we need to know how they work. If talking about situations is no more than a way of talking about things in the world, taking them as things in the world can obscure our need to give an account of them if we are to give an account of truth. Worse, it can lead us to think the wrong things about situations. Warnock, I believe, was led into excess and error. He was concerned (ibid.: 15–16) to defend Austin's account from the charge that there is no conceivable worldly demonstrative correlate for an existential state-ment, such as 'There are white cats'. There is no particular cat which makes that true. Instead of being correlated with some cat, the statement is, according to Warnock, correlated with 'the particular situation of some cat's being (or possibly not being) white' (ibid.: 16). One certainly presumes that Warnock does not mean the situation centring on some particular cat, but rather, the situation of some-cat-or-other's being (or possibly not being) white. Even so, this will not do at all. Setting aside for the moment the question of whether such correlates can do the job demanded of them by the Austin–Warnock account, let us consider them as worldly entities. Warnock clearly considers a particular cat's being white to be something in the world, and it may seem a small step from there to taking some-cat-or-other's being white as some situation (or other) in the world, and so from there to taking some-cat-or-other's being (or possibly not being) white as a situation in the world. Warnock does not actually offer any justification for his claim concerning the identity of the correlated situation, but if we do require a correlate for a statement of this sort, and require it to be a worldly situation, this seems to be about as close as we can come. Even so, it is not coming very close. Some-cat-or-other's being (or possibly not being) white is no more plausible as a particular something to be found in the world than is a particular cat's either-being-or-not-being on the mat. It seems less plausible, if that is possible. Were I to look in the world for such a situation as that, what would I be looking for and how would I know when I had found it? To be sure, I could easily find a white cat – which would make the statement true – but there is no cat such that it is part of the statement's identity that it refer to that cat or to its condition.

Even if we did take the situation of some-cat-or-other's being (or possibly not being) white as the demonstrative correlate, as Ted Honderich points out (1968: 132–3), there is no conceivable type of which such a situation is an instance. A particular telephone's ringing, he points out, is an instance of any telephone's ringing, but of what type could some-cat-or-other's being (or possibly not being) white conceivably be an instance? If it is not of some type, then it clearly cannot make the statement true by being of the type with which the statement is correlated by the descriptive conventions. Honderich does offer a way out for an Austinian account, though an unattractive one (ibid.: 133–4). He points out that we could analyse the truth of 'There are white cats' in terms of 'This is a white cat' being sometimes true. We could make a similar move for general statements, analysing the truth of 'All As are B (or are Bs)' in terms of 'This A is (a) B' is always true. This is not an attractive line to take. For one thing, it seems to shift what we are talking about, from, for instance, the statement that there are white cats, to various other and unspecified statements. And it still seems to be making a general statement – about those statements. Also, it loses the Austinian conception of there being some identifiable situation which, when the statement is true, is as described. My own suggestion is that it would be preferable to stop groping around for some worldly demonstrative correlate. I think it might be more profitable to take the demonstrative correlate not as something or other in the world, but as a way of focusing on what is in the world. I will say more on that later. Now, though, let us note certain other difficulties with Austin's account.

STATEMENTS AND CONVENTIONS

Recall that according to Austin, the demonstrative conventions tie the words (= *statements*) with the referent situation/state of affairs, while the descriptive conventions tie words (= *sentences*) with types of situation – the statement being true if the situation is of that type. Recall, too, that Warnock noted and rectified one apparent 'slip' in

Austin's formulation. Austin, seemingly, cannot claim that a statement is conventionally correlated with a situation if, as we are told, it is part of the statement's identity that it refer to that situation. Accordingly, Warnock rephrased the Austinian account so that what is correlated with a situation by the demonstrative conventions are the 'words as uttered on particular occasions'. On this account, the statement made is not the words as uttered, but a statement made thereby which is identified by the situation referred to and the description applied to it. For my own part, I am by no means convinced that the apparent error really was an error, but Warnock's amendment seems to me to do no harm. Indeed, in terms of my own thinking, the amendment makes no change. I take the statement to be the words as uttered on the particular occasion, and I am quite prepared to accept that it can be part of the statement's identity that it be correlated through the use of conventions with a particular situation. After all, the relevant conventions are part of the identity of the words as then used. Even so, my way or Warnock's, it is still a matter of situations correlating with words as then used. Another alternative would be, as Honderich suggests (1968: 129), to 'abandon the notion of an identified existing situation *which it is a matter of that statement's identity that it refers to* and with respect to which the question arises of whether it is or isn't of a given type'. Abandon it we certainly must if situations are anything like what Honderich takes them to be. Relying on Warnock (1962) he takes them to be circumstances – though the word 'circumstance' does not actually appear in Warnock's account. A circumstance is held to be the circumstance *of* some item being some way. Whether such a circumstance obtains, of course, is a matter of contingent fact. Not only is it not a matter of logic that the statement be correlated with the situation, it may not be correlated with such a situation at all, since that situation may not exist. Even so, the statement could still refer to items and describe them. However, that leaves us with the problem of working out what is correlated with what. (Also, there is the question of how we are to identify statements. Can we do so other than in terms of situations referred to?) A better approach, I believe, would be to develop a workable account of what situations are. Before we turn to that, though, there are some other matters to be considered.

Just why is it that one set of conventions are attached to statements while the other set of conventions are attached to the sentences used in making the statements? The reasoning is that demonstrative conventions tie particular statements – made in particular times, places, and circumstances – with particular situations. The very same sentence (-type) could be used on another occasion to make a different statement concerning a different situation. On the other hand, the descriptions are not tied to particular occasions, but are a matter of which types of situation are standardly correlated with which forms of words. That is the basic idea. However, I believe that Austin's position on this score is ultimately untenable and that, like his doctrine of worldly situations, it creates unnecessary difficulties for his basic account of truth.

This was one of the points of controversy between Austin and Strawson, as the latter (1965: 291–5) denied Austin's dichotomy between fundamentally different sorts of convention. He did not deny that referential and descriptive functions are performed in the making of (at least) empirical statements. Neither did he deny that we can make useful and workable distinctions between differing sorts of linguistic convention. What he did deny was the existence of a duality of rigid and non-overlapping kinds of convention functioning in accordance with Austin's formula. The conventions are similar in kind and overlap. Consider Strawson's examples:

At least one guest will drink no wine at dinner.
This guest is drinking no wine at dinner.
That guest drank no wine at dinner.

These, presumably, are all correlated by the descriptive conventions with the same *type* of situation, that of a guest's drinking no wine at dinner. Were we to substitute the word 'woman' for the word 'guest', we would get three other statements correlated with another type of situation, that of a woman's drinking no wine at dinner. 'Guest' and 'woman' are, apparently, centrally involved in the descriptive conventions. They are important to what is being said about the situations referred to by the statements in question. Just what situations are referred to? Strawson does not tell us what he takes them to be, but he asserts, which does not seem at all implausible, that the terms 'guest' and 'woman' feature in the demonstrative conventions determining what situation is correlated with their respective statements. Perhaps, on the Warnockian model, they are supposed to be correlated with the situation of at least one/this/that guest's/woman's drinking (or possibly not drinking) no wine at dinner – or something along such lines. In any case, 'guest' and 'woman' evidently feature in both the demonstrative and the descriptive conventions. He draws the conclusion that the demonstrative and the descriptive conventions are not discrete, but overlap. I accept his conclusion. However, I cannot accept his argument for that conclusion. Nor, to glance ahead, will I be able to accept the further inference he draws from it.

Perhaps the situation involving the guest or woman is of another type, that of *someone*'s drinking no wine at dinner. Or perhaps it is a matter of the situation at or involving the dinner having as its type that of a guest/woman drinking no wine. We can think of other variations. The point here is that the same term need not show up at both the demonstrative and the descriptive end of things. As well, we have come back to the problem of how we are to specify *the* situation referred to by a statement. Perhaps, I have suggested, a statement may be correlated with a number of situations, each with its associated description. In any case, Strawson has not shown that key terms are involved in both demonstrative and descriptive correlations. Even if he had shown that such words as 'guest' are involved in both the demonstrative and descriptive correlations, it would not automatically prove his point. Just what is the term 'guest' to which the correlations are tied? The demonstrative conventions are said to be tied with the words as then used, while the descriptive conventions are said to be tied with the words as standardly used. Is 'guest'-as-then-used the same as 'guest'-as-standardly-used? It would be absurd to imagine that there are two words 'guest' in any of the above sentences. (Though if there were, Strawson's argument would fail immediately, the overlap being only illusory.) Rather, it must be that the one word 'guest' enters into descriptive conventions by virtue of its standard usage, and also enters into demonstrative conventions by virtue of its use on the particular occasion. In what sense, then, do the conventions overlap? The mere fact, as we take it to be, that both sets of conventions are tied to the same word does not necessarily mean that they overlap in some non-trivial sense. After all, any number of widely divergent correlations can hook up with anything.

What Strawson wants to establish is that referring and describing are both done via linguistic conventions which can overlap in a substantial sense. To do that, we need to establish that describing often takes place as an essential part of referring, or that referring often takes place as an essential part of describing. Both of these things are indeed the case. In Strawson's examples, the term 'the dinner' figures in the descriptive conventions correlating the statement with a type of situation, that of a guest's drinking no wine at dinner. In the very course of taking part in the description, the term 'the dinner' has a referring role, specifying a particular occasion wherein a guest drank no wine. The reference is essential to the description. That person might drink quite a lot elsewhere. Again, the term 'woman' not only has a demonstrative role, it has a descriptive function in establishing the referent. It helps tell us which person we are talking about. Not only are the terms tied to both sets of conventions, the conventions overlap in the very substantial sense that one function is performed *in the course of* performing the other function. Accordingly, it would be best to scrap the dichotomy between demonstrative and descriptive conventions, and just take it that it is the *linguistic conventions* which refer and describe – by no means one to the exclusion of the other. Also, we should take the linguistic conventions as being tied to the words as used on the particular occasion, not just to the words as standardly used. For one thing, inasmuch as reference may take place in the course of description, even the description may be tied to the particular occasion. And if that is not the case for a particular description, then the standard usage is the particular use. Another reason for taking the linguistic conventions as being tied to the words as used on particular occasions is that just how, and whether, a given description fits is generally a matter of just how we are using the language on the given occasion. Standard usage enters in only in so far as we actually employ it on the given occasion.

A FURTHER SUGGESTION

Strawson proposed to strengthen Austin's formulation by redrafting it to take account of the different points he discussed. By doing so he hoped to bypass side-issues, and so to dispose of Austin's theory in its least vulnerable form, forcing the conclusion that this whole line of thought must be abandoned. As yet a further 'improvement' he proposed (1965: 290–1) to revise it by adding the qualifier 'historical' to the term 'statement' in the formula. The term 'historical' is to be understood very broadly, applying to statements about the present or future, as well as to those about the past. As he uses the term, '[s]tatements of totally unrestricted generality may be allowed to fall outside the class of historical statements, but all other statements which can be empirically confirmed or falsified fall within it' (ibid.: 291). In part this revision, a restriction in scope, was prompted by Strawson's belief – evidently correct, given Austin's ideas about facts/situations – that the Austinian formula is incapable of handling general statements. Also, the restriction was in part suggested by Austin's preoccupation with empirical statements. I think, though, that this proposed restriction would not be appropriate. For one thing, it seems to tie us unnecessarily and too closely to verificationism. It is highly debatable whether all truths, or all truths having to do with things in the world, are verifiable, and it would seem unfortunate to restrict our account so as to exclude other truths, if there are any. It is arguable, for instance, that there are scientific theories which are true even if not fully confirmable, and as was discussed previously, it is arguable that there are unconfirmable truths about the very distant past. Unless necessary, we ought not to rule out such possibilities. Again, it seems a deficiency of any account of truth that it could not deal with general truths. To be sure, we could deny that there are general truths, and deny that any of those other things are true, but that would be to shackle our account of truth with considerable implausibility. Yet if we admitted that there are truths which are not covered by this account, this would indicate that the account is at best incomplete and at worst incorrect.

As I have suggested, I think that Austin's account needs improvement, in connection with referential correlates, and elsewhere. Certainly with his insistence on thing-in-the-world referential correlates, Austin has a problem with general statements. I think, though, that there is no need to restrict an Austinian account to statements which can be empirically confirmed or falsified. What is critical is whether a referential correlate is as described, not whether it can be confirmed to be so. It is not at all clear, then, that the formula needs to be restricted to 'historical' statements as defined by Strawson – such a restriction being only one way, I think not a very good one, of ruling out general statements, with which Austin does have problems. In the next chapter I shall offer an alternative account which avoids any need for such restrictions. Here, let us ask why Strawson believes that even this restricted formulation is untenable.

STRAWSON'S DIAGNOSIS

On the strength of the preceding considerations, Strawson rewrites Austin's theory in what he regards as the best possible version which can be salvaged. He employs the qualifier 'historical', he allows for any amount of overlap between the demonstrative and descriptive conventions, and, critically, he offers us a selection based on his conception of what Austinian situations must be. According to Strawson, the least indefensible version of Austin's account would be something like the following:

> A historical statement is true when there exists or obtains a particular historical situation of a certain general type such that the words used in making the statement are, as then used, correlated by semantical conventions with just that particular situation and are, standardly, correlated by semantical conventions with just that type of situation.
>
> (1965: 299)

This is still too vague to be adequate. We need more precisely to specify the *kind* of linguistic[3] conventions involved. As before, Strawson points to difficulties in specifying the demonstrative correlate. He now raises the added difficulty of the way in which the statement is correlated with its referential situation. After all, we must take *denials* into account as well as *assertions*. Consider his example, 'The cat is not in the room'. Is it correlated with the situation of the cat's not being in the room? If, contrary to the statement, the cat were in the room after all, would the statement be correlated with the situation of its being in the room? Must we search the room to know what situation is being referred to? That would be very odd, since it is supposedly part of the statement's identity that it be correlated with its particular situation. Moreover, to continue this line of attack, we might well ask whether 'The cat is not in the room' and 'The cat is in the room' are both correlated with the same situation in the room. If not, with what in the world are they correlated? If so, then seemingly the two statements must be correlated with the same referential correlate in different ways, and it is up to us to specify what those different ways are. (To anticipate, I will go on to suggest that the two statements are correlated, in the same way, with the same referential correlate – roughly, the 'cat-situation'. In the two statements, that situation is described differently, said to be of different types.)

Strawson offers us two ways of getting around the problems which he raises, both of which avoid the difficulties, but neither of which is at all attractive. We must, he claims, settle on one of the following:

A historical statement is true if there exists or obtains a particular historical situation with which the words used in making it are, as then used, so correlated by semantical conventions that the statement is true

or else

[same formulation as far as 'conventions'] as to constitute a statement to the effect that that situation obtains.

(ibid.: 299)

Neither version amounts to much. The former amounts to saying that a statement is true if it is correlated with a situation which makes it true. The latter amounts to saying that a statement is true if there obtains a situation which it says obtains. Not only is it trivial, Strawson tells us, but

the second formulation is misleading or deceptive in just that respect in which it is reminiscent of the original Austinian form. For it blurs the point that *the semantical conventions play exactly the same role* in determining, or helping to determine, *what* the statement is a statement-to-the-effect-that, *whether the statement is true or false.*

(ibid.: 300)

Seemingly we are forced back to the problem, posed previously, that a meaningful statement must be true by virtue of its correlated situation – either that or, contrary to hypothesis, some meaningful statements may lack a correlated situation. At most a truism, the second version may be only a defective truism.

Both options, then, are at best manifestly trivial, each saying that a statement is true in the event that it is true. If the Austin–Warnock account comes to no more than this, it comes to nothing at all. Instead of rejecting an Austinian-style account out of hand, however, I think a better course would be to reject any such account of situations. Situations which are said be *of* so-and-so, situations which *obtain*, are too much like the facts-that, the purely linguistic accusatives, which Strawson warned us against. They pack the whole statement into the supposed demonstrative correlate. I believe that we can find a better account of demonstrative correlates.

Strawson does reject Austinian theories of truth root and branch – and goes on to offer us a postmortem diagnosis. One error, he claims, was in trying to generalize on a formula which applies, if at all, only to statements 'in the making of which a particular item is specified or identified and is affirmed to be (or have been) an instance of some general property or type or kind' (ibid.: 300). (The particular item, on Austin's account, would be the situation.) Strawson's claim, however, does not say anything more about what is wrong with Austinian accounts, but only suggests how one might have strayed into making what is regarded as an error. More substantively, he tells us that an important source of error

> is to be found in what Warnock sees as an unimportant 'slip', calling for minor amendment: viz. Austin's tendency to identify what is, truly or falsely, stated, when a statement is made, with the words uttered, as uttered in making it. In the text of his article, the same word 'statement' is used for both. Statements, in the first sense, are undoubtedly true (or false); statements, in the second sense, are undoubtedly correlated by semantical conventions with items and types of item in the world. If the linguistic term of such correlations is mistakenly supposed to be identical with the subject of the problematic predicate, the bearer of the problematic property, it becomes easier to suppose also that the sense of that predicate is to be analysed in terms of those correlations. What Warnock sees as a minor slip indicates in fact, I think, an important source of error.
>
> (ibid.: 300)

Certainly the Austin–Warnock account has its difficulties. It seems very evident to me that a large proportion of those difficulties arise from this troubling business of situations. Austin and Warnock offer accounts of what situations are which are vague and inadequate at best, and quite often wrong-headed. Strawson does little to rescue them. While situations are an important source of error, it is quite another question whether equating statements with the words used in making them, as then used, is a source of error. I doubt that it is. Strawson thinks that it leads to error because it blurs the important distinction between what a statement says and what it is about – which, given his conception of what a situation is, it does. If that distinction is blurred, then any account in the Austinian style certainly does deteriorate into triviality or absurdity. My own diagnosis, though, is that what we really need is a better account of what situations (to use Austin's problematic term) are – one which does not take them to be situations *of* so-and-so. With a better account of situations, together with a few other improvements, the

Austinian account of truth can, I believe, be made quite presentable. Another improvement which must be made in the Austinian account concerns the correlating conventions. Strawson is quite correct in maintaining that the demonstrative and the descriptive conventions overlap, and must be taken together as linguistic conventions. However, it is not correct that if we do alter the account accordingly, and take the conventions to be tied to the words as used, the account will collapse as a consequence. That follows only if we adopt an incorrect account of the nature of the demonstrative correlate. Indeed, it will turn out that an improved account of the linguistic conventions and their use, and an improved account of the demonstrative correlates will be mutually reinforcing. In the next chapter I shall attempt to develop an account which is adequate.

8

TRUTH

In this chapter I present my own account of truth. In some part it follows on from Austin's account, though it differs substantially. It is maintained that in using language we establish referential foci (which are not themselves entities). These are described in turn. Statements are true when their referential foci are as described. The linguistic conventions, which establish referential foci and establish correlations with descriptive types, do not do so in their own right but only as employed by language-users. The formulation I come to is this:

> *A statement is true if and only if it is correlated with referential foci, established through our use of linguistic conventions, which are of types of referential foci with which we correlate it through our descriptive use of linguistic conventions.*

This account of truth is further explicated and defended, and shown to be applicable to a variety of cases.

It is now time for me to put forward my own account of truth. It will be a somewhat minimal account, as it is intended to apply to truths in all of their divergence and infinite variety. Even so, it is by no means as minimal as many others which have been proposed. The account which I offer is somewhat in the Austinian style, though I would say that my account is a descendant of Austin's, rather than that it is a version of it, for what I shall propose is only partially like what Austin proposed. While it has Austinian antecedents, it has several other antecedents as well, including a measure of Strawsonian influence. Indeed, in some proportion the account is my own. My account of what the truth-bearers are differs from that of Austin, and my account of the conventional correlations involved will differ even more. Most strikingly, I think, we diverge quite sharply on the issue of what the demonstrative correlates are. I shall take that issue as my starting point, working from there through related matters and toward my account of truth. Different ingredients will produce a result which is certainly substantially different, and I believe substantially better.

REFERENTIAL FOCI

Austin took the demonstrative correlate of the statement, or of the words as used in making the statement, according to Warnock's version, to be what he called a 'situation' (or 'state of affairs'). Situations are said to be found in the world. It is part of the statement's identity that it refer to its correlated situation, and it seems to be supposed in all quarters that there is no more than one situation referred to by a given statement. I agree that statements have demonstrative correlates and are true or false accordingly as the correlates are or are not as described. However, I disagree sharply with Austin on both of those other points. A demonstrative correlate which makes a statement true by being as described is not something to be found in the world. Moreover, there may be more than one such correlate correlated with a statement. Accordingly, in discussing them I would prefer not to use either of Austin's terms, 'situation' or 'state of affairs' – let alone that loaded term 'fact'. Dangerous to start with, these terms have acquired too many additional connotations in discussions of Austin's account (and those of others). They all sound too much as if they were intended to be things to be found in the world, and also, they can easily sound too much as if they were what statements stated. In an attempt to avoid misleading terminology, I shall refer to the demonstrative correlate as a *referential focus*. Instead of saying that a statement refers to a referential focus, I shall say that it *establishes* a referential focus. I must now explain what referential foci are and what it is to establish one.

We establish a referential focus when our words, as we use them on that occasion, are correlated with worldly features *as conceptualized and construed by us*. There are several points to be made in this regard. Firstly, when we establish a referential focus we are not talking about something in addition to the world, nor are we adding something to the world. On the contrary, establishing a referential focus is part of how we talk about what actually is in the world. By way of analogy, to establish a referential focus is something like shining a spotlight on a stage: the spotlight may be shifted, narrowed, brought in from another angle, or coloured, according to the nature of our interests in illuminating some patch of the stage. The spot of light is not itself part of the scene illuminated, nor does it create what it illuminates. Our spotlight is not a magic lantern, and what is there was there all the while. Rather, spotlighting is a means we have for addressing our attention to things which are on stage, and to their features. The referential focus which is established by our use of the linguistic conventions is not an item of any sort. It is a means for addressing our attention to things which are in the world, and to their features.

If I say that the cat is on the mat, I am establishing a referential focus concerning the cat in question. It could also be said that I am referring to (and describing) the cat, but sometimes there is no particular thing being referred to, as when I say that some cats are white. Even so, I am still talking about something, even if I am not talking about some *thing*. I am talking about, as it were, 'cat-matters': things having to do with cats. That is my rather broad referential focus. It is, moreover, an instance of a type of referential focus, that of referential foci concerning things some of which are white. In the other case the relevant type is that of referential foci concerning things on the (given) mat.

This account differs considerably from that quite unviable account discussed previously, wherein the statements taken as examples were supposed to be correlated with the situation of the cat's being on the mat, or with that of some cat's being white, as the case may be – and the difference is not just that I have thought of another term in place of 'situation'. On my account, it is not at all a matter of the whole statement being packed into the demonstrative correlate. Nor is the referential focus taken as any sort of a thing in the world. If we did not get carried away by misleading connotations, Austin's term 'situation' could be made to serve. We could say that the (particular) cat-situation is an instance of a situation of something's being on the mat, or that the (general) cat-situation is an instance of a situation involving things some of which are white. We could use either term or some other term, so long as we remain straight on what we are talking about. I prefer not to use Austin's term because what I am talking about is not what Austin was talking about, and more generally, because the connotations are misleading.

An important point is that our referential foci concern things as conceptualized and construed by us. Our language does not simply correlate with, and so represent the structure of, things and combinations of things in the world. Our language does, certainly, correlate with things in the world, but not simply. Wittgenstein, in his *Tractatus* period, and other logical atomists thought that it did so simply, and tried to analyse the world in terms of objective independent units to which we can attach our language in, fundamentally, one right way. That, we now realize, is very incorrect. We differentiate, categorize, and associate according, in considerable part, to our own ideas, interests, attitudes, and general make-up. Reality is not without features in its own right, to be sure, but what we make of it is what we make of it. What is on stage is there, but what we see depends in great part on how we illuminate it. We join, divide, and associate things in ourselves. In establishing our referential focus, we take the world, or some aspect of it, taking it in some way of our own framing, and in going on to take the referential focus as being of certain types, we also proceed in accordance with our scheme of conceptualization and construal. The descriptive conventions as well as the demonstrative ones turn on how we conceptualize and construe things. In considerable part our manner of describing and our manner of establishing the referential focus will be tailored to one another.

PLURALITY OF REFERENTIAL FOCI

Recall, from the last chapter, that Strawson (1965: 297) raised the question of whether 'Jack dined with Jill one day last month' and 'Jack played tennis with Jill one day last month' (same month, same people) are correlated with the same demonstrative correlate. It seems odd that they should be about the same situation, when they might well report quite different events several days apart. Yet it seems odd that they should be about different situations when they are each about Jack and Jill and describing what they did last month. As I suggested, part of the problem arises from taking the demonstrative correlates as things-in-the-world of some sort. In this, of course, he had authority from Austin and Warnock. Another part of the problem arises from the tacit assumption that a statement can refer to, be demonstratively correlated with, only one situation. That is suggested by the assumption that situations are things-in-the-world. Moreover, to recall, Warnock tells us (1964: 67n) that a statement is at least in part identified by the situation to which it refers. That *seems* to suggest that there could be only one correlated situation – the interpretation which appears to be accepted by everyone involved, including Austin. However, as I have previously suggested and shall now elaborate, it might be part of a statement's identity that it be correlated with a whole family of demonstrative correlates.

If we drop the notion of the referential correlate being a thing-in-the-world of some sort, and think in terms of referential foci instead, there need be no difficulty. A statement may have more than one referential focus, and there is no point in asking which is *the* focus. In terms of 'Jack played tennis with Jill one day last month', what are we talking about? Are we talking about Jack? Or are we talking about Jill? Or are we talking about Jack *and* Jill? Or are we talking about tennis matches, or about what happened last month? Etc. These, certainly, are rather silly questions. We are talking about all of these things, and more. We are saying of Jack that he played tennis with Jill one day last month, of Jill that she played tennis with Jack one day last month, of tennis that it was played one day last month by Jack and Jill – and so on. The statement establishes a referential focus on things having to do with Jack, 'Jack matters', as it were, and describes it as being of a certain sort: that of something's (someone's) having played tennis with Jill one day last month. A referential focus concerning Jill is also established and described, as is one concerning tennis, and various other referential foci as well – different foci with different descriptions. This suggests that a statement is true when its foci are as described.

Strawson argued – quite rightly, as we have already noted – that the demonstrative and descriptive conventions are not necessarily discrete, and may well overlap. At the linguistic end they are not correlated with different things (words as then used and words as standardly used). Rather, they are all correlated with the words as then used by the language-user. Instead of distinguishing demonstrative and descriptive conventions, it would be better to say that the linguistic conventions are being used to do different things. We refer to Jack in the process of describing the Jill referential focus, or the Jill-last-month referential focus, and we describe Jack as having played tennis with her in establishing a referential focus concerning their tennis match (which is then described as one of something's having happened last month). And so on. We refer in the process of describing and describe in the process of referring. Strawson rightly points out that 'insofar as the Austinian formula rests on this dichotomy, that formula is defective' (1965: 294). Austin was indeed involved in a muddle there, a muddle which was perpetuated by Warnock.

Instead of maintaining that it is part of a statement's identity that it is correlated with a particular situation, we should recognize that it is part of a statement's identity that it establishes a whole family of referential foci. The referential foci of different statements may partially overlap. Thus, 'Jack dined with Jill one day last month' and 'Jack played tennis with Jill one day last month' are both concerned with the referential focus concerning Jack, though they describe it differently. Each statement is also concerned with referential foci with which the other is not. A statement, then, is not telling us about just one thing – describing just one demonstrative correlate – as Austin and Warnock suggest. Rather, numerous overlapping things are said about numerous overlapping foci.

This requires further comment. To start with, it might well seem counter-intuitive – quite absurd, even – that one statement should be construed as saying so many different things. Rather, we might think that statements just say what they say and that is that. They do say what they say, but there are numerous non-competing ways in which we can describe anything. Not only are there many descriptions which apply to Jack, there are many different ways in which a statement about Jack can be described – and analysed in terms of referential focus and description. The several analyses of a given statement in terms of referential foci and descriptions are equivalent. For every single member of a statement's family of referential foci, the associated description applies – or else, in every single case it does not apply.[1] If the referential focus concerning Jack is not truly an instance of someone's having played tennis with Jill last month, then the referential focus concerning Jill is not truly one of someone's having played tennis with Jack one day last month.

Recognizing that a statement has several referential foci allows us to avoid unnecessary and fruitless questions about which is *the* demonstrative correlate. The conclusion toward which I am working is obviously that a statement is true if its referential foci are as described, and false otherwise. Before I attempt to articulate a fuller account, however, there are some points which I would like to develop about the use of conventions and the nature of communication.

ON THE USE OF CONVENTIONAL
CORRELATIONS

There is an important question raised by what seems like an anomaly in the conception of our words (or sentences) as we use them
on a particular occasion being conventionally correlated with something. Instead of concerning what is at the two ends of the correlation, the question now concerns how they *could* be conventionally
correlated. As I have stressed, we often use language in novel ways
in order to convey the particular meaning we are trying to get over
on that specific occasion. We use the basic meaning-structure of the
language in use as the framework on which we hang our particular
meaning. It is not our words (or sentences) in themselves which are
conventionally correlated with referential foci and types of referential foci, but our words (or sentences) as used on that occasion in
that specific way. This poses the problem: how could a conventional correlation conventionally correlate anything unless it were
there to be correlated? In new uses of language, our words (or
sentences), as newly used, cannot, in general, have acquired conventional correlations, as there is no systematic way of determining in
advance how we *might* use them. Linguistic usage is much more
flexible than that. So long as we recognize that our linguistic usage
does have this flexibility, then, apparently we must conclude that
the linguistic role of words (or sentences)-as-used-on-particular-
occasions cannot turn on established conventional correlations. Can
this result be avoided? If not, this would militate strongly against
any account of truth like that proposed by Austin or like that which
I am in the process of proposing.

We can use conventional correlations all we want to, whenever
we have things to correlate. In formal systems, such as those of
mathematics or formal semantics, we use them extensively and
profitably. We can lay out our correlations precisely and in detail,
making allowances for all possible combinations, since what the
system does and does not allow is implicit within its structure (even
if the system is logically incomplete). For instance, while a formula
of which no one has ever conceived may arise in a formal calculus,
we may be certain that it has a conventionally correlated Gödel
number, since we can systematically make provision for every
formula which may arise in the system. If our linguistic usage were
static and well defined, it would be possible to correlate sentential

functions with satisfying objects. If our linguistic usage were to follow the rigid patterns suggested by the *Tractatus*, then certainly it would be possible conventionally to correlate words with things and facts. However, as the author of the *Tractatus* came to realize, the world does not divide up into atomic units. There is no systematic way of defining how we might care to divide, combine, and describe things. Our actual use of language, therefore, necessarily turns on more than just a structure of conventional correlations. For that reason, a system of formal semantics can only approach, but not reproduce, the flexibility of our actual usage.

To be sure, conventional correlations are an essential element in linguistic communication. Unless there were some conventions, we could not communicate linguistically. There remains the matter of how we use the conventions. Conventions are in large part defined by how they are to be used – and in a formal system, that is that. Even so, in a natural language there is considerable leeway for us to bend linguistic conventions to our own use. Were I to say 'The top of the mountain is covered with dog', people would not understand me, in the absence of bizarre events, and would no doubt think me quite strange. The word 'dog' cannot easily fit there, nor, without detailed explanation, can it convey my intended meaning. The word 'snow' is much more useful for me, since it is recognizable as a common noun standing for a kind of substance rather than a kind of thing, a substance with which we are all somewhat familiar (and which might likely be found covering mountain-tops). Yet as we have remarked previously, what is or is not to count as snow will vary with our intentions and purposes in the matter. A painter, a skier, and a glaciologist might well draw the conceptual boundaries differently. (And 'top', 'mountain, and 'covered' have their own flexibility.) To be sure, the applicable conventions may allow a term a wide range of applicability. Our linguistic conventions may tell us that 'snow' may mean this or that, or something within a certain (and sometimes flexible) range. However, the conventions cannot dictate to us *where* in that range our meaning must fall, nor can they tell us just what use another language-user is making of them. To understand, we must take into account person and circumstance – and often enough we do not get it quite right.

It is not just that we choose an option from a conventional selection. Sometimes we force and quite distort the conventions in order to achieve our communicational purposes. We might refer to carbon dioxide 'snow' on Mars (with or without the scare-quotes), and we might use the term 'snow' for dandruff or for certain sorts of interference on a video-screen. The term can also be used for intentionally misleading verbal obfuscation. These uses have become standard options, but before they became standard they were understandable, at least to a great many people. The first to use them took a standard correlation – 'snow' with snow – and put it to a non-standard use, correlating 'snow' with something *like* snow in certain ways. This relied on us to grasp a certain similarity, and so to get the point of what was said. A metaphor based on simile is then understood, and may perhaps lead to another standard use. Davidson has argued persuasively (1978) that in metaphor we do not use our terms with some special metaphorical meaning. Rather, we use them with their standard meanings employed for metaphorical purposes. Even when there is no trace of metaphor, though, as with 'The top of the mountain is covered with snow', we still use the linguistic conventions to establish and describe referential foci according to our own communicational purposes. On the basis of standard conventions of reference and description we establish referential foci of our own final shaping.[2]

I therefore maintain that Austin's approach requires some modification in this connection. We must take into account the language-user as well as the language used. It does not go far enough just to take the words as then used as being conventionally correlated by the descriptive conventions with certain descriptive correlates. Apart from whatever other shortcomings Austin's formulation might have, we must take account of the fact that the referential and descriptive correlates is done not by the linguistic conventions alone but by the language-user using the language in a particular instance. An adequate account of truth must reflect this, making allowance for the pragmatics of actual use.

ON COMMUNICATION

One must wonder how communication can be possible. If a language-user establishes and describes referential foci according to his or her own intentions and communicational purposes, elaborating on or diverging from the bare-bones meaning-structure of the language used, doing so as convenient or necessary, how is the person addressed supposed to understand what is being said? Are we supposed to be mind-readers? Like Shakespeare (*Henry V*, pro. 1. 23), any language-user calls upon us to 'Piece out our imperfections with your thoughts'. Often enough, certainly, we misunderstand or only partially understand what is being said. Yet communication does occur regularly and successfully. Not only does it occur in spite of the flexibility of our use of a natural language, the utility, efficacy, and, indeed, flexibility of the communication which we actually enjoy *depends* on the flexibility available in our actual use of language.

If we are to be effective in understanding a language-user – as we all are, to one degree or another – we must take into account more than just the words used. We must take into account the person using the language, the circumstances in which he or she is using it, and what his or her likely purposes might be in doing so. Gestures, tone of voice, what went on before, and what is going on around us now may all offer us valuable clues. We must take into account whatever is relevant – and that of course is the problem. There is no precise formula for determining what is relevant or how to take it into account. Certainly I shall not be so foolish as to attempt to provide one. The question is not one of formulae or precision. It is one of communication. If someone tells us 'The top of the mountain is covered with snow', we are not usually called upon to understand this in a vacuum. Instead of being an example inserted into a book, it would normally occur in some more practical context. If the person who said it was contemplating taking a photograph of the mountain, that is one thing. If he or she is planning to climb it, that is something else. In the one case, what is relevant is the visual appearance; in the other, what is relevant is the climbing conditions. In the latter case, visual appearances might well be deceptive. What would then be relevant is whether the route to the summit is snow-covered. If there were a climbable ridge of exposed rock, how it looked from below would be beside the point. Also, for mountaineering purposes one might care to make a sharp distinction between ice and snow, a distinction which would be much less important for the photographer. As it happens we are fairly well able, as a general rule, to make sense of what is said to us, though our ability rests on much more than our command of linguistic conventions.

In interpreting 'The top of the mountain is covered with snow' it is not necessary to know the precise meaning of 'snow' or any of the other words used by the language-user. Indeed, the terms may not be used with any precise meaning. Certainly the language-user may not use the terms with sufficient precision to handle all boundary-line questions. He or she is not trying to handle all boundary-line questions. What is important is that the vagueness around the edges must not obscure what the language-user is trying to get over. In understanding what is being said, not only need we not be able to settle the boundary-line issues, we need not even understand the terms the same way the language-user does. We may draw our conceptual lines somewhat differently, and we may have different areas of precision or vagueness. What is important is that we understand the terms sufficiently well for present purposes. We might draw the boundaries between muddy snow and snowy mud differently, and be vague in different ways, but still sufficiently well understand what was said about the top of the mountain. The differences might not figure in at all. Our communicational goals then may well be, and often are, achieved in spite of our conceptual differences.

To understand what is said in a natural language, then, is not at all like mapping something from one formal system into another. In formal systems, a successful mapping demands that we work out the precise equivalent in one system of what occurs in another. To understand what another says does not demand that we formulate in our mind the exact equivalent of what that person has in mind. Indeed, we *never* conceive of *exactly* what another person has in mind. We cannot, and we need not. Rather, we need to understand *well enough* for present purposes what is being talked about, what is being said about it, and what is to count as its being as described. We can talk about snow on top of the mountain, and understand what is being said, without precisely duplicating or even understanding one another's imprecisions. It is also worth noting, in this connection, that the language-user can convey truths which he or she did not intend. For one thing, what is said might have implications unknown to the language-user. Beyond that, it may be the case, and very frequently is, that a statement conveys meaning for the listener (or reader) which is not present for the speaker (or writer). For instance, A might tell B that C attended a performance of the Choral Symphony the previous night. Let us suppose, too, that A understands what he or she is saying and is not merely repeating something, yet is not particularly interested in premodern music. On the other hand, B, a choir director, is a Beethoven-lover whose favourite piece of music is that symphony. For B, A's statement about what C attended has a *depth* of meaning of which A was only dimly aware. Yet there is no inference from one thing to another thing. It is not another statement which B comprehends. Yet it is not the same statement, either, as it has meaning for B which it does not have for A. It is a different truth.

This sounds like nonsense. If it is not the same statement and it is not another statement, what is it? Part of the answer is that there is no *it*. There is no neat little item being passed from one person to another. It is not neat and there is no item – let alone an item transferred from one person to the next. Rather, there are words – as used, then and there, by *that* person. Other people, in their own ways, make of things what they make of them. The statement which A makes is never identical with the one which B receives. The statements have different identities. Ultimately, we have to say that one has its identity in terms of A and the other has its identity in terms of B. The statements may be equivalent – which must be a matter of equivalence with respect to some standard for saying the same thing. A's statement to B about C's attending the symphony may well be equated with what B understood from A. They are equivalent for many purposes. Yet they are not equivalent for all purposes, and we might wish to differentiate. Whether we do differentiate, and how, depends on what, for us, is riding on it. The identity of what is true or false will depend on that, too.

To return to the simile of the spotlight: while the spotlight illuminates what is on stage, doing so in a way devised by the director, what we see in the spot of illumination may or may not be what the director intended. What we see will in part be a function of our own interests and insights. When a language-user establishes referential foci, how we interpret them will be a function of our own interests and insights, and what we arrive at may or may not be equivalent, according to some standard, to what the language-user intended. Certainly we may attach different importance to things. That C attended the symphony last night might be taken as saying something about C, or about last night – describing different referential foci. Maybe the one who said that was primarily interested in C's doings, while the listener was more interested in when the performance is or was. (Perhaps he or she had thought it was to be tomorrow.) The speaker and the spoken to, then, might address themselves to different referential foci even though they are concerned with what is substantially the same statement.

In point of fact, communication there most certainly is. But no thing is communicated and nothing is communicated absolutely intact. We communicate in spite of, and because of, the vagueness and flexibility of that with which we communicate. We employ conventions in our communication, and their use is quite indispens-able, but the emphasis must be on our *use* of them. Conventions alone form only part of the skeletal framework of language. They do not define what we do with it, or how we do it, or whether we succeed. In framing our account of truth we must take these points properly into consideration.

TRUTH

I now offer my own account of truth:

> *A statement is true if and only if it is correlated with referential foci, established through our use of linguistic conventions, which are of types of referential foci with which we correlate it through our descriptive use of linguistic conventions.*

This is to say that in making a statement we establish referential foci and correlate our statement with certain types of referential foci. As it is a statement, the referential foci are asserted to be of those types. The statement is true if they are of those types – each referential focus being of the type of which it is said to be. All of this is an elaboration on the basic truism that a statement is true if what it says is so.

We should note that this formulation will expand to apply to equivalent classes of statements when we equate them by reason of commonality, for present purposes, of their referential foci and types of which those foci are said to be. Statements are, for present purposes, the same, and are true or false together if, for present purposes, they say the same things about the same things. This is so despite the fact that different people making equivalent statements in different words will use different conventions. The use of par-ticular conventions is not itself a defining characteristic of the equivalence class. What is essential to the truth of a statement, or of the members of an equivalence class of statements, are the referen-tial foci and types of referential foci, not the particular conventions through the use of which they are established as demonstrative and descriptive correlates.

I submit this account of truth in the conviction that it avoids the faults which so fatally undermined previous formulations in the Austinian style, without developing new faults. We do not have problematic entities to create problems for us, and the problem of sorting out which is *the* referential correlate does not arise. As I shall argue in the next section, existential, negative, and general statements are all provided for, equally with statements cast in the affirmative subject–predicate mould. Moreover, and very importantly, the formulation is, I believe, true to the nature of language and our use of it. The account turns on the simple point that when we say something which is true or false we are saying something about something. That is something which is essentially right about the Austinian formulation. However, one of the keys to handling that insight lies in not getting carried away to the extreme of taking the something we are talking about to be some thing. That is one of the points where Austin went dreadfully wrong. According to Strawson,

> It is . . . one of the truisms of logic, to say that, given a statement in the making of which a particular item is specified or identified and is affirmed to be (or have been) an instance of some general property or type or kind, then the statement is true if and only if that particular item is (or was) an instance of that general property or type or kind. . . . what Austin aimed at was a generalization which would cover the whole range [of statements]. But it was a fatal mistake to suppose that the *form* of the limited truism could be preserved in such a generalization.
>
> (1965: 300–1)

Austin's fatal mistake, though, was not in trying to preserve the form he did, but in trying to generalize it in much the wrong way. Once we get disentangled from particular items as referential correlates, and make other necessary adjustments, we arrive at an account which, while somewhat more than a truism, is nevertheless quite true.

NEGATIVE, EXISTENTIAL, AND UNIVERSAL TRUTHS – AGAIN

We have seen that existential, universal, and negative propositions or statements have posed great difficulties for correspondence theories, and particularly so for Austin's version. However, they do not pose one for my account. In each case, the key lies in determining what it is which is being described. Let us consider the problem areas in turn, taking 'The cat is not on the mat' as our first example.

It is incorrect to take the demonstrative correlate as being the situation that the cat is not on the mat, which would be to pack the whole statement into the referent. Rather, we must be applying a description, a negative description, to something. Then, are we describing the cat, as not being on a mat? Or are we describing the mat, as not having the cat on it? If we assume that there must be exactly one demonstrative correlate, this is an embarrassing problem. Instead of concluding, as Strawson suggested, that we must give up on anything like an Austinian theory, the thing to do is to give up on the incorrect assumption that there is exactly one demonstrative correlate. Indeed, two different things – the catless mat and the matless cat – are each sufficient to make the statement true. The referential focus concerning the cat is correctly describable as being one of something's not being on the mat, and the one concerning the mat is correctly describable as being one of something's not having a cat on it. Materially it comes to the same thing, and either way the referential foci are as described.

Existential statements, such as 'There are white cats', need pose no more of a problem. Even though, unlike the last case, there is no particular item involved here at all, that does not mean that nothing is being described. Certainly it does not mean that the demonstrative correlate is the situation that there are white cats. (As Honderich suggested, it would be an absurdity to ask of what type *that* could be an instance.) What is being described is something of a quite different sort from any of those things. That there is something being described, and just what it is, may not be immediately obvious in the normal sort of circumstances. However, consider a case wherein you claim that there are no winged reptiles. You would not feel that your claim had been refuted if the first interstellar expedition found one, though you might phrase the point differently after that. You would feel that your claim had not been refuted because *that* was not what you were talking about. What you were talking about, what you meant, concerned things in this part of the universe. The demonstrative conventions tacitly operative in this case established referential foci concerning earthly matters or earthly reptiles. (Or perhaps we are saying of what is just the reptile referential focus that it is one of something of a sort which has no flying instances – around here.) By the same token, 'It is raining' would not be refuted by someone's pointing out that it is not raining in Timbuktu. Our referential focus does not extend as far as that. (To be sure, a statement might conceivably establish a

190

referential focus on the whole universe, describing it as being of the sort of place where there is/is not something of a particular sort.)

Existential statements establish referential foci which are, or are not, of a type with which the statement is correlated by the demonstrative conventions. The statement that there are white cats establishes and describes a referential focus, one which may have to do with a particular pet shop, a given neighbourhood, or the whole world. The focus is or is not correctly describable as one featuring white cats. Obviously, we could just as well take the statement as establishing referential foci concerning cats, white cats, or white things. Not only is there no particular cat which makes the statement true, there is no thing at all which serves as the demonstrative correlate. We do not need a thing.

In the case of universal propositions or statements, again there is no great problem. 'Cats drink cream' is no more difficult than 'The cat is drinking cream'. The latter establishes a referential focus on things having to do with a particular cat, while the former establishes a referential focus on things having to do with cats. This referential focus is described as one concerning things having to do with things which drink cream. Such a referential focus would create a problem for us only if, for no good reason, we wanted to take the demonstrative correlate as being a thing. Yet there is no more reason to tie the statement to a universal-thing than there is to take the demonstrative correlate of 'The cat is on the mat' as being the cat itself. (If, on other grounds, we wished to maintain that universals of some sort make the statement true, that would be harmless so long as we did not take the universal as the demonstrative correlate.) As it happens, Austin did try to take demonstrative correlates as things. That left his account open to serious criticism, but such criticism does not militate against my account based on referential foci.

SOME OTHER CASES

While we are at it, it would be in order to add a few words about conjunctive, disjunctive, and hypothetical statements, these having sometimes been thought to create problems for a theory of truth. They can adequately be accommodated by my account, but vary widely among themselves and must be treated according to instance. In all cases, we must take the actual communicational role of the statement into consideration, and this is not something which can

191

be done with an all-purpose formula. Conjunctions, for example, do not all work in the same way. 'I have bread and ice' could be treated as the union of statements in each of which we establish and describe referential foci, the overall conjunction being true if in each case they are as described. In one conjunct the referential focus concerning me is said to be of the type of referential focus wherein something has bread, and in the other conjunct it is said to be of the type wherein something has ice. This method, that of treating the overall statement as the union of two discrete statements, is the method usually employed in truth-functional logic. Alternatively, we could treat the statement as one wherein the referential focus concerning me is said to be of a type wherein something has both bread and ice. This would be to unite descriptions rather than to add statements, but in this case it comes to the same thing. It does not come to the same thing in all cases. 'I have bourbon and soda' does not come to 'I have bourbon' plus 'I have soda'. The relationship between the two elements is rather more intimate. It is implicit that the bourbon and the soda are joined in a certain sort of combination. Instead of conjoining statements, it would be better to think of this in terms of an integrated overall description. We could take the referential focus concerning me to be one of the type of referential focus wherein something has bourbon and soda. Superficially, this is similar to the previous case, wherein the referential focus could be said to be of a type wherein something has bread and ice. They are importantly different, however, in that there are importantly different sorts of criteria for being of their respective types of referential foci. Being of a type like that of the 'bourbon and soda' variety requires meeting criteria of a particular sort involving what the two items have to do with each other. Again, 'I read her letter and laughed' follows a different pattern. There is a connection between the reading and the laughing, and certainly the statement cannot just be taken as 'I read her letter' plus 'I laughed', but the connection is different from that between the bourbon and the soda. This time it is implied that there is some sort of a causal connection.

How we are to analyse the widely varying types of referential foci is a matter of cases. In all cases, though, the overall conjunctive statement can be analysed in terms of referential foci being established and being said to be of certain types of referential foci, the statement being true if they are as described. The same can be said with regard to disjunctive and hypothetical statements – and as always, we must take the communicational role of the statement

192

into consideration. 'You may have milk or sugar in your coffee' may be analysed in terms of the referential focus concerning you being of one type, or of the same referential focus being of another type, or one of both of those things being so. This, in the traditional style of truth-functional logic, is to take the statement as 'You may have milk in your coffee or you may have sugar in your coffee (or both)', the truth of the overall statement being a truth-function of the truth of its more basic components. Alternatively, we can take the referential focus concerning you as being said to be of only one type – a type wherein something (someone) may have milk or sugar (or both). We can give other, similar, analyses in the case of what has been called 'strong disjunction', wherein the alternatives are mutually exclusive. 'Smith will win the election or Brown will' may be taken as involving the referential foci concerning Smith and Brown, respectively, with the truth-function being worked out in the manner appropriate for strong disjunction. Or we can analyse it in terms of the election-referential focus being said to be a certain type, one wherein Smith wins or else Brown does. Certainly it is implicit that there is a connection, of a particular sort, between the two alternatives. Just what the connections between them are is a matter of cases. 'World wheat prices must rise or there will be a recession in Australia' implies a causal connection, from wheat-price to recession, while the election example suggests more of a two-way connection. In every case, though, it will be a matter of determining just what is being said about what in a particular case.

There is no need to multiply examples. Any difficulty with conjunctive or disjunctive statements is a difficulty only in working out just what description, according to what criteria, is being applied to what referential focus – that is, in working out just what they mean. The same can be said of hypothetical statements, which also vary quite widely. They too can be analysed in terms of referential foci being of certain types. For example, 'If it had rained, my clothes would have gotten wet' could be taken to establish and describe a referential focus concerning my clothes (under those circumstances). Different sorts of hypotheticals work in different ways, and we can analyse them in terms of truth-functional implication or relevant implication, or we can analyse them in various other ways. With all hypotheticals, however, as with all conjunctives and disjunctives, and all other statements, truth is a matter of what we are using language to do and then of whether the referential foci are, in whatever way, as described.

WHAT MORE?

Perhaps what I have offered seems, if not unsatisfactory, at least incomplete. It might seem that our inquiry into truth ought to lead us to more than the claim, with some little elaboration, that something is true if things are the way it says they are. Is there nothing further to be found? There is more to be found, but there are right and wrong ways to look for more. For one thing, as Strawson pointed out, there is considerably more to saying that something is true than merely giving information. There is legitimate inquiry to be made concerning the non-descriptive performative-like elements which might be involved, and, in general, concerning just what we are doing when we engage in various sorts of truth-related discourse. There is fruitful inquiry to be made concerning the descriptive function of language and how it is made to work, and concerning the conditions, presuppositions, contexts, and purposes of truth-related discourse. Inquiry must be made concerning not only how language is used by the language-user, but also concerning how those addressed understand, indeed, how they are *able* to understand, what is said to them. All of these are worthwhile areas for further investigation. For just one point, there would be room for someone to write a good book on the constructive value of ambiguity in language.

In our investigations of truth, and truth-related discourse, we must bear in mind that there are statements of many and varied sorts, working in different ways for different purposes and used in different circumstances, and the treatment they demand varies accordingly. Our efforts will have to be primarily piecemeal. Instead of trying to find answers with a great deal of content which are yet applicable across the board – a common error in truth theory, leading to defective generalities – it would be better to discuss particular sorts of truth-related discourse. We might discuss how referential foci are established and descriptions are organized and applied in particular ways in particular circumstances for particular purposes. A very wrong way to investigate truth is to become obsessed with discovering *the* nature of truth. That way lies frantic manipulation with theories of truth which do not apply to all cases of truth, if indeed they apply to any. In such attempts the natural tendency is to focus on truth in one of its manifestations and cast our theory of truth accordingly. Cases like that of the cat on the mat might be taken to suggest a simple pictorial or correspondence

194

theory, while certain cases from science or elsewhere might be taken to suggest some form of coherence, and other cases might lend themselves to other approaches. Taking our inspiration from only one sort of case may lead us to create a Procrustean bed on which we would distort truth in general. When discussing *the* nature of truth it would be better to be content with the perhaps disappointingly unspectacular formulation which I have given, and remember that truth takes many different shapes. Just as there is no one kind of statement, but many kinds, so there is no one way for statements to be true, but many ways. There is no such thing as *the* nature of statements, beyond their character as words as used on particular occasions in order to establish referential foci. Each statement functions differently, and is true if its referential foci are as described – according to whatever way in which that particular statement functions. To give a full account of what is involved in a statement's being true we would have to go case by case, for ultimately, each statement bears its own truth-nature with it. Once it goes beyond these simple bounds, the search for *the* nature of truth is a search for a mirage, a search that philosophy would be better off without.

9

ALTERNATIVES II

This chapter investigates more recent alternative theories of truth, and certain further issues concerning truth theory. Dummett's anti-realism and certain important views of Quine are considered. Also there have been further and more sophisticated versions (or at least descendants) of the redundancy theory which must be considered. Of particular importance are those of Prior, Mackie, and Williams, and what has become known as the prosentential theory of truth. My own account is reconsidered in the light of these alternatives.

In this chapter I shall discuss some further alternatives. In some part they will be further theories of truth, though for the most part they will be improved versions of theories which we have previously considered. I shall incidentally discuss some closely related issues. Among the theories to be considered are more modern versions (or at least descendants) of the Ramseyan theory, and also those of Michael Dummett and Quine in what might well be considered to be continuations of the pragmatist tradition. It is by no means my purpose to present a history of recent truth theory, and I shall not attempt to be comprehensive. In spite of what I believe are their serious shortcomings as accounts of truth, I think it important to consider and assess these alternatives, both for the purpose of finding what we can learn from them, and for the purpose of further assessing whether the account which I have presented is still viable.

DUMMETT AND TRUTH

In connection with the pragmatists we raised the question of what practical consequences have to do with truth. Taking as an example something from the inaccessibly far-distant past, I suggested that

196

some things are true or false, one or the other, even though which it is makes no difference to any conceivable practice and even though it might be quite impossible (even in principle) to determine which is true. I concluded that while pragmatism offers us useful criteria of truth, it does not offer us an adequate account of truth. On the assumption that one thing rather than another thing is true of the far distant past, we still had to work out an account of what their truth amounts to. Some, however, such as Dummett (1959), maintain an approach to truth in the pragmatic style, and accept the consequence that some (seemingly) meaningful statements are neither true nor false.

Following in the tradition not only of the pragmatists but of Wittgenstein as well, Dummett puts the emphasis on our use of language. He points out (ibid.: 95) that 'the sense of the sentence is not given in advance of our going in for the activity of asserting'. On the most fundamental level we must, he maintains, explain the meaning of a statement in terms of its use, rather than in terms of its truth-conditions. He tells us,

> *We no longer explain the sense of a statement by stipulating its truth-value in terms of the truth-values of its constituents, but by stipulating when it may be asserted in terms of the conditions under which its constituents may be asserted.* The justification for this change is that this is how we in fact learn to use these statements: furthermore, the notions of truth and falsity cannot be satisfactorily explained so as to form a basis for an account of meaning once we leave the realm of effectively decidable statements.
>
> (ibid.: 110, his italics)

It is this stance which led him to a bold conclusion:

> We are entitled to say that a statement P must be either true or false . . . only when P is a statement of such a kind that we could in a finite time bring ourselves into a position in which we were justified either in asserting or in denying P; that is, when P is an effectively decidable statement.
>
> (ibid.: 108–9)

And so,

[T]he law of excluded middle . . . is rejected, not on the ground that there is a middle truth-value, but because meaning, and hence validity, is no longer to be explained in terms of truth-values.

(ibid.: 110)

Many statements, according to Dummett, are neither true nor false. 'Jones was brave' is a concealed conditional which fails of either truth or falsity if Jones never faced danger. 'A city will never be built here' is of unlimited generality and could never be established as true.

There are separable issues here. One is that of whether meaningful statements can yet be neither true nor false. Another is that of whether truth and falsity is a matter of effective decidability – or, in the tradition of Dewey, of warranted assertability. If statements must be effectively decidable in order to be true or false, and if some meaningful statements are not effectively decidable, then it follows that some meaningful statements are not either true or else false. Conceivably, one might hold that conclusion for other reasons. That meaningful statements might be not either true or false may or may not strike one as grossly counter-intuitive, but it is an issue on which I can remain neutral, and prefer to do so. I shall say a few words about that before I go on to the more important issue of effective decidability. Of Dummett's two examples, the first seems to me to be far less persuasive than the second. It would seem to me that Jones might have been brave even though he never faced danger, just as a diamond might be hard even if it never met the test. Bravery like hardness is a dispositional property founded on the internal character of that which is in question. Jones's character might have been such that he would have met danger bravely, or such that he would have failed to, even though he never faced it. More convincing is the example about a city never being built here. 'Never' covers a long time. The problem is not just that we are dealing with infinity and unlimited generality. We know it to be true that no one will ever discover a greatest prime number or an even prime greater than two. What is a problem about the case of the future city is that there is no way in which its unlimited generality can be checked out. Another problem with this case is that it deals with the future, which may be indeterminate. It may be that statements about the indeterminate are neither true nor false.

We might decide that neither a description nor its negation applies in certain cases of statement-making. Again, it may be that putative statements about the future lack referential foci or genuine descriptions and so are not statements at all. There are different ways we could go here. (Other examples of statements, if that is what they are, which are neither true nor false might, arguably, be found among theoretical statements, which are neither analytic nor empirically verifiable. I shall say a bit about scientific statements in the next chapter.) Whatever we might decide about these matters, however, my claim remains that truth is a matter of whether referential foci are as described.

I am not at all persuaded by Dummett's claim that only effectively decidable statements are either true or else false. I should think that in some cases a referential focus might be as described even though there was no way, even in principle, in which we could decide the matter. One thing or another is true about antidiluvian Lucy's mother, or so I am inclined to believe, even if there is no way we could ever know. It is true that I am writing this now, and it will remain true that I was doing so now – or so I am inclined to believe – even if the heat death of the universe were to obliterate all traces by which even the greatest intelligence could determine the matter. (Or do we posit an eternal, omniscient, and perfectly reliable observer to record the truth? That might be to define effective decidability in terms of truth, rather than vice versa.)

If we can effectively decide an issue, what we can decide is whether things are a certain way. That things are that way, that a certain something is true, is a necessary condition for our being able to decide the matter, if we can decide it, but our being able to decide it is not what makes things that way. To hold the contrary, to hold that things are not, or were not, any way at all unless which way they are (were) can effectively be determined appears to me to make reality too dependent on the knowing mind. But, then, Dummett willingly accepts the title 'anti-realist'.

As it happens, my own conclusions about what I called 'factual statements', discussed in chapter 6, are fairly closely compatible with Dummett's concerning effectively decidable statements as well as, I believe, with Dewey's (1938) concerning warrantedly assertable statements. The primary difference is that I maintain that statements are not true or false because we can decide the matter and that they may be one or else the other (though not 'factual') even if we can never decide the matter. Instead of tampering with the notion of truth to suit particular aims in developing an account of meaning, as I believe Dummett does, it would be better to develop an account of meaning on the basis of that part of truth which one finds useful, without denying the rest of truth.

Dummett's conclusions about truth appear to me both to be unnecessary and to fly in the face of established usage, but he is quite at liberty, philosophically, to use the word 'true' in that way if he wishes to. There is nothing incoherent about Dummett's highly sophisticated position, and indeed, his overall position handsomely repays the effort spent investigating it. Certainly I shall not attempt the formidable task of criticizing it. I merely point out that if it is accepted as correct, this would require not a major but only a very minor revision of my own account in order to accommodate it. Instead of holding that a statement is true if its referential foci are as described, I could hold that it is true if its referential foci could be effectively determined to be as described. I might even take my cue from Dummett and claim that no revision at all would be required, on the grounds that to be as described would be to be effectively determinably to be as described. Truth would still have the same meaning by that account, it is just that fewer things would be so.

QUINE AND TRUTH

Sooner or later, here as in many areas of contemporary philosophy, the work of Willard Van Orman Quine must be taken into account. Certainly it has significant relevance for our current inquiries. For our purposes, let us start with his famous attack on the *analytic–synthetic* distinction. It had long been held that some statements were true or false by virtue of their meaning alone, while other statements were true or false not by virtue of their meaning alone but by virtue of their material content. The latter were said to be synthetic and the former to be analytic (analytically true or false). Not only was the distinction not doubted, it did not seem like the sort of thing which *could* be doubted. Either we can settle the issue of a statement's truth or falsity by checking on the meanings involved, as in the case of 'No bachelors are married', or else we cannot do so and have to look further than just to the meanings. And that, seemingly, is that.

That, however, is to take a truth-bearer as an isolated unit rather than as an expression of a cognitive system in use. As Quine sees it, that is the fundamental defect of any attempt to defend or develop a firm and viable analytic–synthetic distinction. Statements do not and cannot occur on their own:

> our statements about the external world face the tribunal of sense experience not individually but only as a corporate body
> . . . .
>
> The idea of defining a symbol in use was . . . an advance over the impossible term-by-term empiricism of Locke and Hume. The statement, rather than the term, came with Bentham to be recognized as the unit accountable to an empiricist critique. But what I am now urging is that even in taking the statement as unit we have drawn our grid too finely. The unit of empirical significance is the whole of science.
>
> (1951: 41–2)

No statement can be analytic in terms of its own self-contained meaning, for no statement ever has fully self-contained meaning. It is always part of a system. That is the basic reason Quine finds for the impossibility of validating the analytic–synthetic distinction or of developing a viable definition of analyticity. That in point of fact it *is* impossible to provide a viable definition of analyticity he persuasively argues on the grounds that whether we appeal to meaning, to definition, or to the self-contradictoriness of the negation, all such appeals either tacitly presuppose the concept of analyticity or else are otherwise inadequate. In particular, we cannot appeal to synonymy, as the concept of synonymy is as much in need of definition as that of analyticity, and tacitly presupposes it. To be sure, we could define analyticity for a formally defined artificial language in terms of its semantic rules. At most, though, that would only give us a definition for 'analytic-in-L'. It would not even tell us *what* we were defining for L. Much less would it tell us what analyticity is for a natural language in actual use. Of course when it comes to natural languages it is possible to draw on their empirical content. It is tempting to try to define statements to be synonymous when they have the same empirical content, which would then allow us to define analyticity in terms of synonymy. Unfortunately, there is (in general) no way to interpret a given statement in terms of a unique range of possible sensory events constituting its content. Like the belief in analyticity, then, reductionism is another dogma in need of being abandoned, a dogma which also rests on the mistaken belief that statements can be confirmed or disconfirmed in isolation.

All statements in a natural language, even the most seemingly analytic, are subject to revision. At one time, certain supposedly analytical truths about motion, taken together with the obvious facts, yielded the conclusion that the sun moves around the earth. Anyone could see that. However, certain less obvious facts and the utility of overall economy for our conceptual and cognitive systems[1] gradually forced us to alter our conception of motion and to recognize that the earth moves. What had been conceived of as analytically true became, in some cases, contingently false. No longer could we appeal with simple confidence to the principle that things moved if they changed position while one was standing still. Indeed, that belief, which once was held as analytically true, was in need of careful redefinition even to be intelligible. We had to further change our conception of motion in the light of Einstein's work, and we might well have to do so yet again. Our language, as we use it, is used for dealing with things. As we find out more about those things, and as we develop further and other purposes in dealing with them, it may become convenient or necessary to modify the way in which we apply language to reality. So long as our concepts are presumed to have to do with reality, then, we may from time to time be led to revise our conceptual system so as better to fit the facts, better to fit together internally, and better to serve our purposes. For all we know, even something so seemingly bomb-proof as that no bachelors are married may turn out to be other than analytically true.[2]

Even so, while any statement whatsoever is vulnerable, we are not absolutely forced to abandon one to which we might feel strongly attached – if we are willing to pay the price. In some cases the price might be very high indeed. Instead of being able to explain facts we may have to explain them away, and to rely on conceptual and cognitive systems which are otherwise unnecessarily arbitrary and lacking in utility. Without being logically inconsistent or denying the observed facts, we might join the International Flat Earth Society and posit various optical illusions, epicycles, and *ad hoc* forces interfering with the order of events. This would be logically viable, though pragmatically dysfunctional save for the purpose of maintaining that which we are so desperate to preserve.

What we come to is this:

> The totality of our so-called knowledge or beliefs, from the most casual matters of geography and history to the profoun-

dest laws of atomic physics or even of pure mathematics and logic, is a man-made fabric which impinges on experience only along the edges. Or, to change the figure, total science is like a field of force whose boundary conditions are experience. A conflict with experience at the periphery occasions readjustments in the interior of the field. Truth values have to be redistributed over some of our statements. Reëvaluation of some statements entails reëvaluation of others, because of their logical interconnections – the logical laws being in turn certain further statements of the system, certain further elements of the field. Having re-evaluated one statement we must reëvaluate some others, which may be statements logically connected with the first or may be the statements of logical connections themselves. But the total field is so underdetermined by its boundary conditions, experience, that there is much latitude of choice as to what statements to reëvaluate in the light of any single contrary experience. No particular experiences are linked with any particular statements in the interior of the field, except indirectly through considerations of equilibrium affecting the field as a whole.

If this view is right, it is misleading to speak of the empirical content of an individual statement – especially if it is a statement at all remote from the experiential periphery of the field. [For that reason, as he says just prior, p. 42] . . . it is nonsense, and the root of much nonsense, to speak of a linguistic component and a factual component in the truth of any individual statement.

(Quine 1951: 42–3)

According to this view, those statements are true which fit optimally with experience and – which is by no means a separate matter – with our overall cognitive system. As truth is underdetermined by experience, there is room for us to shape our cognitive system, and our view of what is and is not true, in a way which is congenial to us, and we may even assign some statements arbitrary truth-values or none at all. This seems much like an account of truth which is a combination of the coherence theory, minus its usual metaphysics, together with the pragmatist theory. What are we to make of it?

Is it a theory of truth at all? Often enough it is taken to be such. If it is not, what does it offer us? To start with, it offers us, in broad form, a useful criterion of truth – offered as part of an encompassing theory concerning the nature and scope of our knowledge of the world. I question, though, whether it does amount to a theory of truth. Just what is to be required of a theory of truth is not a matter of unanimous agreement, but as I have been pursuing the inquiry, a theory of truth, or an account of truth, must explain what truth is, or explain what is said about a statement when it is said to be true, or explain how we use the word 'true' or explain what we use it to do. It would be *possible* to interpret Quine's position as a theory of truth, one which maintains that to be true is to fit optimally with experience and our cognitive system, or perhaps the claim is that 'true' is a word we apply to such statements.

While a possible theory of truth, it would be an inadequate one. What is it for a statement, or a system of them, to fit with experience? Like the coherence and pragmatist theories, such an account would have great difficulty in giving us more about truth than a criterion of it. Consider the query we posed in connection with the pragmatists: did (prehistoric) Lucy's mother see Lucy's father the day the mother died? One thing rather than another is true there – or so we have an overwhelming inclination to believe – though we have no way of knowing which. Either answer would fit equally well with our experience. If one answer better fitted our cognitive system, or if we arbitrarily assigned it 'true' as a truth-value, would that make it true? Even if the historical, though unknowable, case were to the contrary? That does too much violence to our conception of truth. Without any stretching of the relevant terms, including the term 'true', one thing or the other is true of Lucy's mother, whatever our cognitive convenience might be. While, as Quine points out, we may under certain circumstances accept a statement as true, this does not mean that all true statements enter into those circumstances, nor does it tell us – unless we adopt a most bizarre view of truth – what we accept a statement as being when we accept it as being true. Accordingly, it would be better to accept Quine's account as offering a useful though not necessarily decisive criterion of truth and as being a valuable part of a valuable theory which is not a theory of truth.

Quine himself did not present it as a theory of truth. What, then, did he take truth to be? The answer lies in how he took the term 'true' to be used. On Quine's view it is *not* used in connection with propositions, as there are no such things. Certainly propositions are not the common contents of synonymous sentences. Quite apart from difficulties about what 'contents' are, no two sentences are ever entirely synonymous, synonymy being as much a will-o'-the-wisp as analyticity. Nor can we take two sentences to express the same proposition when they have the same empirical content. As we have just noted, experience underdetermines truth. Two sentences may each be responsive to quite the same observations, yet be incompatible with one another. Truth, according to Quine, is a matter of the empirical world and sentences having to do with it, propositions being no part of the story. What part of the story does the word 'true' play, then, and what does it have to do with sentences and the world? He tells us:

> This ascent to a linguistic plane of reference is only a momen-tary retreat from the world, for the utility of the truth predi-cate is precisely the cancellation of linguistic reference. The truth predicate is a reminder that, despite a technical ascent to talk of sentences, our eye is on the world. This cancellatory force of the truth predicate is explicit in Tarski's paradigm:
>
> 'Snow is white' is true if and only if snow is white.
>
> Quotation marks make all the difference between talking about words and talking about snow. The quotation is the name of a sentence that contains a name, namely 'snow', of snow. By calling the sentence true, we call snow white. The truth predicate is a device of disquotation.
>
> (1971: 12)

To be sure, a simple sentence can be affirmed simply by uttering it, but the more we need to generalize – as in dealing with large or infinite lots of sentences – the more we need the truth-predicate. We must still recognize, according to Quine, that as a device of disquo-tation it really refers truth not to language but to the world.

Here, Quine and I start to draw well apart. I quite agree with him that truth-bearers, which are sentences rather than propositions, have their identity only in terms of a whole cognitive system, that they are true or false accordingly as they, within the whole system as used then, fit reality, and that no truth-bearers can be true beyond the reach of criticism and conceptual revision. I even agree that the truth-predicate is *a* disquotational device. However, it is not just any device for going from quoted sentences to unquoted ones. We could do that much with correction fluid. The truth-predicate is a particular device, with desirable features, which allows us to go from quoted sentences to unquoted ones, thereby saying something about the world. Its way of doing so turns on the fact that our words as used on a given occasion fit into our then conceptual fabric, which in turn relates to the world in a particular way. Calling the sentence true is to say that it relates to the world in a certain way and, thereby, is to say that snow is white. The device of disquotation refers truth to both language *and* the world. By calling the sentence true, we call snow white. Quine, though, of all people should not have concluded that the two are synonymous.

While I dismiss the contention that the truth-predicate is *merely* a disquotational device, I certainly do not dismiss Quine's considerable contribution to truth theory. That our cognitive schemes do function and fit the world as wholes rather than as collections of separate units is a very important truth. Quine served us well by pointing that out and by stressing that there is enough play in the system that we can rig and use our cognitive schemes in different ways to fit the world. Whether and how a sentence is true is a matter of how it fits into our cognitive scheme as used and of how it relates to the world. We may, as convenient, rig our system so that a given sentence must be true, or we may allow things to work out in some other way. In one use a sentence may be analytic and in another it may be contingent, and it may be contingent in different ways, all accordingly as we shape and use our cognitive schemes to suit our theoretical demands and practical purposes. In my own account of truth I have tried to allow for flexibility and cognitive holism.

There is a further topic concerning truth theory about which Quine's views have assumed considerable importance. This concerns quantification over truth-bearers.

QUANTIFICATION, TRUTH, AND QUINE

The semantic conception of truth could be thought of as an extensionally specified version of the redundancy theory, telling us that each sentence is true if its specified truth-conditions are met. As was noted in our discussion of that account of truth, it is tempting to try to generalize Tarski's requirement (T) into

(p) ('p' is true if, and only if, p)

which, as an account of truth, would offer us a more direct version of the redundancy theory. It would have the advantage over Tarski's version of not being so rigid, as it would not require us to precisely pre-specify into the structure of the language the truth-conditions for each sentence. We could then hold that for all p, 'p' – as used on that particular occasion in that particular way – is true if, and only if, p. In spite of its apparent advantages, however, there is serious doubt whether it is legitimate to proceed in this way. There is also question about whether it could give us an adequate account of truth even if the procedure were legitimate. Before we inquire further into Ramseyan-style theories and their adequacy, though, we shall first look into the issues of whether we can legitimately quantify over statements (or whatever they are) in the way required by the proposed generalization.

Tarski, as we recall, and Davidson as well, held that such procedure is illegitimate in that it requires us to quantify through quotation marks, as if a name and its object were not very different things. As it happens, 'p' is not a proposition at all but is just a letter of the alphabet, though it can be used to name a proposition. However, if we could treat naming, in some suitably contrived system, as a function of what is named, as has sometimes been proposed, then the problematic generalization would be quite as well in order as is the unproblematic

$$(x) \, (f(x) = 2x+1)$$

No one has yet successfully shown how to do this, and I very much doubt whether it would be possible to do this to cover the generality of actual instances. It might be better to side-step this particular problem by casting our generalizing in such form as

$$(p) \, (\text{the statement that } p \text{ is true if, and only if, } p)$$

Certain more recent versions of theories in the Ramseyan style (see below) do take such a line. While doing things this way does get rid of the quotes, it still leaves to dangle some questions concerning the legitimacy of the required quantification.

Some of the issues concern quantification into an *opaque context*. An opaque context is one in which it is not possible to substitute one thing for another thing which has the same extension (or extensional meaning) without risking affecting the truth of the result. Typically these are intensional contexts. Thus, to use a standard example, while it might be true that Paul believes that a certain thing is the Morning Star, it may not be true that Paul believes that it is the planet Venus, even though it happens that Venus is the Morning Star. Suppose Paul *said* that it is the Morning Star. Did he say that it is the planet Venus? In a sense he did and in a sense he did not. He made a statement *we* might take to be equivalent, but he might strongly deny it. The point is not that we might call on different senses there, but that the '*p*' in 'that *p*' might not have the same role it has as just '*p*'. As just '*p*', it serves directly to say something about the world. As part of 'Paul said that *p*' it, seemingly, serves as part of a report of what Paul said, without saying anything in its own right. That is, it seemingly serves to report the content of a statement rather than to make one. Whether '*p*' in what appears to be two different roles can be covered by the same quantifier is a matter of some debate. Quine (1960: sections 30, 31, 35) argues that 'says that', being as much an expression of propositional attitude as 'believes that', constitutes an opaque context into which quantification is improper. Others, such as Mackie, disagree:

> We should indeed be in difficulties if we had to find a single category of entities which can occur both on their own, as parts of the world, and as the contents of beliefs, assertions, and so on. But these quantifications do not require this. . . . It is the sameness of sense between these two occurrences that we are using, not of reference. . . . These quantifications apply to sentences rather than to any entities that sentences might be held to designate, but to sentences used, not mentioned: we are not to read '(φp)', for instance, as 'There is a sentence "*p*" . . .'.
>
> (1973: 60–1)

Williams (1968, 1976) agrees with Mackie. For further comment on their views on truth, see the next section. For now, a few more words on the legitimacy of such quantification.

A central issue here is that of the *objectual* interpretation of quantification versus the *substitutional* interpretation. (Whether it has to be *versus* is one of the issues.) According to the objectual interpretation, '$(x)Fx$' is interpreted as 'For all objects, x, within a given domain, Fx'. According to the substitutional interpretation, it is interpreted as 'All substitution instances, of a given sort, of "F–" are true'. Whatever we fill the blank with, 'F(whatever)' obtains. Quine is committed to the former, objectual, interpretation as the correct interpretation of quantification. That is the interpretation which fits in with his ideas about ontological commitment:

> *an entity is assumed by a theory if and only if it must be*

counted among the values of the variables in order that the statements affirmed in the theory be true. [His italics. He goes on to add that] . . . What there is does not in general depend on one's use of language, but what one says there is does.

(1953: 103)

That which is is that which we talk about in true statements. 'To be is to be the value of a variable' – when our true statements have been reduced to their basic logical level. What a theory talks about, and presupposes the being of, are those things which it calls upon from the domains of its quantifiers.

Aside from its utility for his account of ontological commitment, what reason have we for believing that the objectual interpretation of quantification is the proper one? Against the substitutional interpretation, Quine points out that not everything has a name. That being so, filling in the blanks with names, as per the substitutional interpretation, would not allow us to quantify over things we should be able to quantify over. By way of example, Quine points to the real numbers (1969: 65; 1970: 92–3). We cannot draw up a list, even an infinite list, and assign them all names (or serial identification numbers). It can be shown mathematically that no matter how one draws up an infinite list of real numbers, there will be numbers – an infinity of them, in fact – which are not on the list. Therefore, we cannot quantify over the real numbers using the substitutional interpretation, as some truths about numbers would require filling blanks with names which cannot be supplied. Instead, we must quantify according to the objectual interpretation, calling on the domain of real numbers. Quine's conclusion, then, is that the substitutional interpretation of quantification is inadequate. We therefore have to rely on the objectual interpretation and assess formulations such as '(p) (the statement that p is true if, and only if, p)' accordingly. That means that we must reject any version of it, for 'p' does not designate the same object in its different occurrences. (A more general conclusion is that objects of propositional attitudes and any other intensional entities are to be ruled out categorically.)

What should our own conclusion be? The debate about quantification continues. Others (e.g. Marcus 1961) have maintained that it is possible to defend the substitutional interpretation as the general interpretation of quantification. We can side-step that debate, as we are not concerned with quantification in general. It may perhaps be that the substitutional interpretation is not adequate for dealing with quantification over the real numbers, and it may be inadequate for dealing with various other subject-matters. We are not dealing with numbers or the like. The relevant question for us is whether the truth theorist following the Ramseyan tradition can legitimately use quantification, as substitutionally interpreted, for '(p)(the statement that p is true if, and only if, p)' or whatever similar thing they may wish to claim. We need not be tied by the tacit assumption that there is one and only one way in which to interpret quantification, that we cannot use objectually interpreted quantification in one application and substitutionally interpreted quantification in another. Mackie argues (1973: 61–2) that we use rather than mention 'p', and that we are free to use the substitutional interpretation in quantifying over it. Certainly I shall not rule out versions of '(p) (the statement that p is true if, and only if, p)' as being unintelligible. It seems quite plausible to me that they are intelligible and even that they are true. What I wish to argue is that theories based on them – which I consider to be theories in the Ramseyan tradition – do not provide an adequate account of truth.

REDUNDANCY AND THE RAMSEYAN TRADITION REVISITED

It will be recalled that in chapter 4 I argued that Ramsey's redundancy theory was inadequate, and that to say that a statement is true is to predicate truth of that statement. Since Ramsey's time, however, attempts have been made to develop a theory which overcomes the difficulties faced by his account and which yet rejects the truth-predicate, denying that we predicate truth of a statement when we say that it is true. I believe that none of these attempts, by Prior (1971), Mackie (1973), Williams (1976), and Grover *et al.* (1975), give us any adequate account of truth. They do raise important issues even so, and as I am offering a more full blooded account of truth, it is important for me to explore those issues and to indicate where I find their accounts to be inadequate or incomplete.[3]

I shall start with Mackie, who holds what he calls a 'simple theory of truth', maintaining that

> The truth-condition for anything introduced as the statement, belief, and so on, that p is simply p. And to say that a certain statement S is true is to say that, for whatever p we can

identify S as the statement that p, p. [As he puts it some pages later, p. 50, his italics] . . . *To say that a statement is true is to say that things are as, in it, they are stated to be.*

(1973: 22)

He denies that this is to be interpreted as a redundancy theory. While the terms 'true' and 'false' are eliminable,

> this does not commit me to a re-affirmation [i.e. redundancy] account rather than to one of comparison. A comparison account might be summed up by this equation:

> (1) 'S is true' $= (\exists x) ((S$ is the statement that $x) \,\&x)$

> The word 'true' is here eliminated, but truth is not eliminated but displayed: the relation in which it consists is made clear. What I have called the extreme Ramseyan or pure re-affirmation account might, contrastingly, be summed up thus:

> (2) $(x) ((S$ is the statement that $x) \gg ('S$ is true' $= x))$.

> And this would eliminate truth by equating the statement that S is true with the statement that x, i.e. with S itself.

> But it is clear that (1) and (2) are not equivalent. I maintain that (2) as it stands, with '$=$' as a sign of analysis or meaning, is mistaken. But the somewhat similar formula,

> (3) $(x) ((S$ is the statement that $x) \gg ((S$ is true$) \equiv x))$,

> where '$\equiv$' is the sign for material equivalence, is correct and is derivable from (1). We might be tempted toward a re-affirmation account by . . . a failure to distinguish (2) from (3).

(ibid.: 51–2)

Mackie thus rejects the redundancy theory, on the grounds that while 'S is true' and 'x' are materially equivalent – having the same truth conditions – material equivalence does not establish sameness of meaning. I heartily endorse Mackie's conclusion on that point. More generally, I believe that the core of what he says, so far as it goes, is substantially correct. However, I do see his theory as being a continuation of the Ramseyan tradition – whether or not we are to use the term 'redundancy' in connection with it – in that it is denied that use of 'is true' predicates truth of the statement said to be true. While Mackie's account does not equate the statement that S is true with the statement that S, it takes it only as asserting conjointly that S is the statement that x, and that x, and invites us to compare the two. We can know whether S is true by comparing it directly with what it is about: 'to say that a statement is true is to say that things are as, in it, they are stated to be' (ibid.: 50). That they are, as he says, materially equivalent and that we can so compare I quite agree, but I do believe that this is something which can be given further elaboration in terms of what its truth consists of. I have offered such elaboration.

Basically quite similar to that of Mackie, in its central features, is Williams' account of truth:

> Somewhat simplified, the thesis of this book is that propositions like 'Percy says that Mabel has measles and Mabel has measles' stand to propositions like 'What Percy says is true' in the same relation as 'Michael is coming to dinner' stands to 'Someone is coming to dinner'. In each case the former proposition is a verifier of the latter.
>
> (1976: xiv)

Williams of course gives this considerable elaboration. He does so in the pursuit of his strategic objective, that of providing an analysis of such as 'What Percy says is true'. This focuses the inquiry on truth in connection with statements made by language-users. That much I must applaud, though I do believe that there is considerably more to truth than his analysis delivers.

Williams begins by noting that

> To say that what Percy says is true is to say that things are as Percy says they are, i.e. (at least as a rough approximation) that
>
> (1) For some p, both Percy says that p and p.
>
> (ibid.: 1)

This is duly defended against complaints about improper quantification, his line of defense resting on what evidently amounts to a substitutional interpretation of quantification. From there he goes on to consider whether 'true' properly is a predicate. He agrees that Strawson's performative theory, and Ramsey's redundancy theory as well, fail to eliminate 'true' and 'false' without loss (or tacit reintroduction of the concepts of truth or falsity). He agrees that something is said about a statement when it is said to be true, though he agrees with Strawson that what is said about it is not that it is true. What 'A's statement, that X is eligible, is true' says about A's statement may be only that it states that X is eligible. The

Strawsonian rendering of the quoted statement is 'As A stated, X is eligible' (1964: 78) which, unlike the Ramseyan 'X is eligible', does say something (but not that it is true) about A's statement. However, Williams suggests that 'Things are as A's statement states' does appear to embody a truth-predicate. The apparent predicate, of the form '– is true', is expressible as

(17) For some p, both – states that p and p.

(Williams 1976)

In particular, we are concerned with

(18) For some p, both Percy's statement states that p and p
(ibid.)

which is an advance over (1) in that it provides for there being one unique thing, under consideration, which Percy says.

We still have a way to go. *What* states that p? Percy does, for one thing, and so does Percy's statement. Naturally, we do not want a definition which makes Percy himself true, as well as his statement. So, eventually we come to

(25) For some p, for every q, both the proposition that p is the same proposition as the proposition that q if, and only if, Percy says that q and p.

(ibid.)

Putting it that way is a means, adapted from Prior (1971), of separating Percy from his propositions. In connection with this, Williams makes an extensive side-trip (ibid.: chapter 3) to consider the nature of that which is true. He draws an analogy between 'What Percy says' and 'What the postman brought'. Both are incomplete symbols, which do not refer to anything in particular. Yet, 'What the postman brought' does refer to something (typically letters) indirectly, and 'What the postman brought is on the mantel-piece' has particular verifiers of the form: 'So-and-so is on the mantelpiece'. 'Is on the mantelpiece' is still part of the story. However, 'What Percy says is true' has as a verifier something like 'Percy says that Mabel has measles and Mabel has measles'. 'Is true' is no longer in the story. I would suggest that a verifier would be 'That Mabel has measles is true'. Williams, though, takes up Prior's claim that 'Percy says that Mabel has measles' is about Percy, Mabel, and the measles only. Specifically, it is claimed not to be about the proposition that Mabel has measles. For my own part, I hold that it says of the statement that Mabel has measles that it was made by Percy. Williams, however, claims that 'what Percy says' does not stand for anything, and that 'is true' is therefore only a pseudo-predicate of a pseudo-subject. For my part, I hold that Williams has only claimed but not demonstrated that such as 'what Percy says' does not stand for a statement, and so has not demonstrated that 'is true' does not describe one. (In connection with Prior (1971), and Grover *et al.* (1975), we shall see another conception, congenial to that of Williams, of the linguistic role of such as 'what Percy says'.)

To continue, Williams notes that (25) is open to attack on the grounds that if Percy says nothing at all, we would have to conclude that 'What Percy says is false' would be true, since 'What Percy says is true' would not be – assuming that truth and falsity are contradictories. It is then decided that the analysis must presuppose rather than just state that Percy says some (one) thing. Truth and falsity are contraries, being contradictories only when given that presupposition. As the final analysis of 'What Percy says is true', we are given

(30) '$_2$ Σp $\Pi q E I p q J q$, $\Pi C J r r$

(Williams 1976)

where "$_2$" is used to indicate that of the following two statements, both are asserted and the second presupposes the first, and where 'Jp' stands for 'Percy says that p'. (30) is expressed in Polish notation which, when translated into something approximating English, comes to

> For some p, for every q, both the proposition that p is the same proposition as the proposition that q if, and only if, Percy says q – the preceding presupposed – and for all p, if Percy says that p, p.

or, more directly,

> Percy made exactly one statement (this is presupposed), and for all p, if Percy says that p, p.

This pretty much comes to Mackie's 'to say that a statement is true is to say that things are as, in it, they are stated to be' though it is an improvement that it is taken as being *presupposed* by 'What Percy says is true', rather than as being directly asserted, that Percy made the statement. Like Mackie, Williams follows in the Ramseyan tradition by denying that to say that a statement is true is properly to predicate truth of it. Quite specifically, he argues (ibid.: chapter 5) that truth cannot be understood as correspondence or as any other relational property. According to his conception, 'For some x, x is a fact and Percy's statement corresponds [etc.] to x' is to be understood as 'Things are as Percy's statement says they are', or (30). The relationship is analysed in terms of truth – rather than vice versa – and is seen to disappear in analysis. Propositions and facts, often said to ground the relationship, drop out in analysis as well.

I believe that Williams has not done justice to the basic intuition that truth is a matter of the relationship between what we say and what we say it about. As I see it, truth is a matter of such a relationship, centring on a relation between referential foci and the descriptive types of which they are said to be the instances. There are a number of points where I would question Williams's argument that truth is not a relational property, though I shall content myself with just one objection. Williams takes up the claim that a relational theory cannot accommodate negative facts, a claim which is central to his whole case against relational theories. 'The fact that "Toby sighed" fails to correspond to when it is false is like', we are told (ibid.: 77), 'the "someone" whom a woman fails to be married to if she is a spinster'. For my own part, I maintain that the falsity of 'Toby sighed' is a case of a referent *not* being as described through the descriptive conventions, and that the statement is false by virtue of as specific a referential correlate as would have made it true in the contrary case. I hold this on grounds which I have already presented. I still feel free, therefore, to maintain that truth is a relational property, and that while (30) is no doubt true when 'What Percy says is true' is, Williams has not given us an adequate account of truth.

Prior's account of truth appeared somewhat previously to those of Mackie and Williams and is largely similar, having, indeed, contributed to them significantly. That being so, I shall now be concerned only with what I take to be a very important insight which was not incorporated into those subsequent accounts. Like Mackie and Williams, Prior follows in the Ramseyan tradition, denying that there properly is a truth-predicate. Propositions and facts are also rejected except as figures of speech, truth being merely a matter of how things are and how we say they are. Like others who followed in the Ramseyan tradition, Prior wants to take a line wherein such as 'What Paul says is [always] true' is rendered as something like 'For all p, if Paul said that p, p'. We have already canvassed one line of objection to such an approach, that concerning whether such quantification is formally legitimate. It has sometimes been thought to be a problem, another problem, that 'For all p, if Paul said that p, p' is not idiomatic English, which requires something like 'For all p, if Paul said that p, p is true'. But of course the latter fails to eliminate the 'is true'. Ramsey held that the apparent difficulty was not really a logical problem (1927: 158): 'We have in English to add "is true" to give the sentence a verb, forgetting that "p" already contains a (variable) verb'. The fault, Prior suggests, is with English idiom which has not developed enough terms to use in reference to propositions. The fault is rectifiable:

> Questions to which the answer is a complete proposition are not, in English, introduced by a particular word, but are expressed by an inversion of word order ('Will he come?'); but we *describe* the asking of such questions by using the word 'whether' ('I asked whether he would come'), . . . So we could simply *concoct* the quantifiers 'anywhether', 'everywhether', and 'somewhether', and translate, say, 'For any p, if p then p' as 'If anywhether, then thether'.
>
> (1971: 37)

(Prior proposes this terminology because in English, *th*-words, e.g. 'they', 'that', and 'there', customarily answer to *wh*-words, e.g. 'who', 'what', and 'where'.) If we adopted Prior's tactic we would presumably get something along the lines of 'If anywhether said by Paul, then thether' as a translation of 'For all p, if Paul said that p, p'.

In connection with Prior's or any other version of a Ramseyanstyle theory, I remind us, there remains the question of whether the proposed translation, eliminating the term 'true', can properly be said to say the same thing. The question remains even though the translation is true or false accordingly as is the original. One might still think that the original was not just about those things Paul talked about but about the things he said. Even so, Prior raises an interesting and important point with his suggestion that much of the perceived difficulty with accounts in the Ramseyan tradition is due to the logically irrelevant accident that English does not have enough terms which can stand for truth-bearers. This suggestion has considerable merit, and is developed more fully by the propounders of the next theory of truth to be considered.

Dorothy Grover and her associates (Grover *et al.* 1975) present a *prosentential theory of truth*. Their account is also in the Ramseyan tradition, denying that to say that a statement is true is to predicate truth of that statement, and they maintain that it overcomes the difficulties in Ramsey's own account. One difficulty they see (ibid.: 78–9) with the latter is that it cannot, without augmentation, handle cases of modified quantification and indirect reference, such as

Each thing Mark said might be true.

Or

All that Judith said was true, but none of it is true now.

Of course we cannot evade the issue with things like

(p) (Mark said that $p \rightarrow p$ might obtain)

since 'obtain' just smuggles in 'be true' in a very thin disguise. However, we can easily augment standard formal logic with such things as a possibility connective M ('might') and a past tense connective P. This would give us

(p) (Mark said that $p \rightarrow Mp$)

and

(p) (Judith said that $p \rightarrow (Pp$ and $\sim p$)

which solves the problem without any help from the buttressing which their own account is intended to provide.

A more serious difficulty in their view (ibid.: 79–80) is the pragmatic problem that Ramseyan translations neglect an important feature of truth discourse. For instance, rendering

Mary: Snow is white.   *John*: That's true.

As

Mary: Snow is white.   *John*: Snow is white.

fails to recognize that John is intending to express agreement with the antecedent. This, the only pragmatic difficulty they raise, is held to be a real shortcoming in Ramsey's account, one which is overcome in their own. They dismiss the objection that Ramseyan translations change the subject, from saying something about a statement to saying something about what the statement is about, holding that the statement and its Ramseyan translation have the

217

same assertional content (ibid.: 80). That they do have the same assertional content they maintain, it develops, on the grounds that they have like truth-conditions.

It is the grammatical question which they use as a springboard for their own account. They quite agree with Ramsey that while English usage does not permit us to assert just 'p', requiring that a verb be attached to it, the difficulty is only a grammatical superficiality rather than a logical fault. We should, they maintain, properly be able to assert things like

> For each proposition, if John said that it, then it.

Though English usage strongly insists on things like

> For each proposition, if John said that it is true (or asserted it), then it is true.

The problem is that English, while having a quite adequate system of pronouns which can stand in for individual variables occupying nominal positions, does not have an adequate system of *prosentences* to stand in for propositional variables occupying sentential positions. While English does not contain any generally available atomic prosentences, they note that sometimes words like 'yes' and 'so' serve in that capacity (ibid.: 88). Their ultimate claim is that 'It is true' and 'That is true' are prosentences, and that 'is true' is a fragment of a prosentence *wherever it occurs*. The diagnosis of the problem by Grover *et al.* thus approximates that of Prior, and what they propose extends the idea.

Let us start by asking what English would be like if it did contain a generally available atomic prosentence (ibid.: 88ff). Imagine a language English + 'thatt', which is standard English plus such a prosentence 'thatt'. 'Thatt' can stand in for (rather than refer to) antecedent propositions, and permits us such constructions as

> For every proposition, if John says *thatt*, then *thatt*.

And

> *Bill*: There are people on Mars. *Susan*: If *thatt*, we should see signs of life very soon.

English + 'thatt' manages to avoid what they recognize as the difficulties with Ramsey's account. It escapes the pragmatic difficulty in that the use of 'thatt' does recognize the antecedent. Moreover, it is grammatical without requiring a significant conceptual revision of English. The next step is to suggest that 'It is true' and 'That is true' serve the prosentential role, doing what 'thatt' was said to do. If so, then in constructions like

For each proposition, if John said that it is true, then it is true.

we would not be saying anything about propositions. We would be contingently affirming them.

Consider now English*, which is a fragment of English containing 'That is true' and 'It is true' as prosentences but which does not permit a predicative use of 'true' (ibid.: 92ff). Thus, in English* constructions such as 'What Barbara said is true' are not permitted and the verb 'is' in 'that is true' cannot be modified. We can draw on English itself, however, for such connectives as

it was true that, it will be true that, it is possible that, it might be true that, it is necessary that, it is not true that, it is false that [etc.]

(ibid.: 93)

in order to handle modification cases.

Upshot: in English* 'true' can only be used *either* in one of the prosentences 'that is true' or 'it is true' *or* in a connective employed in order to meet difficulties in connection with modification. . . . Now we can sharply state a principle of our prosentential theory of truth: English can be translated without significant residue into its fragment English*. . . . such a translation is perspicuous and explanatory.

(ibid.)

Examples:

English: It is true that snow is white, but it rarely looks white in Pittsburgh.
*English**: Snow is white. That is true, but it rarely looks white in Pittsburgh.

(ibid.: 93–5)

And

English: Everything John says is true.
*English**: For each proposition, if John said that it is true, then it is true.

(ibid.: 93–5)

An instance of the latter is not

If John said that snow is white is true, then that snow is white is true.

But

If John said that snow is white, then snow is white.

The proposers of the prosentential theory continue at some length to argue that the translation can be carried out in all cases without significant residue, showing, they believe, that truth talk in plain English is really prosentential. So why is English the way it is rather than being English*? In brief, English is very much oriented along noun + verb-phrase lines and so presents its prosentences in such form – a feature with the added advantage of allowing us to enter the prosentence to modify the verb as might be convenient in particular grammatical circumstances.

How then are we to assess the prosentential theory? I am not convinced by it. Let us suppose for the sake of argument that we can work out an English* translation for anything which can be said in English. That this is so supports the prosententialist thesis only if the statement in English and the one in English* say the same thing. The prosententialists base their theory on the assumption that 'the assertional content of the translation matches that of the sentence translated. We'll rely on the success [measured how?] of our theory as evidence for the reasonableness of this assumption' (ibid.: 79). Their argument is not specified in more detail but the idea seems to be that the statement and its translation are true or false together, saying the same thing about the same things, and that their theory provides a neat explanation of this. It is on these grounds that they dismiss the 'aboutness' objection that 'is true' statements *also* say something about a statement. I maintain that the objection is not to be so easily dismissed, and that two statements do not necessarily say the same thing when they are true or false together.

Grover *et al.* present and attempt to dispose of a possible counter-example to their thesis. Consider

John: The being of knowing is the knowing of being.
Mary: That's profound, and it's true.

(1975: 104–5)

The 'that' is evidently John's statement, which is characterized by Mary as being profound. Seemingly the 'it's true' characterizes the same referent. The prosententialists claim that 'profound' and 'true' do not apply to the same thing because they *cannot*. If statements are true at all it is only statements (= what is stated) which are true, while statements (= acts of stating) are, they claim, the only kinds of statement which can be profound. That being so, the pronouns in Mary's statement cannot both be referring to the same thing, so we need not take the 'it's true' as referring and characterizing at all. I find their line of defence surprising. Acts of stating can be profound, but it is also true that some features of the world can be very deep, fundamental, *profound*, important etc., and statements (= what is stated) about them can be quite profound. It is, I believe, a profound truth that $E = mc^2$, though my stating it is not a profound act. Given that what is stated can be profound, I see no reason to doubt that Mary characterizes John's statement as being both profound and true. There seems to be reason to affirm it.

Let us return to an example considered in chapter 4:

If that's true, you had better give up.

According to the prosententialist account, that comes to

If (statement), you had better give up.

Of which an instance might be

If the match is rigged, you had better give up.

Giving up would likely be an appropriate response in the event of any number of conceivable circumstances. The *point* of the statement is that a consequent follows given an antecedent. The prosententialists (and the others considered in this section, for that matter) are ahead of Ramsey in that they take account of the fact that there is an antecedent statement. Do they take it sufficiently into account? Let us ask whether the consequent is said to follow given that the antecedent statement has the quality of being true, or is it said to follow given what the antecedent says. The prosententialists must say the latter but not the former. I say both, that if the antecedent statement has the merit of being true – and therefore if things in the world are a certain way – then something follows. What is under consideration is the suggestion, and not just a possible state of affairs suggested. The suggestion, a statement (= what is stated), might be interesting, provocative, absurd, exaggerated, true, or many other things, and certain things may follow. The linguistic force of the example requires not just that there *be* an antecedent statement but that certain responses are appropriate to its having certain qualities. If it is interesting you had better tell Molly. If it is

221

absurd you had better change your mind. If it is true you had better give up. The prosententialists respond, I think feebly, to this line of objection:

> There is another sort of 'tunnel vision' with which we might be charged; namely, we haven't associated 'that's true' with 'that's right' and we haven't contrasted it in an Austinian way with 'that's exaggerated' and its cousins. . . . Unlike Austin 1950 we think, however, that . . . 'That is exaggerated' and 'That is right' are crucially different from 'That is true', since the point of each is different. Expressions like 'exaggerated' and 'right' fit where certain skills and techniques are in question, for example in counting, or possibly language skills. E.g., when you draw a peninsula longer than it should be we say that your map exaggerates certain features . . . But since there is no clear line to be drawn between the learning of language and simply using it, there must be tremendous overlap between 'That is right' and 'That is true'.
>
> (Grover *et al.* 1975: 106–7)

It is quite correct that expressions like 'exaggerated' are used to assess statements in terms of the skills and techniques involved in making them, and it is also correct that they do different jobs than does the expression 'true'. However, it by no means follows that assessments of statements must always be in terms of the skills and techniques involved in making them – as witness 'interesting', 'provocative', and 'absurd'. There are many ways in which we can assess propositions (or statements). That there is the overlap, the existence of which they admit, is most plausibly accounted for on the basis that we *do* assess statements. Sometimes we assess them as being true.

In chapter 4 we considered the argument that '*p* is true' and '*p*' must say the same thing because they are necessarily truth-functionally equivalent, necessarily being true or false together. Such an argument, if valid, would indicate not only that a redundancy theory is true but that it is *necessarily* true, it being logically impossible that 'true' be used predicatively. That is a very strong conclusion from very weak evidence. While '*p* is true' says that '*p*' is true, and so implies that they must be true or false together, it does not clearly follow that they must therefore have the same meaning. Rather, that they are *truth*-functionally equivalent may be a result of what 'is true' predicates of *p*. This argument by no means gives us adequate reason to doubt what is indicated by the balance of English usage, that we do predicate truth of a statement when we say that it is true. All told then I maintain that the prosentential theory and all other versions of the redundancy theory are inadequate as accounts of truth. Even so we should not entirely write off Ramseyan-style theories, for there are things to be gleaned from them. After all, it is not a question of what 'is true'-statements mean in the abstract – there is no such place – but of what language-users use such statements to do. Often enough the point of making a statement that a statement is true is to affirm what the antecedent says, going, incidentally, *through* the 'is true'-statement. Sometimes, as Strawson correctly points out, we make 'is true'-statements with the performative-like force of endorsing the antecedent statement. I think too that the prosententialists have something of merit. We often do talk about statements which we do not directly present, and 'That is true' and 'It is true' and the like can stand in for them truth-functionally, serving a useful purpose in so doing. This can, for one thing, help us for certain purposes to deal with general statements (e.g. about what Paul says). Even so, these consequences do not constitute the nature of truth. They result from it.

10

TRUTH AND 'TRUTH'

This chapter considers whether the theory of truth developed pre-
viously can handle the legitimate demands made on truth theory in
connection with analytic truth, and in connection with such areas of
application as mathematics, scientific theories, metaphysics, and
ethics. It is argued that it can meet the various demands, and that
there are not radically different kinds of truth arising in different
subject-areas. I ask, in very broad terms, how these different subject-
areas are truth-related. Mathematical formulae, it is argued, are
neither true nor false, but have the syntactic property of being true-
under-all-interpretations. When interpreted they may be true but
are no longer purely mathematical. The other areas of discourse do
admit of truth, and are truth-related in their various ways, as is
discussed.

Statements function in a great variety of ways to establish and
describe referential foci, as I have often stressed, and there is also
leeway in the standards by means of which we may assess whether
the descriptions are met. In a way, since each statement functions
differently and so could be said to have its own truth-nature, we
might say that there are many different kinds of truth. I have
claimed, however, that we can give a broad, though necessarily
minimal, account of truth which spans all true statements. Does my
account succeed in its generality, or does it perhaps apply to only a
certain variety of truth? It has sometimes been claimed that a given
theory of truth applies only to a restricted area. For example, Haack
(1978), among numerous others, maintained that Austin's account,
being based on reference and description, applies, if at all, only to
contingent empirical truth. Various claims have been made in connection with various accounts. Whatever may be the case concern-

ing other accounts, would such a claim be correct in the case of the account which I have developed? Does it, for instance, suffer from the limitation, attributed to Austin's account, of being unable to cope with analytical truths? And what are we to conclude concerning the much more abstract truths, if true they be, of formal mathematics? If they are true, does the same account of truth apply to them, or do we need a quite different account of truth for mathematics? We might pose similar questions concerning scientific theories (as distinguished from observation statements), though the issues would be quite different there. We may also inquire concerning truth in connection with metaphysics and morality. I obviously cannot offer a full account of any of these subject-areas, nor do I propose to try. In this chapter I shall be concerned only to make some inquiries into their truth-relatedness. Centrally, I shall be asking whether within their ambit they require a substantially different account of truth.

ANALYTIC TRUTH

If I say that Charles is unmarried I refer and describe, making an empirical claim which is or is not true by virtue of Charles and his past history. One determines its truth as best one can, by investigating the facts. On the other hand, that all bachelors are unmarried is – currently, at any rate – an analytical truth. One does not determine its truth by going out, clipboard in hand, to check the relevant facts. In the case of such statements our referential and descriptive conventions overlap in such a way that the applicability of the description to the referent is determined by those conventions (although, as Quine pointed out, the scheme is always modifiable). In the case of empirical statements, the applicability of the description to the referent, under our conventions, is determined by fact. This, in particular, has led some correspondence theorists to be very uneasy about analytical truth, since they were inspired by the idea that facts made true statements true, that this was the very nature of truth. Are we to say, then, that analytical truths, founded on our conceptual framework rather than on fact, must have some different variety of truth if they are true at all? I maintain that we ought to reject this conclusion. The key difference does not lie in the nature of truth, which remains the same, but in the criteria according to which we determine whether the description applies to the referent. In the case of a true analytical statement as much as in the case of a true empirical one, the focus of reference with which it is correlated by the linguistic conventions will be of a type with which it is (descriptively) correlated by the linguistic conventions. Therein lies its truth. *How* we know whether a statement is true is a matter of cases. *That* it is true, if indeed it is, is as always a matter of whether the referent is as described.

As we have recognized, we must occasionally make changes to our linguistic conventions as we continuously try to keep our conceptual schemes in touch with reality. Accordingly, the boundary between that which is analytic and that which is not – which is more of a grey strip than it is a clear line – will shift from time to time. Even so, truth, as we have characterized it, is the same on both sides of that fluid boundary.

MATHEMATICS AND TRUTH

Granted that analytic statements are true, and not in any deviant sense, let us now turn to the seemingly related topic of truth in mathematics. Certainly there have been a number of theories about mathematical truth. One theory holds that mathematical 'propositions' (as I shall for the moment call them) are true or false in the general sense in which 'The cat is on the mat' may be true or false, rather than in some technical or restricted sense. Once it was frequently held that being mathematically true means being generable (derivable) in a mathematical system, though Gödel's theorem demolished that idea.[1] More promisingly, it has been held that a mathematical 'proposition' is true if and only if it is true (satisfiable) under all interpretations (or all interpretations of a certain sort). Obviously, this is an extremely important property for a mathematical 'proposition' to have, but I shall argue that it is not the same as truth. Others have held that mathematical 'propositions' are not true or false at all. Though we can make true or false statements about mathematical systems or mathematical formulae, and though formulae may be used to construct (or find) true or false statements, the claim is that the formulae themselves are not true or false. I adopt such a view. While there is considerable latitude in the general sense of truth, I shall argue that purely mathematical 'propositions' are not things of the sort which can be true or false in the general sense in which statements at large may be true or false. While it may be useful for certain formal purposes to assign a so-called 'truth'-predicate to such 'propositions', there is no need to look for a different kind of truth for them to have. These conclusions are neither new nor startling. I discuss the matter only in the interests of relating my previous conclusions to the issues of their truth and truth-relatedness.

To ask whether mathematical 'propositions' are true or false is to ask whether they properly are statements at all. To be sure, statements vary greatly, functioning in many different ways. The key question is whether mathematical 'propositions' in some way refer and describe – saying something about something. I argue that they – as distinguished from mathematical 'propositions' given an interpretation of some sort – are not statements at all, but are merely formulae in the context of some formal system. In this, I take what is in considerable measure a *formalist* line. Like many other people, I find the formalist theory of mathematics to be troubling yet attractive. My worries arise from a feeling that mathematics must offer something more than just formulae, mere strings of inscriptions. After all, mathematics seems to be a quite indispensable element of the search for truth in a great many different areas, and has led us to many truths about the world. Indeed, the attempt to find truth, reliable truth, was a principle factor in the genesis of mathematics. What could be more certain than mathematics? It seems quite preposterous that mere strings of inscriptions could offer so much truth which is so reliable. Yet on the other hand, theories which take mathematical formulae to be statements, and true or false, seem suspect, as I shall indicate, because of what they have to say about statements and truth, and because of what they say about mathematics. I believe that we can devise an account which avoids the perceived shortcomings of formalism and which offers a viable account of the actual workings of mathematics, without misconstruing the nature of mathematics, statements, or truth.

If a mathematical formula were indeed a statement, true or false, how (to what) could it refer and describe? What, in reality, is there for it to be about? Could it refer to and describe some aspect of the formal system in which it is a formula? Perhaps a theorem of Euclidean geometry is telling us something about Euclidean geometry, or an arithmetic equation something about the system of numbers. That would give us something for the supposed statement to be about, but this line suffers from logical problems. Certainly it confuses the language–meta-language distinction. Consider: 'That bachelor is 47 years old' is about that bachelor, and, depending on what we take the referential focus to be, it can be taken to say something about, inter alia, the class of bachelors or the class of 47 year olds. 'Bachelors are unmarried' says something about the class of bachelors and about the class of married persons. Yet neither statement is about the English language, though understanding the English language or any other language in which it is expressed is sufficient for us to understand the truth of the statement. Similarly, a formula of pure mathematics is not about the mathematical system in which it occurs.[2] We might give the formula an interpretation, perhaps in terms of adding apples – but then we have a statement about apples, not about either the arithmetic system or the language (English, perhaps) of interpretation. Again, it might be suggested that if 'Two apples plus two apples are four apples' says something (true) about dealings with apples, then '2 + 2 = 4' is a statement which says something (true) about dealings with the number four – that it is equal to, or what one gets if one adds, two and two, or two things and two things. Yet this is to depart from purely mathematical considerations. In speaking of adding, or of matters having to do with four units, we are incorporating an interpretation of sorts, presupposing some method of considering units and addition. There are things having to do with addition or four units only when units of some sort are taken in some way – which takes us beyond the number system itself. The number system may be interpreted in terms of countless other systems, formal or otherwise. There is no such thing as the correct interpretation. To be sure, there are things to be said about the digit '4' and how it enters into various combinations with other inscriptions, but these are syntactic statements about the mathematical system, and could not conceivably be stated by '2 + 2 = 4' or any other formula. What we must recognize is that a formula is not *about* anything, though in view of it we might make a statement about its mathematical system (or about something else) – just as, on the basis of a footprint we might make a statement about the animal which left it, though the footprint makes no statement.

Admittedly, if we choose for some reason to concede that numbers, sets,[3] or such like exist, we might interpret mathematical formulae as making true statements about them. To this end we might, for instance, invoke platonic-style entities, or we might employ the usual sort of technical expedient, doing something like taking '2' to refer to the set of all sets having two elements. (This can yield various conclusions. We could, for instance, take arithmetic as expressing true statements, yet perhaps maintain that in transfinite arithmetic we find only formulae.) Again, we might possibly invoke an ontology of a Quinean stripe, taking the things we talk about – that is, quantify over – to be things. At best, such procedures seem curiously inverted. Normally we seek to make true statements about things, while here we would seem to be seeking (or contriving) things for (what are supposedly) true statements to be about. Moreover, according to this scheme, if we apply the formula to some other subject-matter, instead of just interpreting the formula, we find ourselves interpreting one subject-matter in terms of another and quite different subject-matter. Two quite distinct subject-matters – say, physical things *and* platonic numbers – for one statement seems one subject-matter too many. At best this seems an unnecessary entanglement, and at worst a blunder into an ontological wilderness. I favour a slim ontology anyway, on ontological grounds, and more relevantly, on the grounds that if we can account for mathematics without making ontological commitments, we should do so on the grounds of logical and practical simplicity. Then, if we *add* ontological interpretations to our mathematics, we can accommodate them without being dependent on them.

I take mathematics to be concerned with formulae and formal systems. It is not concerned with *mere* inscriptions, to be sure, but with inscriptions formed into formulae and employed within a formal system. A formula is a string of inscriptions well formed with respect to a given formal system. Mathematics is concerned only with their syntactic interrelationships, but not with any semantic or pragmatic considerations. While a formula has syntactic properties, it does not refer and describe and so lacks truth and falsity. When these formulae have been given interpretations, becoming statements, they are then capable of truth or falsity and have passed out of the realm of pure mathematics.

MATHEMATICS AND SATISFIABILITY

Whatever one calls it, '2 + 2 = 4' has an important property which '2 + 2 = 5' lacks. It is true (or satisfiable) under all interpretations. That is, the formula is such that whenever it is given content in terms of some interpretation, the resulting statement is true. For certain formal purposes, some (e.g. *logicists* who define mathematics in terms of logic and set theory) have chosen stipulatively to define a formula to be true if it is true (satisfiable) under all interpretations.

This expedient undeniably has its uses. Nevertheless, I recommend that we apply some other term to those formulae which are true (satisfiable) under all interpretations. To use the same term for these different properties is not necessary, and may easily confuse the issue. Certainly they are *different* properties, and confusion may be the worse because they are related. Truth in the general sense is a semantic/pragmatic property concerned with reference and description, while 'truth' in the stipulative sense is a property of uninterpreted formulae which say nothing. Being true (satisfiable) under all interpretations is a syntactic property held by certain formulae which have the peculiarity that whenever their syntactic system is fleshed out to become a semantic/pragmatic system, the statements which arise will necessarily be true. These statements, semantically/pragmatically fleshed-out formulae, then describe, and the resulting descriptions necessarily apply to what they are attributed to. While this syntactic property has to do with semantic/pragmatic properties and has semantic/pragmatic implications, it is not itself a semantic/pragmatic property and it is not truth. Compare:

$$\left.\begin{array}{c} \text{F is true (satisfiable)-} \\ \text{under-interpretation-I} \\ \\ \text{F is true (satisfiable)-} \\ \text{under-all-interpretations} \end{array}\right\} \text{ and } \left\{\begin{array}{c} \text{F-under-interpretation-I} \\ \text{is true} \\ \\ \text{F-under-each-} \\ \text{interpretation is true} \end{array}\right.$$

There is no (single) F-under-all-interpretations. While there is an 'if and only if' sort of relationship between the left- and right-hand members, we are yet attributing different properties to different things. Truth (satisfiability) under interpretation is not the same as truth, the former property being syntactic while the latter property is semantic/pragmatic. Neither is formula F the same as F interpreted.

MATHEMATICS AND INTERPRETATION

In the course of interpreting a formal system we give semantic/pragmatic content to the syntactic structure, thereby giving the system material content. The interpreted system has the very structure of the formal system of which it is an interpretation. This is not because the formal system is somehow part of the interpreted system, but because the interpreted system is the formal system – with the terms being given material content through their being correlated directly or indirectly with the world according to our use of some conventions of interpretation. (The conventions employed may, for instance, correlate geometric straight lines with the paths of light rays, or '+' with the combining of things of some sort, '2' with pairs of things, and may use '=' to indicate that one thing and another thing are 'the same' according to some means of reckoning.) Directly or indirectly, the interpreted formula refers to and describes features of the world, is a statement, and is now true or false. It will naturally be true if the formula interpreted is true under all interpretations – as will be the case for all legitimate mathematical formulae.

It may appear that true statements do not necessarily result from the interpretation of legitimate mathematical formulae, as witness such cases as that of the addition of alcohol and water. If one adds two litres of alcohol to two litres of water, the resulting volume of fluid is less than four litres, this being an instance of comiscibility. One can add mass that way, but not volume. Adding volume may at first appear to be an interpretation of the formula '2 + 2 = 4' which is false, but actually it is not a proper interpretation at all. The syntactic structure has been altered, volumetric addition and '+' following different relational patterns. There is only a proper interpretation of a formal system when we incorporate the syntactic structure into a semantic/pragmatic structure – that is, give the symbols an interpretation – without altering their relational pattern. It is not that there is something wrong with applying arithmetic to alcohol and water, it is just that we have to be careful to interpret it properly. If we are to match up a formal system and a material subject-matter, doing justice to both, it is necessary to find a suitable formal system for a given subject-matter, or a suitable subject-matter for a given formal system, but either way, we must develop a non-distorting system of interpretation.

MATHEMATICS: SYNTAX, GRAMMAR, AND INTERPRETATION

According to the above view, formulae such as '2 + 2 = 5', which are not true under all interpretations, are in violation of the rules of syntax of a legitimate mathematical system. Yet one would think that deeming such formulae to be in violation of the rules of syntax would not properly be comparable with deeming the sentence 'The man who to I speaked are my green' ungrammatical. The formula '2

+ 2 = 5' would seem to be more on a par with 'Two apples plus two apples are five apples', which is not ungrammatical, but just makes an analytically false statement. For its part, it would seem that the sentence 'The man who to I speaked are my green' would be ill formed in a similar way to that in which '2 + = + 5' would be ill formed. An interpretation of that, such as 'Two apples plus are plus five apples' *would* be ungrammatical (if we could call it an interpretation at all). The critical point is that, particularly in mathematics, the formation rules are not the only rules of syntax. The axioms and rules of inference are incorporated into the syntax of the mathematical system, though not into its formation rules. We need therefore to distinguish two ways in which formulae can be in violation of the rules of syntax. A formula which is not well formed will have 'interpretations' which are not well formed, and therefore meaningless and neither true nor false. A formula which, though well formed, violated the rules of its mathematical system would (when properly interpreted) have analytically false interpretations, such as 'Two apples plus two apples are five apples'.

That the rules of a mathematical system can extend beyond rules about what are to be well-formed formulae raises questions about what can, or should, be built into the rules of a mathematical system. Some, as we shall see, would put restrictions of various sorts on what is to be permitted, while others would not. It is very important to note in this connection that the rules for a system (formal or non-formal) can, and frequently do, tacitly incorporate presuppositions. In ordinary language, for instance, distinctions, forms of construction, etc., are developed and used which answer to (presumed) features of reality. If we run afoul of these conventions, our statements may be ungrammatical or at least peculiar, and may even appear analytically false, all of which may make it difficult to say anything unconventional – a desirable feature from Big Brother's point of view. I have heard it argued that it is inconsistent of me to maintain that there are prime numbers between ten and twenty, while yet maintaining that there are no such things as numbers. Languages incorporate some occasionally awkward presuppositions about things and nouns. Again, Descartes and many of his successors were led into metaphysical dead-ends through a too naive acceptance of the subject–predicate mode of speech. Alexius Meinong went on to posit golden mountains as objects of thought. It is, to be sure, a matter of cases and applications. Most linguistic conventions, as Austin and others pointed out, are or at least have been useful, which is how they came to be incorporated into their language.

Mathematical systems also often have features built into them to make them more suitable for various purposes. Such features are built into the syntactic structure rather than into any particular scheme for interpretation, and are not directly concerned with truth or falsity. An obvious example is Euclidean geometry, which is very useful for discussing shapes on approximately flat surfaces. We may structure our mathematical systems in particular ways so that they will yield interpretations of the sort we want, and we may even style them for aesthetic reasons. Reality, for whatever reason, often seems to fit better with systems which are more aesthetically attractive. We now ask whether we can properly demand that mathematical systems, to be acceptable as mathematical systems, must incorporate certain favoured features. To be sure, a mathematical system, to be a system at all, must have an identifiable structure of some sort, which requires there to be some definite formation rules and basic syntax. Can we legitimately go beyond that to legislate further features which a mathematical system may or may not properly have, rejecting as not properly mathematical those systems which do not comply? There are those who have urged the imposition of further restrictions. Mathematical *intuitionists*, for instance, have insisted that all of mathematics, to be mathematics, must be generated by construction from the (intuitively known) natural number sequence. *Logicists* have insisted that genuine mathematics must be based on the axioms of logic (with, perhaps, a few special additions). Others have proposed other restrictions. In all cases, non-conforming systems are held to be illegitimate. In contrast, mathematical *Formalists* take mathematics to be concerned strictly with formal systems and their operations, without further restriction.

As I view the matter, the key difference between the intuitionist and the formalist lies in what they take the *aim* of doing mathematics to be. The intuitionist requires that any formula or formal system must admit of consistent (and constructive) interpretation with respect to the natural numbers. This is because mathematics is seen as a search for the truth about this intuitively known subject-matter. Though, for example, the axiom of choice and the bulk of transfinite mathematics might be shown to be (syntactically) consistent – and thus fair game for the formalist – intuitionists would not be willing to admit such things to the practice of mathematics

233

unless and until they can be legitimized by construction in terms of the intuitively known. Without there being a specific difference in their concept of formula or formal system, they accept as mathematical only those which are appropriate to the pursuit of what they see as mathematical truth. Similarly, platonists and others with their own ontological commitments may attempt to ban forms of mathematics which are not productive in terms of the preferred ontology. (Imaginary and transfinite numbers, and even non-Euclidean geometry have, at various times in the past, been subjects of proposed bans.) If we take proper mathematics to be saying true things about something or other, then that mathematics which does not do so is not proper mathematics. For my part, I would prefer not to dispute mathematical ontology with intuitionists, platonists, or anyone else. Rather, I would suggest that we do not think of mathematical formulae as being statements or as being in any sense true. People with varying interests in mathematics can then go their separate ways without branding any branch of mathematics illegitimate merely because it fails to meet their extra-mathematical requirements. While a formula must be true under any legitimate interpretation, we should not fail to recognize a formal system as an instance of mathematics merely because it fails to have interpretations of the sort we happen to prize.

For their part, logicists are not particularly concerned about the sorts of interpretations we might give our formulae, so long as we avoid inconsistency. They hold that mathematics avoids inconsistency and is so productive because, and in so far as, it is founded on the axioms of logic – with a few supposedly minimal additions. Whether the additions to logic really are minimal is highly debatable, but that is beside the point. Certainly I see no reason to quarrel with the logicists in so far as they advise caution about what we are to admit into the practice of mathematics. Inconsistencies, such as Russell's paradox, have arisen in the past, due to poor logic. Whether everything we might wish to include in mathematics can be given the grounding logicists require, and whether departures will necessarily result in inconsistency, are not matters upon which I can express a definitive opinion. However, I do insist that the soundness of mathematics does not stem from its being based on axioms of formal logic which are necessarily *true*. They are not true at all. While the axioms of formal logic may formalize 'the grammar of thought', as it were, they are not true and certainly do not express thoughts. This is so even though, being true under all interpretations, they can be extremely useful means of finding and conveying truth.

Formal conceptions such as satisfiability, being true-under-all-interpretations, and the like, have their uses and are closely related to truth. Yet it is only to confuse the issues to mistake the properties they define with truth, or what these properties apply to with statements. Mathematical formulae do not themselves say anything about anything, so the question of whether things are as they are said to be cannot arise. It is to misconstrue their truth-relatedness to try to find a way in which they are true. That they do not say anything about anything, that they are not susceptible of truth or falsity, is central to their great utility for finding and conveying truth.

ON THE TRUTH OF SCIENTIFIC THEORIES

Another problematic matter is that of the truth or falsity, or, more generally, the truth-relatedness, of scientific theories. The conclusions we come to will depend in considerable part on what we take scientific theories to be and, more broadly, on what we take science to be. As opposed to scientific laws and other empirical statements, scientific theories are characterized by being formulated in terms some of which are neither observational terms nor (logical or syntactic) connectives. In quantum theory, for instance, reference is made to such properties as 'strangeness' and 'charm', which are strange properties indeed, and cannot (as yet, anyway) be given an interpretation in observational terms. In contrast to theories, other statements in science, even the most general laws, rely only on terms which are empirically (observationally) interpretable. (For example, the general gas law deals with pressure, temperature, and volume, all of which are observable properties.) Even so, while scientific theories rely on terms which are empirically uninterpretable, or at least are uninterpreted, they are still connected with empirical matters. They may serve to predict and in some way explain them, and it is on such a basis that we arrive at our theories. Evidently they have some connection with truth, but their having recourse to uninterpreted terms has led some to question whether scientific theories can be characterized in terms of truth and falsity.

It has been suggested that scientific theories, instead of being truth-bearers, are merely instruments or devices by means of which we are able to manipulate or infer other statements which do have empirical content. They would thus be similar to rules of inference, such as *modus ponens* in elementary logic (though they need not be relegated to a meta-language). This, in brief, is the *instrumentalist* account of the nature of scientific theories. According to this account, scientific theories are still subject to assessment – as are rules of inference in logic, or hammers and chisels in woodworking. Good instrumentalities are those which serve their purposes well. Some theories are much better than others at organizing and explaining our empirical knowledge, and at generating accurate predictions about further findings. We might yet ask why a good theory works as well as it does. It seems unlikely that this would be merely a happy accident. We can arrive at explanations, in terms of what they are and what they are applied to, of why hammers and rules of inference work as well or as poorly as they do. Why, we then ask, do good theories work well?

The simplest possible explanation of why scientific theories work as well as they do is that they are true, or at least approximately true. They say something which is correct about something in the world. As opposed to instrumentalism, this is the *realist* account of the nature of scientific theories. The non-observational terms are held to refer to real things and properties, though ones which have yet to be characterized observationally. Until they are so characterized, they can only be described in terms of their relations with other things. As it happens, theoretical entities and properties have often become observable because of improvements in our observational techniques (such as the use of the electron microscope). Until it became identified in terms of the DNA molecule, the gene was known only theoretically. Examples might be multiplied. It would seem that various scientific theories have been shown to be true observationally, often after having been given a great measure of support by their instrumental success. One would naturally think that they had been true all along, prior to their being given an interpretation in observational terms.

There is yet another account of scientific theories, one which also purports to account for the success of good scientific theories. The idea is that the non-observational terms serve as convenient and concise mechanisms for describing observational entities and their properties and interrelationships. According to this *descriptivist* account, a scientific theory is an elliptical compendium of observational statements which could, in principle, be broken down into a

large or infinite class of such statements. The primary problem with
the descriptivist account is that it represents what is at best only an
unrealized programme, for no one has ever succeeded in treating
any theory to such an analysis. As we saw in connection with
Quine, an important reason why reductivist schemes are suspect is
that they treat statements as if they had precise well-defined identity
in their own right, rather than as having their identity as expressions
of a broader conceptual system. If – as I am very much inclined to
doubt, to say the least – the reduction-programme could be
achieved, then a scientific theory would amount to a mass of true or
false observational statements, and the realist theory would take
over. On the other hand, if the programme could not be achieved,
the descriptivist theory could not be a contender. Our choice would
then be between the realist and instrumentalist alternatives. I am
pleased to note that the descriptivist theory is not widely accepted
these days.

Perhaps we should not ask for a general account of scientific
theories. As a rule we should be suspicious of accounts in the 'one
size fits all' style. When we stretch something to fit we too often
distort. I would not care tacitly to presuppose that one account
would fit all of the great variety of scientific theories. It may,
perhaps, be that an instrumentalist account would fit some scientific
theories while a realistic account would better suit others. Certainly
I would by no means feel comfortable in taking the position that the
central claims of gene theory had not really been truth-bearers at all
until genes became identified or identifiable in terms of the DNA
molecule. A hard-core instrumentalist would have to accept such a
conclusion. Yet while we did not know what a gene was, the claim
that there are things of an indeterminate nature within the cell
which produce certain observable effects would seem to have been
both meaningful and true. Certainly there is no need to know all
about something in order to know something true about it. (We
may know it to be true that someone is coming this way when Peter
is coming this way, even if we do not know it to be Peter who is
coming.) Clearly, we can describe something, and describe it truly,
without giving a description which is sufficient for all purposes. I
should think that some scientific theories anyway are true or false in
so far as they assert something – in so far as they in some way,
however limited, describe some referential focus, however vaguely
delimited. Even so, while we might accept that gene theory, for
example, had been substantially true all along, and that various

other theories could equally well be said to say something about something, and so to be true or false, we might yet question whether such would apply to *all* scientific theories or even to all good ones.

Some theories, such as those of quantum mechanics, touch on the observable only lightly around the edges, with a very complicated structure in the uninterpreted middle to explain what goes on at the observable edges. Perhaps such theories, useful as they may be, are incapable of being given an interpretation in terms of observable matters. And perhaps there are in-between cases, of whatever sort, as well. What are we to conclude now? All good theories, of course, have to do with truth in so far as they predict, explain, and organize observable facts. Good theories answering to the realist account may be said to be true directly. But if there are other sorts of good theories, could they be said to have truth-content, to be in some perhaps limited way true? Instrumentally useful theories, which were observationally uninterpretable yet helped us to handle observational facts, undoubtedly would have some analogy with the formal systems of mathematics. Each would be a case of something which lacked observational content but which could be used to yield results which were assessable in terms of their material content. Even so – which is my point – there is a fundamental and critically important point of difference. Good mathematics is good mathematics because of the syntactical properties of the system. Mathematical formulae can be true-under-all-interpretations only because they do not say one thing or another about reality. Reality does not pass judgement on mathematics. In contrast, reality most certainly does pass judgement on scientific theories. Good theories must somehow be appropriate to the observed facts, and if the facts had been substantially different we would have needed different theories to accommodate them. Yet this is not necessarily to say, with the descriptivists, that they are appropriate to the observed facts because they redescribe them. Nor is it necessarily to say with the realists that they are appropriate to the observed facts because they express true statements about unobserved real things which are the basis for the facts. These may not be the only alternatives. Perhaps there are instrumentally good theories which are somehow appropriate to the observed facts without being true or false. After all, hammers and chisels may be more or less appropriate to that to which they are applied, yet they are only tools and not truth-bearers, and they say nothing about their field of application.

Even if they are not truth-bearers, we may learn something from tools. The tools of a carpenter are different from those of a dentist, barber, or pipe-welder, and by inspecting them we can gain some idea of what they are applied to. (Indeed, studying their tools is one of the ways in which we find out about the life of prehistoric cultures.) If we know how the tool is applied, we can learn even more about that to which it is applied. If we knew nothing of wood there is much we could find out from investigating a set of carpenter's tools and observing how they are used. As tools, scientific theories can indicate to us something about reality – if only the mere fact that some aspects of it are amenable to treatment of a certain sort with that kind of tool. Is it a matter of learning about reality through observing the successful use of theories, much as we learn through observing the successful use of hammers – or is it that theories, unlike hammers, can be said to have some sort of truth-content?

Instead of considering only whether *a* theoretical statement (or pseudo-statement) which is instrumentally good has truth-content, though, we would do better to consider it as one component of a whole system plus mode of application. After all, while even analytic statements have an empirical interpretation, theoretical statements are at a remove from the experiential boundaries of our conceptual system and have no direct interpretation at all. Individual theoretical statements cannot even touch reality on their own. They can be evaluated only as components of the whole theoretical system. Sometimes the whole system proves to be very useful indeed, organizing and explaining experience, and serving as the basis of successful predictions. In such a case the whole system can be said to have empirical truth-content in the sense that what it does say about empirical reality, including its predictions, is so. What, then, are we to say of the truth-status of those individual statements which lack an interpretation? One option would be to decide that they have truth-relevant utility, though not truth, as components of a successful system with truth-content. That would give them in effect a somewhat similar truth-status to that of mathematical formulae, as leading to but not being true statements. They would be less trustworthy than mathematical formulae, though, in that their strength is not based, or solely based, on syntactical considerations.

Another option would be to take them as being statements which, while having no empirical interpretation, are designated as true by virtue of their role as part of a conceptual system that fits well with empirical reality. As Quine points out, we need not and should not take such statements as necessarily and eternally true. At best they are contrivedly true, being contrivances useful for our cognitive purposes. As science moves on we may replace one scheme of contrivances with a better one. In that it recognizes that good theories have to do with truth, that we rig our theories so that they work out well in practice, and that we change the rigging as seems appropriate, this option has its attractions. It has its drawbacks as well. One major drawback is that it would lead us to posit existential statements as being true by designation. That they would be only mutably so makes it little the more palatable. I can accept that the theory that there are genes which do such-and-such was a hypothesis which turned out to be true. However, it seems too much to accept that it was a useful truth-by-designation which evolved, through theoretical and empirical advances, into a contingently true fact. Would we accept statements about unicorns as having been truths in a system which turned out not to fit reality usefully (the statements therefore not evolving into contingent truths)? I would take them never to have been truths at all. Statements, or pseudo-statements, about genes or unicorns do have a truth-bearer-like role in their respective systems, and certainly it would be wrong in the midst of a story about unicorns to describe one as having two horns and scaly wings. That they have such a role in their system does not mean that they are about anything, however, and that they have such a role is thus not a reason for taking them to be true, by designation or otherwise. There is a certain amount of leeway in our conceptual systems, and we can adjust our definitions and interpretations accordingly, as Quine pointed out so well, but we no more than St Anselm can define things into existence.

As it turned out the gene-story, with a few adjustments, was true while unicorn-stories were not. The gene-story was actually about something, eventually being capable of empirical interpretation, while unicorn-stories are not capable of such interpretation. What is the truth-status of statements (or whatever they are) in an instrumentally useful but uninterpreted theory? It may be that, as in the early days of gene-theory, they are *capable* of interpretation even though the right interpretation has not yet been discovered. In such a case it would seem to be appropriate to maintain that they really are about something and so are, as the case may be, true or false. It may even be that a scientific theory says something about something real, attributing qualities and relations of a sort, and even existence, even though, due to our inherent limitations, we would necessarily forever be unable to find an empirical interpretation for the theory's statements. A statement in such a theory would *have* content – perhaps we could say it has an interpretation which is not empirically knowable – and having content, unlike mathematical formulae, it could properly be said to be true or false. It could be false. A theory might be useful for many purposes, and perhaps even the best we could ever arrive at, while still not having things right. The theories of quantum mechanics might perhaps be true or false in any of these ways. Again, a theory might be instrumentally useful while having no content whatsoever, serving only as a mechanism for organizing what is observable and generating empirically verifiable conclusions. One might think it unlikely that a theory could do this consistently unless it somehow captured some of the unobserved or unobservable reality, but it is at least conceivable that there might be instrumentally useful theories of such a sort. Perhaps some of the theories of quantum mechanics are like that. Such a theory would be only a truth-related instrumentality on my account since, not saying anything about anything, it would be neither true nor false. For all I know, there might be instrumentally useful theories of any or all of the above sorts, which would or would not be true or false accordingly.

Whether theories are true is a question which is important only to a point. If we could find an interpretation in observational terms for our theoretical statements, and so determine their truth or falsity, that would be quite a valuable result. Failing that, they can still have quite an important role concerning truth. Scientific theories, true, false, or otherwise, are useful to the extent that they serve to organize data and serve as the source of useful predictions. That of course is the sort of thing which may lead to their being given an interpretation in observational terms. Until and unless that happens though the question of whether their statements are true or false or only instrumentally useful is not of overwhelming importance. What is important is whether they are useful in finding or organizing truth. Whether a scientific theory is true or false, or only of truth-related utility in some other way, though, truth remains a matter of whether a statement says something which is so about something. There are some further points which I would like to raise concerning the truth-related role of scientific theories, which I shall approach through considering science in relation to metaphysics.

METAPHYSICS, SCIENCE, AND TRUTH

Metaphysics is an inquiry into the nature and modes of being. That same broad definition applies to physics as well, since it too aims to find out about the basic nature of reality. Do the same considerations and conclusions about truth apply to metaphysics as to physics? Or is there an important difference between them which entails that metaphysics has to do with truth in some different way, if it has to do with truth at all? Many have held that there is an important difference, and a considerable proportion of them have gone so far as entirely to dismiss metaphysics as meaningless twaddle, not at all to be compared with science which offers us a model of knowledge. Kant took such a line. According to him, science studies phenomenal reality and is capable of truth, whereas metaphysics presumes to inquire into things-in-themselves. Since all we can ever know are phenomena, metaphysics is a futile and meaningless inquiry into a realm necessarily closed to the intellect. Subsequently, however, science has wandered far from the direct investigation of phenomena, as when it pursues particle physics or investigates viruses with an electron microscope. No one has ever seen a neutron, though we may see what we take to be evidence of them in a Wilson's cloud-chamber or at Hiroshima. No one has ever seen a virus, though we might see an enhanced visual representation produced by our electron microscope. Indeed, it is only inference that what we see through an ordinary optical microscope is really there, as we cannot look directly and compare what we see with what the microscope shows us. If it is within the province of science to inquire into non-phenomenal matters which are associated with and can in some way explain phenomena, this suggests that science (at least those parts of it) and metaphysics are in approximately the same line of business. If science is legitimate when it inquires into such matters then perhaps metaphysics also can have legitimacy.

This suggestion was welcome to some and scandalous to others. Attempts much more recent than that of Kant were made to distinguish between science and metaphysics in such a way that the latter might be rejected with impunity. The logical positivists, archantimetaphysicians that they were, tried to do so with their various versions of a verifiability theory of meaning. It was hoped to show that the truths of science were verifiable while metaphysics was empty nonsense. As is notorious, there were numerous (and I think insuperable) conceptual problems with this attempt – some of which concern the question of whether the verifiability theory itself has meaning. One of the problems in connection with science is that general statements can never be verified, no matter how many confirming instances we might find. Nor can we even raise the question of whether there might be an unobserved reality answering to such-and-such a description and grounding particular pheno-mena – such questions being dismissed as metaphysical. On such grounds the descriptivist and instrumentalist accounts of scientific theories were developed. We might *try* to reduce theories about atoms and sub-atomic particles to descriptive statements about things we can observe, or we might just think of such theories as useful forms of discourse. If we go to extremes we can extend the like treatment to anything having to do with sub-visual matters. Such reactions accept the presumption that, to be legitimate, science must deal only with empirically verifiable matters, and attempt to explain science's legitimacy accordingly. Even so, this allows the possibility that metaphysics can be held to be legitimate on similar grounds. Perhaps the *yin-yang* metaphysics of Taoism is a compen-dious description of observed polarities and continuities in nature. Perhaps Whiteheadian process-metaphysics has its uses as a scheme for organizing our knowledge of the world on a very general level.

The logical positivist's attempt to validate science and demolish metaphysics is generally regarded as unsuccessful, and not just because of its internal difficulties. That science should be only an instrumentality which is not *about* anything, or that it should only be about meter-readings and the like phenomena, has provoked considerable opposition even on the part of many with little sym-pathy for metaphysics. The price seems too high, and even at that price the attempt to get rid of metaphysics fails. Much more suc-cessful as an account of meaningful theories has been the Popperian view that meaningful theories are those which can be falsified and good ones are those which, while falsifiable, have successfully withstood falsification (as discussed in Popper (1963) and else-where). The march of science, on this view, has been characterized by the continuous criticism and falsification of theories and their replacement by theories which are more successful and more com-prehensive (by virtue of being able to accommodate the facts which falsified the previous theory). This view is compatible with realism about scientific theories and would allow their statements to be true or false in the way that other statements are, this being the stance which Popper himself took. Does this approach allow us to distinguish between science and metaphysics, with the latter being rejected as unfalsifiable and therefore meaningless?

Before we attempt to answer that question we should note that the complex scientific theories of the modern age are not as straightforwardly falsifiable as the old phlogiston theory of combustion or simple empirical statements about cats being on mats. If we have a complex theory dealing with a complex subject-matter, evidence to the contrary may not be decisive or may not seem to be decisive. For example, while the Newtonian theory of physics had been quite successful, having resisted falsification for many years, there were certain anomalies. The orbit of the planet Mercury consistently showed departures from that predicted for it by the Newtonian theory. Our first reaction in the case of an anomaly in connection with a well-entrenched theory of course is to write the whole thing off as being due to observational error – though that became impossible in the face of Mercury's consistent aberration. Next, one assumes that the theory has been incorrectly applied. Since the calculations had been correctly done, it was thought that perhaps Mercury had been influenced by some unknown body or force operating in the solar system. This would allow that while the theory was correct, our factual knowledge of the composition of the solar system was inadequate. (The planets Neptune and Pluto were discovered through assuming that our physics was correct and searching for a cause of the observed irregularities in the orbits of the known planets – the one before, the other after the problem with Mercury was resolved.) Even when no explaining factor is found it is assumed that there must be *some* explanation. The explanation, when it comes, may lie in a previously unknown fact consistent with the theory, or it may come in the shape of a new theory. A new theory may take the form of a minor extension or re-shaping of an old theory or, as Kuhn points out (1962), it may take the form of a whole new theory thoroughly reorganizing our understanding of an entire subject-matter. Such was the case when Einstein developed his theory of relativity, solving not only the problem about Mercury but several others which were seen as more important.

Scientific theories and the problems which they encounter can be very complex indeed, often much more so than in the preceding example. Complex and very abstract bodies of theory deal with complex bodies of fact, and there is even room for disagreement about what is to count as observational data. Only rarely can a theory be demolished by one contrary finding of fact. Very much is it a matter of the sort Quine described, wherein an intricate conceptual scheme is attached to the world of experience only around the edges, and somewhat flexibly at that. Theories confront reality only as wholes and must be assessed in terms of their overall fit with the world as a whole. Moreover, as is notorious, even the very best of theories are underdetermined by reality.[4] Whatever our observational data, there is more than one way – in principle an infinity of ways – in which we can provide a theoretical explanation of the data.

This is by no means to say that any theory which can explain the given data is as good as any other. Some theories may be unsatisfactory in terms of their fit with reality as a whole, however well they may handle a given portion of it. Others may be given an observational interpretation and so be promoted, as it were, from being theories to being facts (though as we have noted, even observational facts cannot be entirely free of theoretical dependence). For other theories, neither falsified nor observationally interpreted, there are still reasons for recognizing some theories as being better than others. Theories are better if they have greater predictive power and can explain a wider variety of observational data, and if they manage to avoid ad hoc assumptions or have fewer of them. They are thought by scientists to be better if they have the hard-to-define qualities of elegance and simplicity. Like works of art, scientific theories are valued as they offer us order in complexity, and, as with works of art, there is no precise and universally effective way by means of which we may evaluate them. Indeed, scientific theories *are* works of art of a sort. Deciding between them becomes a matter of which view of things we find preferable.

Can a metaphysical theory be falsifiable? Like other theories, metaphysical theories can evade falsification if we are prepared to stand by them in the face of any amount of cognitive inconvenience. Short of that, though, metaphysical theories can sometimes properly be said to fail to fit with reality, and so to be falsified. Cartesian dualism is dead not simply because it has gone out of fashion but because it just does not fit with the world as we know it. There is not much call for Leibnizian monads these days, either. On the other hand, various metaphysical theories have shown some utility. Various versions of materialism have shown some utility at least in connection with science, though perhaps not for all purposes. Again, scientists, and the rest of us, regularly rely on the metaphysical assumption – which is what it is – that the world, by and large, is an orderly place. (To be sure, it can be claimed that we do not really *believe* that. We just act as if we do.) Certain other metaphysical theories seem to be at such a remove from empirical reality that they do not make any appreciable difference one way or another.

It seems to me that the difference between scientific theories and metaphysical theories is really not one of kind but one of degree. Scientific theories, good, bad, or mediocre, are somewhat closer to the empirical periphery of our cognitive framework, and so have more to do with that which is empirically true or false. They are more falsifiable, and they serve more directly as bases for predictions and more directly to form our referential foci and schemes of description. Yet to a degree, which may or may not range down to zero, in particular cases, metaphysical theories can also serve to do these things. They too can serve, at the outer periphery, to shape our cognitive frameworks and so to shape the form truth takes for us. They might, to a degree, lead us towards or away from truth. Conceivably, since reality might actually (if not demonstrably) be ordered in a way indicated, a metaphysical theory might even be true.

TRUTH, BEAUTY, AND GOODNESS

I shall close this chapter with a few brief remarks concerning the large and difficult subject of whether and how truth and value are related. Is there truth about value – or vice versa? At the very least, we must recognize that truth and value seem to have something to do with one another. When we ascribe goodness, or rightness, or beauty to something, what we say (or utter) functions as if it were a statement. That is not to say that such an ascription *is* a statement, but at least it is cast in such a linguistic role. Some have held that such ascriptions are literally meaningless. Others have held that such ascriptions have a different linguistic role from that of statements, perhaps acting as performative-like utterances serving to express our attitudes toward certain things, or serving as imperatives telling us to do so-and-so. Indeed they do serve to express our attitudes – but is that all there is to it? Certainly not. Consider, for one example, a hypothetical utterance: 'If x is good/right/beautiful, then such-and-such (follows)'. If causing unnecessary pain to innocent beings is wrong, quite a lot follows. If 'x is wrong' serves *only* to express an attitude or convey a command, then nothing follows because attitudes and commands on their own do not have implications. Whatever other linguistic devices might be involved, statements are what have implications. Other examples tending to the same conclusion might be added, but the point is already apparent: while attitudes and imperatives or such like may well be part of the story, in using them as we do we treat ascriptions of value as if they served a statement-making function.

Granted that ascriptions of value do function as if they were statements, the question remains of whether they actually are statements. Do they say anything about anything – and if so, what do they say it about? What is value? It may perhaps be that being valuable is (only) a matter of being valued. Or perhaps certain things (justice, happiness, or whatever) are valuable and ought to be valued, whether we value them or not. These are often seen as being the only available alternatives though as I shall suggest, that assumption may warrant some scepticism. Let us consider the first alternative, that being valuable is (only) a matter of being valued. Taking such a stance by no means commits us to the view that ascribing value to something is only to express an attitude, or that such ascriptions can be neither true nor false. While our attitudes may lead us to have certain standards, that we do have such standards is a fact, a fact on the basis of which we can make assertions. If we have arrived at some standard of value, some statement of that which is valued, to say that something is or is not of value is to make an assertion about whether it meets that standard. To say that something is good might, for instance, be to say that it promotes pleasure or the satisfaction of preferences, or that it promotes our general wellbeing. To say that an act is wrong might be to say that it fails to treat people as ends-in-themselves. To say that something is beautiful or ugly might be to say that it does or does not meet some critical standard. And so on. If our values are defined in terms of what is valued, then ascriptions of value are true or false in the normal way so long as we can intensionally or extensionally specify, in non-evaluative terms, whatever it is which is valued. It might be quite factually true, for instance, that something is good if that *means* that it affords pleasure. Whatever our standards might be, it is factually true whether or not certain things meet those standards.

On the other hand, if things are valuable not because they are valued but because they *are* valuable, whether we value them or not, then the question of truth, if not those of ethics, is fairly straight-forward. If moral or aesthetic values are real features of the world, then true or false statements can be made concerning them. Of course that still leaves us with the problem of identifying value. If what is believed to be valuable can be identified in meaningful non-evaluative terms, our ascriptions of value can still be true or false in the normal way. Unless we settle for something seemingly arbitrary and tightly circular, though, there does not seem to be any convincing way in which we can so identify the valuable. If, for instance, the morally valuable is held to be x, then to say that we ought to value x would be to say that doing so promoted x or had the quality of x. Such a claim would not be persuasive to one who did not already think that we ought to value x. Accordingly, many have concluded that value terms can only be defined in terms of one another. Some, such as Moore and his followers, maintained that values were intuitively known real qualities had by some things and not by others, but undefinable (except perhaps in terms of other values). Others have sought to identify the valuable (whether or not valued) in other ways. Those with such convictions certainly treat ascriptions of value as if they were true or false. It may perhaps be that they are just talking nonsense. However, it is conceivable that they are making statements which are true or false, and to recognize this possibility it is not necessary to call on a conception of truth which is in any way aberrant. If they are able to consistently refer and describe on any basis whatsoever, what they say is true if there are standards for meeting that description which are then met. If one intuits (or whatever) goodness in something and says that it is good, that which is said is true if the thing does meet the intuitive (or whatever) standard intended. Those with similar standards may well understand what is said. We may understand values differently or deny them altogether, but that would be because we have a different conception of value, not because there are radically differ-ent sorts of truth with which we might be concerned.

As I have suggested, I am doubtful that our choice is only between taking the valuable to be the valued or else taking it to be the valuable in its own right. I shall explain why shortly. To start with, I would point out that truth cannot be disconnected from values for it is contingent on values, be they only our own.[5] It is also contingent on brute reality to be sure, but truth is not a direct feature of reality. There is truth only where there is a statement, and statements are made and shaped by us. Out of what James (1911: 50) called 'a big blooming buzzing confusion' we distinguish things, events, and relationships of interest to us, and think of and describe them in terms of features we take to be important. It is not just that we choose to focus on certain things and their qualities. We frequently do choose, but what we pay attention to, what we *can* pay attention to, is shaped also by our pre-conscious mind-sets. Some of those have been acquired through past choices, or through cultural or other environmental influences. It may even be that some of our mind-sets arise from, or at least are influenced by, genetic factors acquired through our long evolutionary background, some traits being more conducive to survival than others. Moreover, as Kant showed us, our perceptions as well as our conceptions are pre-consciously shaped and organized within our self. There are any number of causal chains of any number of sorts impinging on us from the world around us and we have our particularly human modes of receiving and organizing inputs. Were we bats using echo-location, or sharks perceiving via electromagnetic fields, we would experience the world quite differently. Even with the same material input, beings of an alien species might well form a perceptual world of quite a different sort. We perceive the world and deal with it according to what we are and, which is not a separate point, according to our interests in it.

Values come in at least on the level of consciousness, the level whereon we focus on one sort of thing rather than another as being important. According to James,

> The conception of consciousness as a purely cognitive form of being, which is a pet way of regarding it . . ., modern as well as ancient, is thoroughly [wrong]. Every actually existing consciousness seems to itself at any rate to be a *fighter for ends*, of which many, but for its presence, would not be ends at all. Its powers of cognition are mainly subservient to these ends, discerning which facts further them and which do not.
>
> (1910: vol. 1, 141)

It is on the conscious level that we make choices, and we value certain things on the conscious level. Conscious beings certainly are fighters for ends, but there is more to it than James tells. There is more to us than our consciousness, and our values run deeper than our valuing. Beneath the conscious surface of our minds we have ends which lead us toward some choices and away from others. Our whole being as living entities has *well*-being needs which orient us toward or away from various things. The same is true for other living beings, including the non-conscious ones. A grub burrowing through a log, or a plant struggling toward the light, is, though unconsciously, pursuing its own ends.

At this stage we should reconsider the assumption that something's being valuable must be a matter either of its being valuable in its own right or else of its being consciously valued. We should consider the possibility that values can be our values without this being so by virtue of our actually and consciously valuing them. I shall here address only the restricted topic of what is good for us in our own right, the morality of our dealings with others being, while very important, an issue too complex to pursue here. What I suggest is that our well-being needs define what is good for us. Is that so, or does what we need become good for us only when we value it? Let us take a closer look at the theory that being valuable means being valued. In the past, attempts were made to identify our good (= valued), identifying it as pleasure, happiness, or whatever – attempts which ran aground on the empirical fact that not everyone values any one particular thing. These days it is fashionable to define what is valued, our good, in terms of prudent desires: what we desire when we are well informed and thinking clearly, or what we would desire were we in that condition. With admirable liberalism, this view allows us to define our own good, weighing one thing against another according to our own choices. Of course we can make mistakes, through ignorance of relevant facts or through confused thinking. Our actual desires may not be prudent desires, and our prudent desires may not actually be desired. This position is a retreat from equating the valuable with the valued to equating it with what is, or would be, valued under ideal conditions. It rests on some tacit presuppositions about ideal conditions. Since we can never know all the facts, being well informed can only be a matter of knowing the ones relevant to our choice, the ones which might affect our decision. If choice in the face of facts were arbitrary, no fact could be ruled out as irrelevant. The presumption must be that relevant facts are relevant because they are in some significant way tied to our interests. Again, what is to count as clear thinking? Is it just being logical? Lunatics can be that. We are thinking clearly only when we respond to the facts sensibly and appropriately. Ultimately, what is sensible and appropriate has to have due regard for one's interests, and anyone who's thinking diverges from that too far is regarded as malfunctioning mentally. The prudence of desires, the relevance of facts, and clarity of thinking have to be based on interests – not vice versa.

I maintain that what is good for individuals is a matter of their interests – which I understand as that which contributes to the effective coherent functioning of their life-process as a whole. Like physical health, that admits of flexibility and is hard to define, but, like physical health, it is basically a factual matter. What we choose is important – and it is contrary to our interests to have frustrated desires – but, like our reason, our values spring from deeper sources. Our consciousness does not define our ends, though it gives us some. Our consciousness is an adaptation which allows us better to pursue our ends. There is obviously much more to be said on this subject than I have said here, though this is not the place to pursue the subject. I do have very much more to say elsewhere (1991).

Certain points, I believe, emerge. One is that the shape of our values and the shape of truth as we know it both rest on what we are. Nor is the connection only coincidental. The way in which we think and experience the world is shaped by our nature and by our inherent interests, and, flowing on from that, by the interests which we have developed. Our values are not on the other side of some impenetrable fact-value barrier from the facts of what we are, or of the world we are in, but spring from them. Truths shape our values, values shape our truths, and truths about our values are not true in any esoteric or non-standard sense.

11

CODA

In this concluding chapter I review some of the historical theories of truth and the associated issues in the light of the preceding discussion. This is for the purpose of developing an assessment of our present position. The account of truth which I have presented is general, but no general account of truth can have very strong content. This is because statements state in a variety of different ways, for many different purposes. Certainly there is much more to be said in connection with truth, depending on what the connection is and what our interests in the matter are. I suggest, though, that rather than pursue truth theory past the point of diminishing returns, it would be more profitable to investigate different ways of referring and describing, for various purposes, and to investigate different ways of being true.

People frequently say things which are true or false, or perhaps are something else, and often it greatly matters whether or not what we say is true. But what matters? In developing an account of what truth amounts to, one of the conclusions I came to is that we say something about that which is true or false when we say that it is true or that it is false. I then developed an account of what we say about it when we say that it is true. In the course of doing so I have investigated some related issues and developed tributary conclusions. Various other theories of truth have been discussed along the way, considered from the point of view not of rejecting them but of learning from them. I hope to have shown that we can learn from their strengths as well as their weaknesses. In coming to our own conclusions, we must profit from what has gone on before, attempting to focus on the problem-area as clearly as possible, so that we can develop an account which is viable and neither attempts too much nor settles for too little. In this final chapter I shall review some of this material, and our developing conclusions, working toward an assessment of our present position.

LOOKING BACK, AND LOOKING FORWARDS

It has been fashionable in recent times, though it is becoming less so, simply to dismiss the coherence theory of truth. A major reason for the low estimation in which the theory has been held is its association with idealist metaphysics, though to a great extent it is possible to separate the truth theory from the metaphysics. As a purely practical matter, however, considerations of coherence offer us useful tools for working with incomplete or inconsistent data. Any time we are concerned with things of which we do not have direct knowledge, we must proceed on the basis of how that which we are wondering about fits in with what we know. As a criterion of truth the coherence theory has considerable utility. Beyond that, as an account of the nature of truth, it offers us insights well worth retaining. For one thing, it reminds us that we live in a world of highly interconnected complexity. Parts of the world are only parts, and, at least to a considerable extent, they have their identity in terms of their wider context. Also, our cognitive scheme by which we understand the world forms an interconnected web. The coherence theory also reminds us that there are many different ways in which we can conceptualize or describe some aspect of reality – none of which exhausts what is there. Quite correctly, we are told that truth is relative to our cognitive scheme – and any cognitive scheme has its limitations. From that, many of the coherence theorists drew the conclusion that truths are only partially true, and are therefore partially false. Only the universal Absolute, encompassing every feature of reality, is absolutely true, and that we can never attain. I believe that taking this line was a mistake. While any attainable truth is limited – and distorting, if we foolishly imagine that our conceptualizations are exhaustive of reality – it can still be entirely true, in terms of what we are saying about reality within the framework of our cognitive scheme. Like the metaphysical doctrines, the doctrine of degrees of truth is not an intrinsic feature of the coherence theory of truth, and therefore is not an intrinsic fault. A serious and central fault of the theory is that it tries to take truth as being purely a matter of conceptual interrelationships. At some point, though, in some way, we must rely on the alogically given. I believe that the account of truth which I have presented avoids these faults. At the same time, it adopts the virtue of recognizing that reality and what we say about it – and I distinguish between the two more than do most of the coherence theorists – can be conceptualized in any number of different ways. With this, it recognizes that the identity of what is true, and the criteria of its truth, are relative to our conceptual scheme.

The correspondence theory of truth, unlike the coherence theory, most certainly does rest its account on the the alogically given. Therein lies its greatest attractiveness. There is what we say, and what we say it about, the former being true if it fits the latter. Nothing could seem simpler nor more evident. The complexities and the problems come in when we try to work out what fits what, and what fitting amounts to – yet if we just leave it unanalysed, we have no account at all. The classical correspondentists tried to explain it in terms of structural isomorphism. However, it was not possible to develop a viable account in terms of structural isomorphism between things so disparate as what we say and what we say it about. For one thing, we can contrive an explanation of the correspondence relationship supposedly in the middle only at the price of loosing our moorings to what should be at the ends. We wind up with entities, propositions and facts, which are tailored to fit each other, but on the one hand we cannot adequately account for what propositions have to do with what is said, and on the other we cannot adequately account for what facts have to do with reality. We can dismiss propositions and facts as linguistic substantives useful, if at all, for, respectively, talking about our words as used in asserting and for talking about certain sorts of assertions about reality – but that does not leave us with anything which we can fit together in a useful structural isomorphism. In any case, structural isomorphism on its own is not enough. We can contrive some description according to which *any* two things are structurally isomorphic. To solve the problem, those things which fit together have to be *relevantly* structurally isomorphic. The correspondence theory must, but cannot, allow for an explicit or implicit element of assertion about *how* this fits that. Yet another problem with the correspondence theory is that, particularly in anything like the version of the *Tractatus*, it tends to divide the world, and also what we say about it, into discrete well-defined units. That does violence both to the world and to what we say about it. The account of truth which I have presented avoids these faults, I believe, while yet retaining the basically correct intuition that true statements, except perhaps for analytical statements, are true by virtue of external reality – and even analytical statements are true *about* external reality. In place of structural isomorphism with external reality, we look to referential and descriptive correlation.

Pragmatic accounts of truth, as well as those of the correspondence theorists, ground truth in the alogically given, that external reality about which what we say is or is not true. Whereas the correspondence theory has rather less merit than first glance would seem to indicate, the pragmatic conception of truth has more. It is easy – too easy – to dismiss the basic idea, that truth is that which works out well in practice, as offering us only a criterion of truth rather than a proper account of what truth is. There is much of value in their linking of meaning with criteria. That which is true or false does not occur in the abstract. It is shaped by us in terms of our conceptual scheme. On this point of agreement, the pragmatists and coherentists have it right. Going somewhat beyond the coherentists, the pragmatists correctly stress that whatever is true or false is so with respect to the purposes we have in considering the matter at hand and the criteria with which we proceed. Any statement is meaningful only with respect to the explicit or implicit criteria, well or poorly defined, which we have for its successful application to reality. That is true, they maintain, which works best in practice, in terms of those purposes and criteria. Here, I believe, the pragmatists falter. Working out well is not enough. It has to work out well in the right way. There are a great many criteria according to which we can assess whether a statement works out satisfactorily, not all of which are indicative of truth. According to our criteria, it may suit us to believe that something is a certain way, but there is still the question of whether it is that way. It is truth-expediency which counts. Our criteria must determine what it is to be a certain way, the statement being true if things are that way. In my own account of truth I have sought to give proper recognition to this necessity.

Redundancy theories of truth as well can too easily be dismissed, and they can also too easily be accepted. In their various versions they offer inadequate accounts of truth but they do have features of merit which ought to be recognized. Much of their allure stems from the vain hope of finding a quick and easy way of disposing of an otherwise frustrating subject of inquiry. Generalities along the lines of '[the statement that] p is true if and only if p' seem simple enough and obviously true, but they only sweep the problem under the rug. While '[the statement that] p is true' and 'p' are truth-functionally equivalent, there remains the question of whether the former but not the latter is used to make a statement about p. Critical cases suggest that this is indeed so, and various ways of making the word 'true' disappear do not make the problem disappear. We must give an account of what is said about p when it is said to be true. Even so, redundancy theories have at least the merit of reminding us that the truth of p is a matter of p and whatever p is about. Instead of calling on extraneous entities or looking to lame general answers about what it means for any statement to be true, we look to what is involved in *that* statement's being true. Again, the prosententialists do well to remind us that, in spite of appearances, our often complex linguistic paraphernalia is frequently used merely to facilitate talking about an initial subject-matter, and not then for the purpose of discussing statements about it.

If we turn our attention to the function and use of particular statements, we find in some cases that stating is not all that is involved. The performative theory of truth, in part derived from the redundancy theory, draws our attention to the fact that ascribing truth to a statement at least often serves the function of adding one's own endorsement to it. That is all to the good, as it directs our attention toward what a language-user is using language to do on a particular occasion of use. It is not just a matter of words and world somehow having something to do with each other, but of our use of language in certain ways in particular contexts to achieve certain results. We need to concentrate on that. Even so, as an account of truth the performative theory cannot explain away those cases which indicate that something is said about a statement said to be true. We must ask what is said about it, which leads us to look more closely at what is involved in making the statement which is said to be true.

The semantic conception of truth also owes a considerable debt to the redundancy theory. To be sure, the adequacy condition (T), which requires that the semantic system entail, or at least be consistent with, all sentences of the form ' "p" is true if and only if p ', is not offered as a definition of truth, though it is sometimes taken to be such. Even so, as Tarski points out, each (T)-sentence provides a partial definition of truth, telling us of what the truth of its particular p consists. It is a virtue of the semantic conception that it directs us to the truth-conditions of particular sentences. It is inadequate, though, in that it takes the truth-bearer to be the sentence as it occurs in a formalized language, rather than taking it to be the statement, the sentence as it is actually used by the language-user on the particular occasion. The semantic conception of truth, then, attempts to define truth purely in terms of the semantic structure of a language, without taking into account the pragmatics of actual use. What are true or false, though, are not sentences in the abstract, but sentences in use and as used. To a point, semantic theories can take this into account – but only to a point. We can specify truth-conditions for any particular use of language. Yet when we have done that, we have only specified truth-conditions for *that* particular use of language. The language-user might use language in a somewhat different way subsequently, and that is not something which can be pre-specified into the structure of the language. Only *ex post facto*, and on a purely *ad hoc* basis, can a formal system accommodate the fluidity and vagueness so vital to our linguistic usage.

Here it will perhaps seem that I am objecting to the semantic conception of truth on grounds which apply equally well to my own account of truth. I have claimed that a particular statement is true when its referential foci, as established in that particular use of language, are of the requisite types, according to our criteria in that use of language. That may not sound any better than the claim that a sentence is true if its specified truth-conditions are met. There is a very important difference, though. According to the semantic conception, once the satisfaction-conditions for a language have been specified, whether a sentence is true is a matter which can be determined solely by checking its formal structure and the attached list of specifications. What is true or false is defined into the language itself. On my account, on the other hand, what is true or false is so according to whether or not what is talked about is as described. Does that make a real difference? It may seem that it does not, as on my account truth depends on whether the truth-conditions for that use of language are satisfied on that occasion, which can easily be specified into our semantic system for that occasion. But that is for *that occasion*. Other occasions require other specifications. It all depends – and the semantic conception cannot help tell us what it depends on. If we are going to apply it to a natural language we must first decide whether particular sentences are true and then specify it into the structure of that language as the language is to be used on that occasion. On my account, however, taking the pragmatics of the situation into consideration, we can say that what is said about something is true or false, as the case may be, according to whether that something satisfies our intensional criteria, as then employed, for being that way. Circumstance and intention might even combine to make it appropriate to state that snow is green. Not having this dimension, the semantic conception of truth cannot tell us what it is to be true, but can only record what is true. In recording that, it does not do justice to the pragmatics of actual usage in truth-stating, with its continuously varying flexibility and constructive vagueness. It only presents frozen cross-sections of it.

The semantic conception of truth cannot properly be taken as vindicating the correspondence theory. In particular, requirement (T), contrary to the claims of Popper and some others, does *not* require true sentences to be true by virtue of any sort of relation to an independent objective reality. It makes no claims whatsoever about what makes true things true. *Any* serious account of truth, to be serious, can and must be consistent with requirement (T). It is quite neutral. Moreover, the satisfaction-specifications can be made on the basis of any reasons whatsoever which we might have for believing that certain things are certain ways. It does not provide us with an account of what it is to be true. It can, at best, record only an extensional account of what is true. Ultimately, this is the problem which defeated Davidson's attempt to develop a corre-spondence theory. Going far beyond Popper, he attempted to develop a theory relativized to speaker and time of utterance, working on the basis of the meaning-structure of the language. While he is able to shed informative light on the meaning-structure of our language, his attempt to find a semantic theory of truth finally foundered because the notions of meaning and translation which he developed were themselves dependent on the notion of truth. It would be quite circular to specify our truth-conditions in terms of those truth-conditions. The moral must be that for seman-tics, truth is a starting point, not a finishing point.

The semantic conception of truth does have its uses and has considerable value. It can be a helpful conception in devising arti-ficial languages useful for certain technical purposes. Also, and very importantly, we can use it as a valuable tool in the investigation and analysis of natural languages. This we do on the basis of our given satisfaction-specifications. As Davidson points out, we can start from things of the form 'Such-and-such is true if and only if so-and-so' and, rather than trying to generate a theory of truth out of it, instead use it as a tool for analysing the 'so-and-so' end of it. As he so ably demonstrates, *given* a pre-analytical conception of truth we can investigate various kinds of usage, analysing and coming to better understand their meaning-structure. While this cannot yield a theory of truth, it can help us better to understand what is involved in a particular statement's being true.

I have criticized the semantic conception of truth on the grounds that it cannot tell us what it is to be true. Yet I have also held it to be a virtue that it does not give us some sweeping formula about truth in general, but concentrates on what is involved in truth in individual instances. It may seem that in my own account of truth I present a sweeping formula about truth in general. But what I am saying about truth in general is that each statement is true in its own particular way, in terms of how *it* says something about whatever it says it about. I claim that the term 'true' is applied to those statements which, in their own way, say something about something where the something is as it is said to be. That is far from being a sweeping generality which casts all truth in the same mould, but it is to say what it is to be true.

From their different points of view, Strawson and Austin both agreed that truth theory should develop an account of what the term 'true' is used to do, rather than search for a theory of truth in the abstract. For Strawson, the role of the term is not descriptive but performative or performative-like. To say that a statement is true is not to make a statement about the statement, but is to perform an act endorsing it. No doubt such an act is at least often performed, and Strawson performed a valuable service in calling this to our attention, and, more generally, in directing our attention to our overall usage of the term. Even so, there is reason to believe that saying that a statement is true is to make a statement about that statement, and not just to endorse it, a conclusion which Strawson himself came to accept. According to him, though, what is said about the statement is only something about its actually or hypothetically having been stated. There is question about whether that is stated or whether it is presupposed – the latter seeming much more likely – but in any case there remains the unanswered question of *why* the statement (whose identity we may not even know) is to be endorsed or rejected. That it is true, or that it is false, can be a reason if truth or falsity are attributes of statements. Certainly it seems that it is not just that the word 'true' is a vehicle for endorsement, but that the truth of the statement is a *reason* for endorsement. On such grounds I hold that truth and falsity can meaningfully be predicated of statements. It is therefore appropriate to explain what we say about a statement when we describe it as being true.

A problem which Strawson raises is that there is no analysis of what we say about a statement when we say that it is true which will be accepted by all of those who ascribe truth to statements as being a valid analysis of what they are doing when they do so. Whatever we may offer, many will say that that is not what they are saying/doing when they say that a statement is true. But does a correct account of what people use the term 'true' to say have to be one with which they will all agree? If so, we must abandon our attempt, and we would even have to abandon the redundancy account, for by no means all would agree that they were saying only that p when they say that p is true. We would have to abandon any attempt to give an account of what people say when they say anything at all, for we could never get unanimous agreement. Moreover, as Quine points out, there is no rendering of anything which is synonymous for every purpose. Any description of anything – statements included – captures only certain features. Even so, within the limits of the mode of description, a description can be correct and illuminating. While we can never hope to capture every nuance of someone's statement that a statement is true, and can never arrive at an account which will be accepted by absolutely everyone who makes such statements, we can still aspire to develop a correct and illuminating account of what we use the term 'true' to say and do.

Austin set himself to provide such an account. He took the point of view that we say something about a statement when we say that it is true, and attempted to explain what we say when we do so. This he did via a discussion of the descriptive use of language. He took it that statements say something about something, the true ones doing so correctly, and that the true ones are true by virtue of how they relate to what they are about. The relationship he proposed might perhaps be considered to be one of correspondence but it is not one of structural isomorphism, being based on conventional correlation. Thus far I am in agreement with Austin. However, I maintain that his account soon goes astray through insufficient responsiveness to our actual linguistic usage and its flexibility (this being an unusual charge to make in connection with Austin). The primary problems concern the demonstrative and descriptive conventions and their correlates. He took the referential correlate of a statement to be a situation (state of affairs, fact). Thus, while 'Cats drink cream' is correlated with no particular cat, it is correlated with a situation (or whatever) concerning cats, which is then subject to description. However, he assumes that a statement has one and only one demonstrative correlate, and, as we are informed by Warnock, it is part of the identity of the statement that it have *that* demonstrative correlate. As if that were not bad enough, the situation/fact which stands as demonstrative correlate is held to be itself a thing-in-the-world of some sort. However as Strawson points out, if demonstrative correlates are things-in-the-world, then it is absurd that statements, of a sort which Austin's account would require to have the same demonstrative correlate, might yet concern quite different things, events, times, and places. More generally, there are many sorts of statement such that we cannot plausibly identify a thing-in-the-world demonstrative correlate for them. Also, examples indicate that statements can (and must) be taken as being correlated with various different demonstrative correlates, depending on how we analyse what is being said about what. This brings us to another set of shortcomings with Austin's account.

According to Austin, the demonstrative conventions are sharply distinguished from the descriptive conventions, even being tied to different things at the linguistic end. The former are tied to words (= statements), our words as used on that occasion, while the latter are tied to words (= sentences), our words as standardly used. This is a mistake, for three important reasons. Firstly, as Strawson suggested, reference and description overlap substantially. We refer in the course of describing and describe in the course of referring. Our linguistic conventions have both dimensions, and cannot be separated into radically different types of convention. We use them both ways in establishing either sort of correlation. Secondly, Austin is incorrect in taking the descriptive conventions as being tied at the linguistic end to words (= sentences) – to our words as standardly used. Whether we are using language demonstratively or descriptively, what we say (and do) is a matter of how we use language on *that* occasion. Standard usage counts only to the extent, often a considerable one, that we employ standard usage. Both demonstratively and descriptively, then, our linguistic conventions connect, at the linguistic end, with our words as used then in those circumstances by us. Thirdly, it cannot just be a matter of their being conventionally correlated with certain correlates. That particular use of language might be quite novel, and so not involved in any conventional correlations. Rather, we use conventions on the particular occasion to establish correlates. It is not the linguistic conventions themselves but our use of them on the occasion which is critical.

In my own account I have attempted to avoid the faults which I identified in Austin's account, and those of other accounts, while yet retaining the conception that statements say something about something, the true ones doing so correctly. We may not be talking about any particular thing, or arrangement of things, in the world, but we do talk about some subject-matter. We establish referential foci, which are said to be of certain types, but they are not to be considered as things-in-the-world. What ties together that which we are talking about is not the world on its own, but our interests in it and our means of conceptualizing it. The question of which is *the* demonstrative correlate is not to be answered but rejected. Not only can the world be described in many ways, our conceptualizations of it can be analysed in many different ways. Moreover, the account I have presented recognizes that truth does not occur in the abstract, and does not apply to truth-bearers in the abstract. In all cases, truth is a matter of a particular use of language in a particular way for our then purposes. Austin falls short by taking the descriptive conventions as being tied to our words (= sentences) as standardly used, and falls short again by taking the correlations as being established by conventions rather than through the use we make of conventions to suit our purposes for the occasion. Language as we use it does not come in precise pre-delineated units of standard issue. Rather, we use language with great flexibility in establishing and describing referential foci, according to our purposes and criteria. What we say is true if our referential foci are as they are said to be.

Concerning the question of what it is that we say about something when we say that it is true, I believe that this is about as far as we can go with a general answer. More adventurous theories go astray while redundancy theories fall short by not going that far. Statements are made in an enormous variety of widely differing ways, establishing and describing different sorts of referential foci according to various criteria for various purposes. It would be foolish to attempt to offer a characterization which was both very strong and very general of how statements state and what it is for them to do so correctly. Even so, there is much to be explored. In the manner of Davidson we can of course explore meaning and the structure of language, *given* truth. Beyond that, on the basis of logic and what we can find out about meaning-structure, and many other factors, we can explore diverse applications of the descriptive use of language. We must investigate criteria and the purposes for which we use language and assess what is said. So far as they went, the pragmatists were quite correct in maintaining that truth is in large part a function of what we are trying to find out or communicate.

Exploring the workings and use of our conceptual and cognitive schemes repays our efforts. It is, for instance, an interesting and worthwhile study to investigate the criteria according to which we do or do not deem certain things or actions to be good, and to investigate our purposes in so doing and the circumstances which are relevant. There are several patterns there, and such a study can tell us more not only about our linguistic usage but about our valuing. Also, by studying other applications of descriptive language we can find out more about our conceptualizations of the world around us and about, in those terms, our knowledge of it. Thereby we may come to know the world better. There are many ways to describe, and so we find that there are many ways for a statement to be true. I suggest that it would be more profitable to investigate ways of being true, and certainly more profitable to investigate what is true, than to pursue beyond the point of diminishing returns the question of what it is to be true.

TRUTH AND *THE TRUTH*

A senior friend of mine, a scholar who has achieved some eminence in a different though related field, some years ago remarked that when discussing my research I pronounced the word 'truth' as if I were personally acquainted with it. I was horrified. My mind raced to those media evangelists who pronounce the word 'God' in a particular way. Indeed, that tone so pervades their oratory that one can easily identify them even when they are doing the station-break. Certainly I do revere truth, but I made a strict resolve to be more careful of my pronunciation thereafter. The dear man assured me that he found my tone charming rather than offensive, but, I hope redundantly, I would here like to quite disclaim any first-hand knowledge of *The Truth*. Indeed, I believe that no one can properly claim such knowledge, and that no one could. Truths we can know, some more useful or informative than others, but not *The Truth*. Truths there are, many of them, but there is no such thing as *The Truth*. I will explain why I believe this to be so.

Reality *is*, obviously, and we are part of it, though we can know it only partially. Even the most complete knowledge of reality, such as none of us could possess, would not be knowledge of *The Truth*. Even reality itself is not *The Truth*. 'Truth' is an epistemological term which applies to the things that we do or could say *about* reality. Truth is (roughly) a matter of whether descriptions fit what they are asserted of – but our conceptual schemes are not mandated by reality. There are any number of conceptual schemes in terms of which we can truthfully describe the same reality. Any of those conceptual schemes will divide reality along some lines, but not others, and describe with respect to certain criteria and purposes, but not others. Even the most complete description of reality according to one scheme will ignore distinctions and descriptions which would be prominent under some other alternative scheme. We cannot even take *The Truth* to be the logical sum of all truths under all possible conceptual schemes, for there can be no sum. Our conceptual schemes depend on our purposes and criteria, and the possible variations of that are indeterminable. Instead of there being *The Truth*, there are only truths which reflect and are limited by our conceptual schemes. This is not to claim that truth is arbitrary, that it is only a consequence of our prevailing conceptual scheme. To a limited extent, certainly, that is true, but only to a limited extent. As Quine points out, we can gerrymander our conceptual schemes so as to protect certain favoured truths, and where the applicability of a description is indeterminate we can make an arbitrary assignment of truth-values. Even so, there are severe limits on how far we can stretch our conceptual fabric, and to the extent that truth is about reality, our statements, while formed and having their content *in terms of* a given conceptual scheme, will be true or false *by virtue of* the reality which they, in their way, describe.

Even the most complete account cannot capture all of anything at all, let alone all of reality or any appreciable portion of it. For that reason, I counsel scepticism concerning any theory or dogma which claims to tell us everything important about something. Indeed, I offer the following as my nomination as Thinking Person's Axiom One:

> If you think you have *the* answer –
> you are wrong.

Many specific questions can be given a definitive answer, to be sure, but we can never say everything worthwhile about any given subject-matter. Whether or not telling everything about the flower in the crannied wall would tell us everything about everything, telling all about the flower would be beyond even theoretical possibility. Reality is more complex than any account could capture, and no matter what we say about anything, and no matter how true what we say is in terms of its conceptual scheme, that thing has undescribed features and relationships which might be important to someone for some purpose. Those features and relationships do not go away because they do not suit our conceptual scheme or theoretical convenience. Dogmas which offer us *The Truth* posit a shrink-to-fit reality.

A FINAL WORD –
THOUGH NOT THE LAST WORD

I do not presume to offer *The Truth*, not even The Truth about truth – which would hardly be less presumptuous. Recall, as we noted previously, that the word 'true' has an etymological connection with those ancient words which also gave rise to our word 'tree'. Truths, it is suggested, are in some way like trees. What is a tree like? Some trees are symmetrical, straight up and down, and fit a certain pattern. One suspects that such trees are well represented around Oxford, Cambridge, and Vienna. Again, some trees, like Australian gum trees, are quite irregular in shape, each tree expressing the peculiarities of its own character, environment, and history. They too are firm, reliable, and durable, with a beauty all their own. You have actually to look at a gum tree to know what it looks like. Gums, I think, offer a better model of truth, as each truth is true in its own way.

As I have tried to point out, truth takes many forms – as many forms, ultimately, as there are statements. What we might wish to say of the forms of truth is not something which could possibly be captured by any once-and-for-all theory. I have not sought to capture truth. Rather, I have sought to present an account which is faithful to our actual usage of the term 'true' and which recognizes the freedom of truth. That is the freedom with which we shape and use language to serve our diverse interests and purposes in saying things about things – or in otherwise thinking about things. As we use the terms, 'true' and 'false' apply to that which is or might be stated, be it actually stated, or be it believed, doubted, wondered about, or whatever. Whatever we do, though, it involves *us*. Truth is never divorced from the language-user (speaker, listener, thinker, . . .), and the freedom and flexibility of truth is our freedom and flexibility in shaping our use of language to fit the world and to fit our purposes and interests in it. That which is (or might be) said is a matter of what we do (or might) say *about* whatever we (might) say it about. A referential focus of whatever sort is established, in whatever way, and in saying (believing, doubting, . . .) what we do, the referential focus is said (believed, doubted, . . .) to be of a particular type. When it is of that type, when things are as they are said (etc.) to be, the statement is true. The formula we came to is this:

> A statement is true if and only if it is correlated with referential foci, established through our use of linguistic conventions, which are of types of referential foci with which we correlate it through our descriptive use of linguistic conventions.

Needless to say, this is not the last word. Much remains to be said in connection with truth, depending on what the connection is and what our interests in the matter are. There could never be a last word, so long as there is thought and truth. I offer this account as a point of reference on a never-ending road to truth.

NOTES

1 INTRODUCTION

1 In the German language, quite different words, *treu* and *wahr*, are used to distinguish quite different ways of being what in English we would call true. A true pearl is *treu*. A belief, when correct, is *wahr*. It would be rash, though, to conclude that there were no more than two ways of being true.

2 COHERENCE

1 In particular, I am referring to those post-Kantian idealists, mostly German or British, who developed the coherence theory of truth. Hegel, Bradley, Blanshard, and Joachim are among their number.

2 I always have to stress to the unwary that the terms 'ideal', 'idealism', etc., as used in this context are not to be taken in their popular sense, as having to do with optimism, lofty standards, or the like. As used here the reference is directly to *idea*, having to do with things mental (or mental-like).

3 There are some complex side-issues here about whether observations and experiences are themselves true or false, or whether it is only sentences or statements about them which are so. Fortunately, we need not go into all that, since the point remains in any case.

4 A major worry I have about Rescher's approach is that it deals only with sets of presumptive data which are already in propositional form. The formulation of propositions in itself presupposes theories and orderings of importance. Often as we attempt to pull a gestalt into focus, one of the things we are doing is finding a *way* of describing things. If we build a story out of parts, we also form parts to fit our stories. I suspect, then, that Rescher is neglecting important aspects of the problem.

3 CORRESPONDENCE

1 Subsequently published in Moore (1953). Some of the ideas had been anticipated by Russell as early as 1906.

2 One may note that I glossed over this issue in my presentation of

Russell's account in the first paragraph of this section. Should I have said '. . . (2) believes that (3, 4, . . .) whatever', or should it have been '. . . (2) believes (3, 4, . . .) that whatever'? Where does the '*that*' go? The former version is appropriate if it is the believing which ties the components together. The latter version is appropriate if terms (3) and following are knit together by their own binding relation. We cannot even formulate the multiple relation theory without cutting across the ambiguity in the status of the problematic term.

3 So, if I believe that Jack is taller than Jill, this must not be understood as 'I believe (that Jack is taller than Jill)', where 'that Jack is taller than Jill' is used to name what is believed, but as 'I believe that (Jack is taller than Jill)', where 'Jack is taller than Jill' is used to state what is believed. See note 2.

4 Ordinary language philosophers, for their part, urge that linguistic 'improvers' often neglect important subtleties and nuances which have been built into a language over centuries of practical use. We may be well-rid of golden mountains, but we must be careful about what else we set aside and about what we set in its place.

5 In this connection, I would note that while a true proposition about an object is (supposedly) structurally similar, in some important way, to the object, with the object therefore similar to the proposition, it is the proposition which is true, and not the object. Neither are two structurally similar objects true or false of one another. While a true proposition may in some sense be a true picture, asserting is fundamental to its being a picture, to its being a picture *of* something, and certainly to its being a true picture.

4 ALTERNATIVES I

1 Actually, Russell was directing his remarks there against John Dewey, though Dewey, as in his 1938 book, was less inclined than James to take truth as being a type of expediency. Sometimes Russell's criticisms of other philosophers are more interesting than accurate.

5 THE SEMANTIC CONCEPTION OF TRUTH

1 Tarski (1956), and a less formal presentation (1944).

2 For a further discussion, see chapter 8, 'Paradoxes', in Haack (1978). Also, Kripke (1975) and Mackie (1973).

3 For a further discussion, again see chapter 8 of Haack (1978).

4 Whitehead and Russell (1910). The detailed formal development is presented in Tarski (1956).

5 For those unfamiliar with the notation, '(p)' is a universal quantifier indicating that what follows holds for any p (here understood to be a sentence). The above line can be understood as

For all (sentences) p, the sentence p is true if, and only if, p.

An instance of this would be

'Snow is white' is true if, and only if, snow is white.

The sixteenth letter of the alphabet is used to stand for any arbitrary sentence, and when we put quote marks around it, that names the sentence.

6 See Haack (1978), chapters 7 and 8.

7 In the case of 'Snow is white', we have made a sentence of a sentential function by replacing an unbound variable by the name of an object. One can equally well turn a sentential function into a sentence by binding the variable by a quantifier, in which case the situation concerning satisfaction-conditions is essentially the same. For instance, the sentence 'For some x, $x > y$' is satisfied by all sequences, since the sentential function '$x > y$' is satisfied by some sequences, while 'For all x, x is not x' is satisfied by no sequence, since 'x is not x' is satisfied by no sequence.

8 It evidently surprised Donald Davidson, since he came to change his opinion between his 'Semantics for natural languages' (1970) and his 'Radical interpretation' (1973).

9 That is, in the semanticist's use of the term, a specification of the satisfaction-conditions. It is not a theory of truth as I would use the term.

6 INTERMEZZO

1 The following material on facts is adapted from my 'A matter of fact' (1977).

7 AUSTIN AND STRAWSON

1 The term 'world' must be understood as that which we can meaningfully talk about – whatever that includes.

2 As we will recall, Strawson came to accept (1964) that to say that a statement is true is to make a statement about a statement. It is to say that the statement has been made (at least hypothetically). Truth, however, according to Strawson, is not a property which statements have, and when we say that a statement is true we do not say that it has such a property.

3 I prefer the term 'linguistic' to Strawson's 'semantic' since the linguistic conventions involve what are, according to our use of the terms, both semantic and pragmatic factors.

8 TRUTH

1 These claims need to be modified somewhat in the face of Donnellan-type examples. Suppose Jack and Jill are playing shuttlecock and battle-dore. As it happens, that is an early version of what is now called badminton, but it is a different game. I tell you that the couple playing

badminton are Jack and Jill. Now you know that those two over there are Jack and Jill. I have succeeded in establishing a referential focus. I have used an incorrect description in doing so, but I correctly describe the referential focus as one of the ones playing being Jack and Jill. I have also incorrectly described the Jack and Jill referential situation. Maybe now you incorrectly believe that the game in progress is badminton. Whether the statement is true or not depends on whether one is trying to identify the game or the players. The nature of the statement depends on what we are trying to do in the communicational act. Often we do several things, but some are more to the point than others. Faults may affect some aspects of what we are doing and not others, so that then it is no longer true that all of the referential foci will be as described or else they all will fail to be so. Then it becomes a matter of deciding what is important.

2 This is one reason why there are severe difficulties with computer-translation from one natural language to another. A machine can correlate between one formal structure and another, and, after its fashion, indicate material correlates, but there remains the additional factor of how language-users use the structure of a natural language. This is not to deny that sophisticated machines could be developed which could handle such matters. Perhaps we are such machines. Still, any such machine would have to work with the conventional structure of the language *and* be able to take account of the ways in which languages are used in particular instances for particular purposes.

9 ALTERNATIVES II

1 By 'cognitive system' I mean the interlocking system of beliefs, concepts, etc., which go into our thinking about things, while by 'conceptual system' I mean merely our (also interlocking) system of concepts.

2 I have been challenged by students to indicate how 'No bachelors are married' might come to be contingent and perhaps false. Of course in attempting to show how this would be possible we must set aside evasions of the issue such as calling on other senses of the term (e.g. 'holder of a bachelor's degree') or creating new ones (e.g. 'bachelor = person with brown hair'). Such tactics only change the subject. What we must deal with is usage flowing from our current usage concerning marital status. Certainly I cannot prophesy what might develop, but in an age which has rigid plastics the possibility of married bachelors cannot entirely be ruled out. In fantasy it has occurred to me that we might perhaps discover intelligent beings on some distant planet who are somewhat like us. They have an institution of marriage, one which is complicated by there being three quite distinct sexes, all of which are vital to reproduction. The ideal is a happily married triple. Instead of marrying all at once, two of different sexes may marry while looking for the party to complete their marriage. Might one or both of them be a married bachelor? Can we answer that question now?

3 These accounts, in the Ramseyan tradition, may or may not be described as redundancy theories, depending on how we use the term. This is an issue to which I attach little importance.

10 TRUTH AND 'TRUTH'

1 Kurt Gödel established that for every consistent non-trivial formal system there must be well defined formulae such that neither they nor their negations are generable (deducible) in that formal system. Moreover, we can establish independently that some of the formulae are 'true' in the system, in the sense that they are true when interpreted in terms of the system itself.

2 It might be noted that what can be said in English does not *define* the English language, whereas what can or cannot arise in a mathematical system does, in a way, define the system. However, that does not mean that a formula says something *about* its system, any more than milk makes a statement about a dairy cow – though the production figures may tell us something.

3 Sets, that is, as distinguished from their elements. To hold that Jack and Jill exist is one thing. To claim that the set whose elements are Jack and Jill exists as a *third* thing is to make a different claim, which goes much further.

4 Henri Poincaré first made this point in his *Electricité et Optique* (1890). There has been a vast amount of comment since.

5 While taking a somewhat different line on truth, Brian Ellis (1980) points out, I believe correctly, that the term 'true' is not only a descriptive term but an evaluative one, applied to statements which meet important standards. I think that this is worth noting. Unlike James, though, he assumes a sharp distinction between epistemic and moral value.

BIBLIOGRAPHY

Aristotle, *Metaphysics*. I quote from the W. D. Ross translation, which is available in several editions.

Austin, J. L. (1946) 'Other minds', In J. O. Urmson and G. J. Warnock (eds) (1961) *Philosophical Papers*, Oxford: Clarendon.

—— (1950) 'Truth', in G. Pitcher (ed.) (1964) *Truth*, Oxford: Clarendon.

—— (1954) 'Unfair to facts', In J. O. Urmson and G. J. Warnock (eds) (1961) *Philosophical Papers*, Oxford: Clarendon.

Black, M. (1948) 'The semantic definition of truth', *Analysis* 8: 49–63.

Blanshard, B. (1939) *The Nature of Thought*, 2 vols, London: Allen & Unwin.

—— (1962) *Reason and Analysis*, La Salle, IL: Open Court.

Bradley, F. H. (1883) *The Principles of Logic*, London: Oxford University Press. Revised edition, 1958.

—— (1893) *Appearance and Reality*, London: Swan Sonnenschein. Reprinted by Clarendon, Oxford, 1946.

—— (1914) *Essays on Truth and Reality*, Oxford: Clarendon.

Carnap, R. (1947) *Meaning and Necessity*, Chicago, IL: University of Chicago Press.

Davidson, D. (1967) 'Truth and meaning', in D. Davidson (ed.) (1984) *Inquiries into Truth and Interpretation*, Oxford: Clarendon.

—— (1969) 'True to the facts', in D. Davidson (ed.) (1984) *Inquiries into Truth and Interpretation*, Oxford: Clarendon.

—— (1970) 'Semantics for natural languages', in D. Davidson and G. Harmon (eds) (1975) *The Logic of Grammar*, Encino, CA: Dickenson.

—— (1973) 'Radical interpretation', *Dialectica* 27 (3–4): 313–28.

—— (1974) 'Belief and the basis of meaning', in D. Davidson (ed.) (1984) *Inquiries into Truth and Interpretation*, Oxford: Clarendon.

—— (1977a) 'Reality without reference', *Dialectica* 31 (3–4): 247–58.

—— (1977b) 'The method of truth in metaphysics', in D. Davidson (ed.) (1984) *Inquiries into Truth and Interpretation*, Oxford: Clarendon.

—— (1978) 'What metaphors mean', in D. Davidson (ed.) (1984) *Inquiries into Truth and Interpretation*, Oxford: Clarendon.

—— (1990) 'The structure and content of truth', *Journal of Philosophy* 87 (6): 279–328.

272

Dewey, J. (1938) *Logic: The Theory of Inquiry*, New York: Holt, Rinehart & Winston.

Dummett, M. (1959) 'Truth', in G. Pitcher (ed.) (1964) *Truth*, Oxford: Clarendon.

Ellis, B. (1980) 'Truth as a mode of evaluation', *Pacific Philosophical Quarterly* 61: 85–99.

Ezorsky, G. (1967) 'Pragmatic theory of truth', in P. Edmonds (ed.) *The Encyclopedia of Philosophy*, New York: Macmillan, Free Press.

Geach, P. T. (1965) 'Assertion', *Philosophical Review* 74: 449–65.

Grice, H. P. (1957) 'Meaning', *Philosophical Review* 66: 377–88.

Grover, D. L., Camp, J. L. Jr. and Belnap, N. D. Jr. (1975) 'A prosentential theory of truth', *Philosophical Studies* 27: 73–125.

Haack, S. (1976) 'Is it true what they say about Tarski?', *Philosophy* 51: 323–36.

—— (1978) *Philosophy of Logics*, Cambridge: Cambridge University Press.

Hempel, C. G. (1935) 'On the logical positivist's theory of truth', *Analysis* 2.

Honderich, T. (1968) 'Truth: Austin, Strawson, Warnock', *American Philosophical Quarterly*, Monograph Series No. 2, Studies in Logical Theory.

James, W. (1907) *Pragmatism*, London: Longmans, Green.

—— (1909a) *The Meaning of Truth*, London: Longmans, Green.

—— (1909b) 'Ten unpublished letters from James to Bradley', with introduction and notes by J. C. Kenna, *Mind* 75 (1966): 309–31.

—— (1910) *Principles of Psychology*, London: Macmillan.

—— (1911) *Some Problems of Philosophy*, London: Longmans, Green.

Joachim, H. H. (1906) *The Nature of Truth*, Oxford: Clarendon.

Johnson, L. E. (1977) 'A matter of fact', *Review of Metaphysics* 30: 508–51.

—— (1991) *A Morally Deep World: An Essay on Moral Significance and Environmental Ethics*, New York: Cambridge University Press.

Kirwan, C. (1971) *Aristotle's Metaphysics ΓΔE*, Oxford: Clarendon.

Kripke, S. (1975) 'Outline of a theory of truth', *Journal of Philosophy* 72: 690–716.

Kuhn, T. S. (1962) *The Structure of Scientific Revolutions*, Chicago, IL: University of Chicago Press.

Londey, D. (1969) 'On the uses of fact-expression', *Theoria* 35: 70–9.

Macdonald, M. (1954) *Philosophy and Analysis*, Oxford: Blackwell.

Mackie, J. L. (1973) *Truth, Probability, and Paradox*, Oxford: Clarendon.

Malcolm, N. (1958) *Ludwig Wittgenstein: A Memoir*, London: Oxford University Press.

Marcus, R. (1961) 'Modalities and intensional languages', *Synthèse* 13: 303–22.

Moore, G. E. (1953) *Some Main Problems of Philosophy*, London: Allen & Unwin.

O'Connor, D. J. (1975) *The Correspondence Theory of Truth*, London: Hutchinson.

Partridge, E. (1958), *Origins: A Short Etymological Dictionary of Modern English*, London: Routledge & Kegan Paul.

Peirce, C. S. (1878) 'How to make our ideas clear', in J. Buchler (ed.) (1955)

Philosophical Writings of Peirce, New York: Dover.

Poincaré, H. (1890) *Electricité et Optique*, Paris: Carré.

Popper, K. (1963) *Conjectures and Refutations*, London: Routledge & Kegan Paul.

—— (1979) *Objective Knowledge*, Oxford: Clarendon.

Prior, A. N. (1971) *Objects of Thought*, Oxford: Clarendon.

Quine, W. V. O. (1951) 'Two dogmas of empiricism' in W. V. O. Quine (1953) *From a Logical Point of View*, Cambridge, MA: Harvard University Press.

—— (1960) *Word and Object*, Cambridge, MA: MIT Press.

—— (1969) *Ontological Relativity and Other Essays*, New York: Columbia University Press.

—— (1970) *Philosophy of Logic*, Englewood Cliffs, NJ: Prentice-Hall.

Ramsey, F. P. (1927) 'Facts and propositions', *Proceedings of the Aristotelean Society*, suppl. vol. 7: 153–70.

Rescher, N. (1973) *The Coherence Theory of Truth*, Oxford: Clarendon.

Russell, B. (1907) 'On the nature of truth', *Proceedings of the Aristotelean Society* 7: 28–49.

—— (1908) 'Mathematical logic as based on the theory of types', in B. Russell (ed.) (1956) *Logic and Knowledge*, London: Allen & Unwin.

—— (1910) *Philosophical Essays*, London: Allen & Unwin. Revised edition, 1966.

—— (1912) *The Problems of Philosophy*, London: Williams & Norgate.

—— (1918) 'The philosophy of logical atomism', in B. Russell (ed.) (1956) *Logic and Knowledge*, London: Allen & Unwin.

—— (1924) 'Logical atomism', in B. Russell (ed.) (1956) *Logic and Knowledge*, London: Allen & Unwin.

—— (1946) *History of Western Philosophy*, London: Allen & Unwin.

Strawson, P. (1949) 'Truth', in M. Macdonald (1954) *Philosophy and Analysis*, Oxford: Blackwell.

—— (1950) 'Truth', in G. Pitcher (ed.) (1964) *Truth*, Oxford: Clarendon.

—— (1964) 'A problem about truth – a reply to Mr. Warnock', in G. Pitcher (ed.) (1964) *Truth*, Oxford: Clarendon.

—— (1965) 'Truth: a reconsideration of Austin's views', *Philosophical Quarterly* 15: 289–301.

Tarski, A. (1944) 'The semantic conception of truth', in L. Linsky (ed.) (1952) *Semantics and the Philosophy of Language*, Urbana, IL: University of Illinois Press.

—— (1956) 'The concept of truth in formalized languages', an English version from the Polish (1933) and German (1935), translated by J. Woodger, in *Logic, Semantics, and Metamathematics*, Oxford: Clarendon.

Tillman, F. (1966) 'Facts, events, and true statements', *Theoria* 32, 116–29.

Warnock, G. J. (1962) 'Truth and correspondence', in C. D. Rollins (ed.) *Knowledge and Experience*, Pittsburgh, PA: University of Pittsburgh Press.

—— (1964) 'A problem about truth', in G. Pitcher (ed.) (1964) *Truth*, Oxford: Clarendon.

White, A. R. (1967) 'Coherence theory of truth', in P. Edwards (ed.) *The*

Encyclopedia of Philosophy, New York: Macmillan, Free Press.

—— (1970). *Truth*, London: Macmillan.

Whitehead, A. N. and Russell, B. (1910) *Principia Mathematica*, Cambridge: Cambridge University Press.

Williams, C. J. F. (1968) 'What does "*x* is true" say about *x*?', *Analysis* 29: 113–24.

—— (1976) *What is Truth?*, Cambridge: Cambridge University Press.

Wittgenstein. L. (1921) *Tractatus Logico-Philosophicus*, translated by D. F. Pears and B. F. McGuinness (1961), London: Routledge & Kegan Paul.

—— (1953) *Philosophical Investigations*, Oxford: Blackwell.

Woozley, A. D. (1949) *Theory of Knowledge*, London: Hutchinson.

INDEX